WILLIAM LUNELL'S HOUSE, 19 FRANCIS STREET

Growing Up
So High

Growing Up So High

A Liberties Boyhood

SEÁN O'CONNOR

HACHETTE
BOOKS
IRELAND

First published in Ireland in 2013 by
HACHETTE BOOKS IRELAND

First published in paperback in 2014 by
HACHETTE BOOKS IRELAND

10 9 8 7 6 5 4 3 2 1

A CIP catalogue record for this book is available from the British Library.

ISBN 978 1 4447 4309 8

Typeset in Cambria by redrattledesign.com

Printed and bound in Great Britain by
CPI Group (UK) Ltd, Croydon, CR0 4YY

Hachette Books Ireland policy is to use papers that are natural, renewable and recyclable
products and made from wood grown in sustainable forests. The logging and manufacturing
processes are expected to conform to the environmental regulations of the country of origin.

Hachette Books Ireland
8 Castlecourt Centre
Castleknock
Dublin 15, Ireland
A division of Hachette UK Ltd
338 Euston Road, London NW1 3BH
www.hachette.ie

This book is dedicated to my dear wife Viola for her constant patience and support and for the many blessings of the quiet home she created for us nearly forty years ago.

Contents

PART 1:

Small Don

1. THE ADVENTURES OF
SMALL DON

'Go out and play,' Mam was saying, her face so close to mine that I could smell her Ivory Velouté face cream. 'I told you before. You can't go to the Army Tattoo in Ballsbridge. If your Uncle Joe wants to take your brother Tommy, then that's his business. You'll just have to get used to the fact that you can't be number one all the time.' I longed to see the Tattoo because it was the talk of the school. Comfortable boys from the suburbs, who were in my class because of their Liberties connections, bragged how their dads had brought them to see the soldiers driving motorbikes in formation, standing to attention on the crossbars with rifles on their shoulders. I was not going to miss out on these wondrous sights if I could help it.

Just as I was about to ask when I was *ever* number one, the door suddenly opened and Aunt Dené came trotting into the room, her arms waving and her head enveloped in a cloud of Woodbine smoke. 'Nellie,' she moaned, 'there's a squatter in me grave. I have to talk to you.' She turned to me. 'Shonny, are you causing trouble again? I know you arrived on the anniversary of the Black and Tan truce, but you're crying since you were born. Will you go out and play because I have to talk to your mammy.' Before I had a chance to depart she was into a tirade about an unfeeling member of her clan who had come home from England and put an urn of someone's ashes in the family grave in Glasnevin Cemetery without a word of permission.

I left them at it, grabbed my short coat, and made haste to leave the parlour of Nannie O'Neill's house, at the back of her pork butcher's shop. Mam called out to close the front doors if there were cattle being driven down Francis Street. I needed time to get around her to let me go with Joe to the Tattoo, and I had to get on Joe's good side so it would strike him that he should take me. Even then it was becoming clear that life was full of such situations, where you had to use your head to get where you wanted. I left in a hurry because Aunt Dené was a person I did not want to cross. She was from Benburb Street, a foreign land on the other side of the River Liffey, and I couldn't make her out.

She had been courting my Uncle Paddy for many years and there had been no sign of marriage. The heat of ardour had gone from Paddy, and Mam told me later in life that on the night before they finally did get married he confided to her that he hoped he was doing the right thing. Dené was a nice person: she and her mother were generous on Holy Communion Day and Hansel Monday, but for me she suffered from two serious defects of character: she was not from the Liberties and she was a grown-up female. My plea to be allowed to go to the Tattoo had been interrupted, but I could return to the subject another time.

This particular day was a holiday from school while the teachers were considering strike action. Mam had told me to use my own discretion in how I might spend it. That was her way of saying I should spend the day outdoors, but not get into trouble. I had arranged to go for a walk to the quarry pond in the brickworks dump on Crumlin Road, a few miles away, with my pal, Tom Byrne. My idea was to try again to catch a nice pinkeen, like the one I had just missed the last time I was there. It was a lovely redbreast in colour, a real beauty that had slipped over the edge of my net.

I sat on my imaginary mustang with the reins in one hand and galloped out, slapping my flanks. As I thundered over the horizon of our front door, I nearly collided with old Mrs Welsh on the way to her fish stall in the Iveagh Market. She was dressed entirely in black, as usual, following the Liberties custom of mourning a dead husband for life. 'Hello, Seán,' she smiled. 'Are you coming in to see me later?' We were pals because I had found her purse on the footpath outside Nannie O'Neill's a few years before, and she never forgot that I had handed it over to Aunt Molly in the shop. Across the road, I could see a couple of boys rooting through the sweepings of the Tivoli Cinema from the night before, looking for sweets, coins or jewellery and about to be evicted by Harry, the usher.

Tom was waiting for me in the front porch of the Iveagh Market, leaning against the huge wooden doors that kept out the street sounds and smells from the vast market hall where used clothes were sold. He was telling his cousin that the carved face on the second arch on the front of the market was Cochise, the Apache chief, while the cousin was busy relying on an old cure in allowing Spot, the Carrolls' ardent but unfaithful dog, to lick a scab on his knee.

I reared my mount on his hind legs, neighing loudly, and stopped, breathless. We were all set for the day out. I liked horsemanship, but couldn't abide playing Cowboys and Indians. All that *dar-dar* stuff left me cold, and playing dead and wounded reminded me of my sisters' games of 'Statues', where you were given a push and had to come to a stop, frozen.

Tom and I were in the bunts, meaning we played cards as partners on the street. In particular, we pooled our buttons for a game called Don. Tom was a real shark, but we had been caught reneging on a trump the day before, so there was no chance of being let play in the usual school for the moment. I called him Big Don, and he called me Small Don, but this had nothing to do with our height: it was just because we were pals. Big Don was actually the nine of trumps and Small Don was the five. Both counted double in a trick when you played Don. In the Liberties, to be called Small Don was a compliment.

My pal was a bit older than me, with a bowl haircut, a pale face and bandy legs. His other distinguishing feature on this day was a boil plaster ready to fall off the back of his neck. He wore grubby white runners, like my own, and a Sloppy Joe shirt over his longers. Tom had a great imagination. He'd been brought up by his father since his mother had died. The dad worked as a washerman in the engine shop of CIÉ, the national transport company, and filled Tom's head with the small talk of men whose job was a sort of captivity.

People used to say that my pal was a little man cut short. I slapped my horse on the rump and sent it home as we started out on the trail. Tom said that first of all he wanted to tuck his longers into his socks, because he heard that the rats near the quarry could easily dart up the leg and cause harm. He was like that.

He goes, 'Me dad told me last night that he once hoped to be a priest but it didn't work out.' I stared at him, surprised by this new and unlikely information, and asked what had happened. He sighed, then said seriously, 'The bread didn't change.'

I laughed my head off. Good old Tom, always innocent and making me feel better than him, even if he *was* older. Kindly Mrs Doyle was standing at the door of her dairy shop, talking to her neighbour, Jimmy Lynch, the shoe repairer. I was often in both places. The boys on the school Gaelic team said that Jimmy Lynch made the best waxed end in the Liberties, with a strong fine needle and plenty of length in the thread, making it easy to stitch the burst panels of a leather football back together again.

Mrs Doyle sold jammy Mikado biscuits, and I had to buy a quarter-pound of these for Uncle Joe's tea most days. Joe lived a regulated life. He had his dinner when I came home for the lunch break at half past twelve from school. After that he would fall asleep for a while, sitting at the table with his head on his hand, just as he had been trained to do when he was on twenty-four-hour call as a Marconi wireless operator on his first voyage to Argentina.

We loped down sunny Francis Street. Women were busy shopping. Delivery vans and horse cars claimed their space on the roadway. A packed herd of cattle suddenly came into sight round the corner from Thomas Street, moving quickly, the drovers shouting encouragement and hitting them with sticks. We ran back to the shop and just got the doors closed in time before we continued on our way. The smell of cows filled the air. Now and then one would rear up in fright, and put her hooves on the back of the beast in front for want of space. They would take any escape route they could, and it was no joke to open the kitchen door behind the shop and find a frightened cow staring at you, mooing and dribbling, almost unable to turn around to get back out. They were on their way to Kehoes in Garden Lane to be slaughtered, having been driven from the cattle market on the North Circular Road a few miles away. I could imagine them in a country field sometimes, their coats shining and tails swishing, not like the mucky victims they had now become.

I saw Mallo coming in the distance. That wasn't his real name, and was short for 'Mallethead'. He had got the nickname because his parents kept him permanently shaven-headed due to the presence of head lice among his friends. Mallo stopped us, shouting, 'Mandrake gestures hypnotically,' and pointing in the manner of the cartoon magician in the *Evening Mail*. He boxed in the schoolboys' league in the stadium, and was highly regarded. He was pally, but he said, 'Hello,' by giving me a playful deadener on the arm, then turned to my friend. Dropping his head on Tom's shoulder, he unleashed a fusillade of light uppercuts to the solar plexus in a smart display of in-fighting. In conclusion, he stepped back and gave him a friendly cross to the temple, none of it in the real, of course, just in the cod. He was only showing off. Tom didn't say a word. Nobody would stand out with Mallo.

We said goodbye and headed for the Coombe, which was closed to traffic as workmen were replacing the timber cobbles. Dad had told me before that the wooden surface was to quieten the noise of the horse traffic, but the smooth timber was an icy trap for them in winter. I remembered having a nightmare one night after I had seen a poor fallen horse, with a shaft of the dray broken, struggling in full harness, its rolling eyes bloodshot and full of terror.

There was a stream of dirty water flowing under the road, so we made boats from pieces of paper we found blowing around and watched them disappear from view and come into sight again at the next excavation. We went on up the Coombe and called into my Uncle Mick Whelan's shoe-repair shop at the corner of Reginald Street. He was married to Dad's sister Mary, and never stopped telling old jokes. There he was, working on the last, mending shoes and smiling away. I had heard Mam say he was famous for singing 'Show Me the Way to Go Home' backwards, and that his name had been mentioned by Man About Town in the *Evening Mail* for it, so I asked him to sing it for us. He did, but I was a bit disappointed because he kept the same melody, and only sang the *words* backwards. Everyone knew that song because it was usually the last one to be sung at a Liberties party. When you heard it, it was time to go.

We set off again and May Kelly cycled past in Ardee Street, wearing slacks. Jeers all round, and not just from us. 'Let yer father out of bed' and 'Give us a crossbar on your girl's bike' brought no response. I shouted, 'Sell it and buy an ass,' trying to be smart, but Tom went too far.

He tried, 'Hey, May, who died and left you the trousers?'

She stood up on the pedals and roared at him, 'Yeh little bread and tea harrier, Thomas Byrne! What you have wouldn't fill them.'

We went silent knowing that to continue would invite May's next scale of invective, which would be unpleasant and possibly memorable.

On Ardee Street there was a gang of boys playing combo with a tennis ball – Three an' In, to be exact. Bellew was in the goal, which was chalked on the wall, and had already let in two, so he was preparing to surrender the goalkeeper's job when the third was scored. I was all for playing with them for a few minutes, but when I said, 'Hello,' Bellew just grunted and said, 'Get lost. Don't know yeh.'

Just then, an open lorry with the Jacob's Biscuits logo displayed on the front trundled around the corner from the Coombe. A roar went up. 'It's the Jacob's load!' The game broke up immediately, with boys grabbing their short coats and running after it. They knew that it was on its way to the brickworks dump to unload a cargo of biscuits that had been damaged in the making at the factory in Bishop Street. This was a movable feast day, and we had well learned to act swiftly if we wished to glut ourselves. We were going in the same direction as the lorry, but today I did not feel like exerting myself in a scramble over half-baked Cream Crackers or the like, so we watched the caravan disappear up towards the dump.

At the bottom of Cork Street we called in to say hello

to Ken Barber, who had been in my class in Warrenmount
School and he pointed out where Miss Kavanagh, one of
our teachers, lived beside him. We passed the house in
respectful silence, hoping that the door would open so that
we might see her again, but our curiosity was in vain.

Congley the farrier was nearby in Cork Street. We stood
as far inside the door as we dared, ready to exit quickly.
The action was set in a lofty enclosed forge, poorly lit, with
sawdust thrown on the cobbled floor. A big carthorse was
waiting to be shod and a huge fire was being blown with
the bellows by the blacksmith. In front of him a horseshoe
was taking shape on the anvil. Two young men, standing
on the same side of the horse, held its reins. The air was
smoky, but in the dim light we could see that the animal
was beginning to stir restlessly. The next thing was that he
started to pee with mighty force, the sawdust having little
effect in soaking up the downpour. We heard a few curses
then, nothing new, but these got worse when the horse
started to cack. The smell was terrible, but smells were
never a consideration for us. There was movement in the
cack and we took stock of a new phenomenon. It was filled
with long, fat worms, writhing and crawling in the steaming
dung. It was terrific. Tom said afterwards that it was better
than the zoo. However, it was all too much for the men
holding the horse, one arguing with the blacksmith, and the
other asking us what were we gawking at, and inviting us in
plain language to get out, which we did.

We reviewed the way we might shorten the road. One
possibility was to go into a shop and ask them if they had any
broken biscuits. If they said they had, we could roar, 'Well,

go and mend them,' and run out. Another method practised by the boys in the Liberties was to call a passing policeman 'Bluebottle', but you had to be in a crowd for that one so as to avoid identification, and you also had to be familiar with the local alleyways as escape routes. In the end, we decided just to go on and enjoy whatever we found on our ramble. As we continued up Cork Street, we passed Paddy Whelan's shop. He had the O'Connor warrant to supply us with bikes and prams on a mysterious credit system known only to Mam and himself. I knew him well from calling in with her as she often seemed to need repairs to her chariot, as she called it. Paddy was always nice to us, and I was fascinated by the fact that he could write very well despite missing a thumb due to some accident.

A horse and car went by, carrying two barrels. The driver was looking for kitchen slop. He sang out, 'Slop! Slop!' every few minutes, and the women in the houses called him in to take the waste away. As he called, 'Slop! Slop!' we intoned after him, 'The pigs are dyin',' in perfect rhythm, litany style. He was well used to it. It was harder with the coal man, as we had to anticipate his melodious call of 'Coh-o- il! Coh-o-il!' with our question, 'What do you feed your mother on?' If we got it right, he would obligingly call out, 'Coh-o-il! Coh-o-il!'

We met Cashman walking on the road, pushing a handcart and carrying a shovel. He had been sent out by his dad, who had a potato plot on the canal bank at Sally's Bridge, to collect horse manure, which meant that he had to patrol Cork Street taking a watchful interest in any dray that went past.

Coming up to Dolphin's Barn Bridge we stopped to watch the boys swimming in the murky canal. Some were diving off the bridge in a belly-flopper, which meant that they were either winded, if they were lucky, or else made contact with the bottom of the shallow canal, which could be very unlucky, as it was the last resting place of any junk thrown over the bridge. 'It's like soup,' one boy shouted. 'Terrific! The real gowdle harbour! I'm crossing on the dog's paddle.' A broken sign floated in the water, saying, 'CYM demands a swimming-pool for Crumlin.' The body of a pig was mouldering in the shallow water where the towpath went under the bridge. I looked on without envy. Like most Liberties folk, I had little interest in learning to swim, and the state of the canal was no incentive.

A boat loaded with Guinness barrels passed by, being pulled by a horse on the towpath. As it drew away, a man directed his terrier in pursuit of a water rat disturbed by the backwash. The dog kept throwing looks at his master, and wherever the owner pointed with his stick, it followed, the rodent barely escaping in the reeds on the other side of the canal. We looked on with approval, shouting encouragement, and hoping that the dog would catch the rat and kill it for our pleasure.

Close by, we saw a woman tying up a small sack that was writhing with life. We asked her what was in it and she said they were kittens she did not want. Then she threw them into the middle of the canal without a further word. The sack floated on the surface for a while, moving and shaking, then slowly sank out of sight. In the custom of my tribe, I thought little of it and we went our way. On the corner opposite Dolphin's Barn Bridge, we called in to an old widow in a little country house with an orchard in the back garden. The boys from the Liberties knew her well and never boxed the fox there: they would not rob apples from a widow. She, in turn, gave them to us for nothing, so honour was maintained all round.

As we passed Maher's pub on Crumlin Road, a shower of rain started. An old man stood in the porch, as we did, in silence. Suddenly a young couple jostled past us. 'What's the place coming to at all?' he said to us. 'If they're drinking before marriage there'll be trouble afterwards.' He stared at us, demanding agreement, but I thought he was just another hard chaw, and we left our shelter the minute the rain stopped.

Tom knew that some money could be earned from the cyclists using Kilmartins betting office next door. 'Can I mind your bike, mister?' he asked, when the next man arrived to place a bet.

Not having a lock for his racer, the man said, 'OK,' and went into the bookies. Bikes were being stacked against each other by the new arrivals, so Tom busied himself keeping his client's racer on the outside of the pile by way of extra service. The owner was well pleased when he came out a few minutes later, commending Tom and handing him a penny with a smile, just right for two Cleeves Toffees.

Our next action was in Whitneys, a busy shop beside the bookies. Mr Whitney sold groceries and newspapers, and allowed his customers to trade in their empty bottles and jam jars. These were kept on a shelf at the door. Tom was a natural robber, who sharpened his skills by secretly adding his own requirements of cigarettes to his father's grocery account at Nortons in Francis Street. I think he just loved the excitement. He told me to go to the counter and keep nice old Mr Whitney busy, so I asked the price of a large jam jar. I could see Tom in the Bisto mirror on the wall as he took a bottle off the shelf side-handed without breaking stride, and placed it on the counter. Mr Whitney smelt it for paraffin oil, then gave him a halfpenny. On the way out, Tom reached over to a rack of comics on the back of the door and, in a swift pounce, had six exactly similar copies of *Film Fun* under his top. I settled for a jam jar to hold my fish, if and when I caught it, promising myself to return it another day.

We pushed on up the Crumlin Road. I was beginning to get more excited about the fishing as we got nearer the quarry. The brickworks was long gone, and all that remained was a huge chimney and acres of undulating hills of stony soil created by the dead industry. The whole area was slowly being reclaimed by Nature and the corner of the site nearest the road was in use as landfill, with Dublin Corporation bin lorries in a queue waiting to unload.

There was great life around the site. One group of boys pushed an old, wheeled bogie along on what was left of the rail tracks. Others were catching bees as they landed on the flowery weeds, with a jam jar in one hand and a piece of cardboard to cover it in the other. Bellew was rubbing a dock leaf on a bee sting, and I had to turn my back when he started preparing to blow up a frog. We knew all about bees. The bumbler bee with the white bum was useful for starting your own hive. Some of them could be put into a buried biscuit tin half filled with flowers, with holes made in the lid at ground level. They would fly off after a short while, and come back laden with pollen. We often did this in the grassyard, the plateau of soil that lay over the ruins of Handkerchief Alley next door to us in Francis Street, and marvelled at the sight of their return. How and why did they come back? The brown bee, called the teddeyer, was the work bee, and the name of the black bee with the red bottom was the docteyer, which kept them all healthy. But today was for fish, not bees.

Some boys had climbed over the abutting palisade fence of the Iveagh Grounds, looking for fancy beer-bottle tops from the waste bins that had been tipped over the grass mowings. Another gang, older than us, was inspecting the barbed-wire defences that protected the boundary wall to the K&S factory, where they made jam and had a large stock of jars. More were interested in what they could salvage off the dump, and were rooting around with their hands in the jumble. The boys who had run after the Jacob's load were foraging in a diminishing pile of crumbling biscuits, competing with seagulls and crows, as the professional scavengers raked into the slope and drew out bottles, pieces of aluminium and cinders. There was a great demand in the Liberties for the latter as they acted like coal slack and kept a fire glowing for ages.

One of the scavengers, Brennan, who knew me from school, told me that he had trapped a couple of birds on the dump. He was hoping to breed off them, but did not know their sex. Could I sex them? I was known for my love of birds, and couldn't say no, although I didn't think I could do what he asked.

Near the dump, a quarry sloped down a long way into a shallow pond and that was my target. It abounded with pinkeens, and I knew exactly where I wanted to go. On my previous visit, I had come across a half-buried tar barrel lying on its side under the water in the middle of the pond. I had noticed that the fish swam into this cul-de-sac if they were disturbed, and it was there that I had just failed to catch the lovely redbreast the last time. I got a battered basin from the dump, with the bottom split but not open, useless for any purpose except mine. I wanted it to act like a sieve. When I waded into the pool in bare feet, I disturbed some pinkeens. They were quite small, but I knew they would all zoom to the shelter of the buried barrel.

A woman standing in the water beside me was trying to catch a fish in a net for her little boy. She had no chance, and I felt like giving her a lesson in how it was done. She seemed to think that pinkeens would simply wait to be caught, so she was bringing the net under them slowly and, just as gently, lifting it out of the water. Now, no self-respecting fish is going to surrender that easily. The correct way, as known in Liberties lore, was to get the net under the fish by stealth and strike upwards with great speed, concentrating on clean movement. Only then did you inspect the net for the result and, if you were quicker than the pinkeen, there it was. This messing with faulty technique I couldn't understand, so I waded towards the barrel and watched the pinkeens flash into it. That was ideal, and I chose a nice one from my first haul. I put him in my jam jar, and as I climbed back up the hill, I couldn't help noticing how a raiding party over from Aughavannagh Road was lighting a fire under the carcass of a pig they had found in the quarry. On enquiry, they told me they were going to eat it.

With my joy safely in the jar, I headed for Brennan's house. It was across the road from the dump, but reeked as if it was part of it. He led me upstairs to a bedroom converted into an aviary, where canaries and finches flew in one big mixed collection. 'I'm hoping to breed mules,' he said, 'so the finches are all cocks and the canaries are all Norwich hens.' So far, so good. Next he pointed at a covered cage hanging on the wall. 'Here they are,' he said. 'I'm trying to get this pair into breeding condition, but all they do is fight.' He pulled away the cover and showed off his captives.

It is true that I had read every book in Thomas Street Library on courtship and display among birds, but this was new. One was a full-grown herring gull with a bill like a scimitar and the other was a black-and-white hooded crow in riot mood. Their cage was an orange box divided by a wire shutter and they were trying to savage each other through this. The gull gave a cry of incredible intensity, a real siren-sound, while the crow cawed him or herself into a frenzy of terrible rage. I ventured to Brennan that, in my opinion, such a pair had never been cross-bred before, and the result would be of great interest. Then I left him in good humour, and headed out to meet Tom and go home. An ambulance sounded in the distance.

On the way back down the road we came to the police barracks. The street sign, 'Crumlin Road', was on the front of the building although it was called Sundrive Road Police Station. Tom thought it was to fool the crooks. The Black Maria was pulling out and the driver asked us if we were on the jare, or on gur, but I told him, showing off my fish, that we had the day off school and we were on our way home, answering both his questions at once.

Across the road, there was a ruggy-up going on at a bus stop outside the Loreto College. Two neatly dressed men stood there, looking frightened. One was clutching a Bible. They were surrounded by a mob of children who were pointing at them and chanting in unison, 'You're a Communist! You're a Communist!' The man with the Bible was calling out to people walking past that he was a Christian, but nobody stopped. The circle of boys was getting closer when the bus pulled in, and the two men got aboard quickly, as the shouting continued. One of the boys resumed his game – scutting on the back of buses. He produced a metal biscuit-box lid, went to the back of the bus, and prepared to squat down with his feet in the lid, gripping the bumper. His timing had to be perfect, as he had to place himself out of reach of the conductor's kicks from the platform when the bus was moving, while knowing that if he made his move too soon, the conductor would get off the bus and take the metal lid. In this case it was done with skill, and we all cheered as they departed down Crumlin Road, sparks flying from the tin, and the rider beyond the arc of the swinging boot.

When we came to Dolphin's Barn Church we stopped to marvel at the monkey puzzle tree just inside the gate. We knew these were far too prickly for any monkey. We talked about the reason for the tree being positioned where it was, and agreed that it was just to make sure, if a monkey ever escaped, that it would be frightened off by such a sight. Then we went inside the church to gape at its second wonder, the stained-glass window behind the altar. The central figure was that of a beneficent Jesus living in a slipper. Between us, we reasoned that this was meant to be a good example for people who could not afford new clothes, and showed there was no harm in being poor. Not only that, but there was a hole in the slipper, and the foot of gentle Jesus could be seen sticking out through it. His arms were outstretched and He seemed to be asking for someone to lift Him up. We knew it meant something special that we had not yet learned in school, and decided to ask Brother Devane about it the following day.

As I gazed with fellow feeling at the picture, Tom was visiting the candlelit shrines in the church. We knew never to take a candle away from a statue, but having discussed the moral dilemma for a few minutes, we thought that it was all right to take the burned candle grease for use as chewing gum. Tom's taste in such matters was not well developed, and we sometimes had conversations about the merits of eating sweets found on the footpath, and the difference it made if the sweet was wrapped. He was also partial to a banana, and thought little of picking up a fresh skin from the footpath and scraping it with his teeth. We took a drink from the holy-water tank behind the church, having blessed ourselves first and said a little prayer, then rested for a while on the stone plank seat at the back door. I topped up the jam jar before we left.

Mangan's hardware shop on Dolphin's Barn was fascinating for Tom. He loved tools and hoped to be able to buy them some time. Mr Mangan was selling a paintbrush to a dubious customer. The shopkeeper had an accent like Charlie Chan. 'The head of this brush is made from a Chinese pike,' he said, and the man looked at him incredulously. 'Yes, indeed, the hair of the Chinese pike,' said Mr Mangan again.

'Chinese pike? How could the hairs of a Chinese pike be turned into a paintbrush? Am I missing something?' said the purchaser. Then he added, with enlightened curiosity, 'How do you spell pike?'

'No need to be acerbic, it's P-I-G,' said Mr Mangan, and the man smiled and bought the brush. Tom asked me what a 'serbic' was, but I didn't know.

We were attracted to the Blanchardstown Mills next door by the van belonging to the rat-catchers parked outside. This was a shop we thought we knew well as they had a branch in Thomas Street. They sold all kinds of seed, millet sprays for the budgerigars and corn for the pigeons, straight from open sacks on the floor. In fact, there were a couple of commoners there, strays from the church steeple, standing on the footpath waiting for the sweepings, and trying to make love as they did so. We inspected the contents of the sacks in wonder, and left directly when the man behind the counter, who was weighing out bags of dried fruit, looked at us and pointed at the door without speaking.

Across Reilly's Avenue there was a Boy Scout hall, and we presented ourselves for possible membership as a means of passing the time. A genial fat man listened to our questions with great attention. There was no hesitation whatever on his part. He asked us where we went to school and told us that there were no vacancies in Dolphin's Barn, and to return to the Liberties if we wanted to join. Mam said afterwards that there was no Boy Scout troop near us, and that we were the very kind of boys who might have been best welcomed, and not to mind the oul' gouger. I did not understand the social import of her message, but I agreed with her conclusions.

Page was standing outside the Leinster Cinema, in his buttoned blue uniform, talking to an enormous handsome man, who looked like the actor who played Tarzan. Tom said that he still had the hanger in his coat, he was so broad. The one blot on his noble head was his ears, which were misshapen, as if he had suffered some trauma. We knew him as Lugs Branigan, a detective in the police force and the pride of James's Street in the Liberties, where he was born. He was the terror of the bowsies and famous as being the heavyweight champion of Leinster. Everyone he arrested wanted to fight him. If there was a mill he could deal very effectively with the culprits, and he was well respected because he often did not turn up in court to give evidence when he felt that the defendant had been punished enough. He and Page were close, and if Page was faced with an unruly situation in the cinema, he could call on Lugs and his heavy gang for help. We stared in wonder at his physique, and I tried to imagine what it might be like to get a smack on the jaw from such a man. I did not intend to find out, and when he saw us looking at him, we darted away.

We spent some time making up our minds whether we would go home by way of the Back-of-the-Pipes or down Cork Street, and eventually settled for Cork Street. As we passed by, we had a good look into the barbershop, where *The Great Oyster Eating Competition* could be seen. This was a set of pictures hanging on the wall showing laughing black people eating amazing plates of oysters. I had often seen them in McDonald's barbershop in Francis Street before it closed, so it was nice to make acquaintance again.

As we passed by St Margaret's Terrace, Tom got hot in his leather and wanted to wait on the corner for a while. Nearby lived a girl he had seen at the pictures by the name of Pauline Kilkenny and he said she was a lovely person. I had my own misgivings because I had seen Pauline on one of my walks on a previous occasion. She was going into a house and, assuming that it would be in order as we were acquainted, I knocked at the door to say hello. Her granddad opened it and called her out, whereupon she gave me a severe telling-off, saying I was making a show of her.

We got fed up waiting and noticed a long queue at the Cork Street Turf Depot across the road. Tom thought his auntie might be there, but there was no sign of her, so we skipped inside to have a look. The depot was one big room, with a high ceiling and no windows, lit badly by a few bulbs. People had sacks for the turf, and gigs, handcarts, wheelbarrows, go-cars and prams to get it home. The overseers were exercising their power in examining each ration book and there was no mercy shown. If you were up to your allowance, no case of the bronchials or soft cough would melt the hearts of ice. One countrywoman was looking for stone turf from the bottom of the bog, but all the peat there seemed made of wet straw. Two young men with bare chests filled the huge Avery scale pan while another changed the weights to suit the ration with the smoothness of a three-card trick man. There was no sign of the aunt, so we carried on down Cork Street as I was getting anxious about my fish.

When we passed Marrowbone Lane a war party from Dolphin's Barn ambushed us. There were four of them and two of us, so fighting was to be avoided, unless one-to-one combat was offered, in which case we would have to do our best. One of them was a rough-looking rossie that I had seen before when we were bunking into the Tivoli Cinema. Her dirty blonde hair was straight, shoulder-length, and her face was pale and threatening. I recognised her as the one who threw open the cinema doors in the side lane during the interval between films. She was reputed to be willing to give the usher a coort if he would ignore the free entry of her gang when this happened.

She was a common rossie and we were in trouble. Her pals were no better. They looked as if they intended to mill us so the only possible saver was to parley. I remembered how it was done in that picture where the crook sells guns to the Cherokees. Randolph Scott goes to face them, saying, 'How! Dohiyi!' holding up his right hand in the sign of peace. We were interrogated by the tallest of the gang, a hungry-looking boy with sunken cheeks and red eyes. He looked as if all his energy had gone into growing tall, leaving the rest of him in want. In fact, he seemed to be squatting inside himself, and not finding it congenial. He asked us where we were from, and what were we doing so far from home, and if we had any ghen-eye-nox on us. As he spoke, one of the other boys, a little hogger with a stick in his hand, was saying, 'Hit him a box,' while the commoner was using bad language to accentuate the threats. We were doing our best and getting nowhere, so I tried a different approach. I cried out, 'I know Ello.'

Now, Ello was the king of the kids in Dolphin's Barn. He was tough and rough but had a good heart, and I had made a point of talking to him on one of his bazz-offs out of his own territory, when he visited the Tivoli. He was appreciative that his reputation made in fights in the Leinster had gone before him. Saying that I knew Ello, the familiar name that only his acolytes would use, stopped the drift towards disaster for the moment. 'You do? How?' said the tall one.

I set it all out in clearly ambiguous terms and the quartet calmed down. By the time I was finished I was one of Ello's best pals and a distant cousin of his girl, Curly, whose name I was lucky enough to remember. I did not hear, 'Pass, friend,' but they stood aside, like the Egyptians we had been told about in school, and let us go.

We soon arrived at the hospitable border of Francis Street. The night watchman on the Coombe corner was sitting in his tiny open-fronted hut, with the brazier in front of it ready for lighting. As we were passing Marks Alley we went in to see Seán Ralph. He was in my class and we were good pals. He had every good look of the Huguenot about him, and we thought that he was like the picture of Napoleon in school. He was out, but we talked to his dad, Jack, who sold in the bird market on Sunday mornings. In fact, he was the one who informed me that the Sunday-morning bird market had been brought to Dublin from France by the Huguenots, and that he had been told by Matt Moore, the butcher in Francis Street, that he had been to such a market in the shadow of the cathedral in Paris only the previous year.

He told me that although you could breed mules by crossing canaries with most finches, the exception was the chaffinch because they mated while flying. I had often seen canaries mating in a bird's precarious way, with the proud breeder urging anyone around to see the spectacle – 'Look, he's treading her.' The very image of the two chaffinches in the air reminded me of a double-winged aeroplane, and I had to ask Uncle Bartle about it another day. He knew all things about birds and he reckoned Mr Ralph might be wrong: he thought the chaffinch was not an ordinary finch, and had a different diet. Right enough, I never saw a chaffinch for sale in the bird market. We said goodbye to Mr Ralph, and when we came to Francis Street Chapel, Tom said, 'Salong,' and went home.

When I arrived back at 15 Francis Street, the light was dying over the Liberties. The street had gone quiet and my dinner was ready to be heated up. I carefully emptied my fish into the big rusty biscuit tin I kept in the backyard with the ones I had caught on previous outings. There was little left of the day and I was really dropping. Soon I got ready for bed. I jumped out of my short trousers and runners, kept on my shirt, and vaulted in, avoiding the red spot on the sheet caused by the attack of a marauding black hopper who had managed to evade the DDT insecticide defences of the bedroom the previous night. Then I moved into position against the wall and pulled the blankets over my face so that the boogie man would not see me. Next, I said my prayers:

> *As I lie down my body to sleep,*
> *I give my soul to God to keep.*

If I die before I waken,
I hope the Lord has my soul taken.
There are four corners on my bed.
There are four angels overhead.
Matthew, Mark, Luke and John,
God bless the bed that I lie on, Amen.

Followed by the coda:

Amen means so be it,
Half a loaf and a thrupenny bit,
Two men, four feet, walking up O'Connell Street,
Shouting out, 'Pigs' feet, two and six a pound.'

The room darkened to the muted music of the Liberties. I had caught myself a fish. I was after having a great day. Uncle Joe could take Tommy anywhere he liked; I was happy again. Anyway, I didn't seriously mind Tomawsho being given a treat because back when I was only five he'd let me be one of his pals, although he was nearly twice my age. I fell asleep thinking of the great gas we used to have then.

2. LADY ANNE'S PROMISE

Tommy and I were leaning out the window over Nannie's shop in Francis Street. I was five. He was shouting in my ear about the Three Stewdies, but I was busy looking at the commotion below me. Mammy had gone downstairs to get change for the phone from Uncle Joe before she went to the post office to talk to Daddy, who had gone to work in Coventry for a few months, and two of my sisters were playing Beggar My Neighbour in the room behind me. Mammy had warned Tommy to mind me because I was so young.

Motor cars, lorries and horse cars going in both directions were being obstructed by a McCarrens lorry delivering meat to Durney's shop in the narrow part of Francis Street where we lived. Cathedral bells were ringing. An old man who had been singing on the street stood looking up at us, pointing his finger in a threatening way. The stench of exhaust smoke and horse dung filled the air. It reminded me of the toilet on the landing of the haunted staircase in our house. Tommy told me that the smell was just the smoke from Uncle Paddy's cigarettes because he spent such a long time reading in there.

A horse-drawn funeral was just about to turn into the chapel yard of St Nicholas of Myra Church, halfway down Francis Street, and I could barely see the bobbing black plumes. When they disappeared from view, my brother and I began to shout out the window in unison, 'Make way for horse traffic.' The stationary vehicles slowly picked up pace again, and when the noise level had died down, the old man took up his place on the footpath and resumed singing 'Waltzing Matilda', looking back in our direction.

He had been doing his best to be heard before the traffic jam, but the women going shopping had ignored him and he could not compete with the tolling of the bells; I had felt sorry for him. I knew parts of the song he was singing because I had heard Tommy practise it when he was learning it for the Feis, but the man stopped when I tried to join in.

A Guinness dray clip-clopped into the street with a boy scutting on the back reading a comic. Tommy told me that it was his pal, Rory Taylor. Just as it was going by, I shouted, for a joke, 'Look behind and lash the whip.' When the driver saw Rory he flicked his long whip and Rory had to jump off. 'You little louzer, Shonny O'Connor,' he roared. 'I'll box your ears.'

A dealer selling cabbage outside the pub at the top of the street was crying out, 'A penny the heada Yawke.' When she heard me imitate her, she just laughed and waved hello. Only the previous week she had given myself and my sister Peggy a slice of melon to try out, saying I was the splitten image of the O'Connors and she could see Bartle in me, and that her name was Mrs Fox.

When I looked across Francis Street I could see Granny O'Connor's house over Durney's shop a few doors up from the Tivoli Cinema. She lived there with Granddad and Uncle Bartle, although I could not see any of them through their bedroom windows just then. It was great having my two grannies as neighbours so close to each other. We lived in Nannie O'Neill's house with Nannie and her two sons, Joe and Paddy. Aunt Molly and her big daughter Eileen came in every day to work with Joe in Nannie's shop below us. I liked Eileen because she pretended to be Kitty the Hare and made up ghost stories to tell me. My favourite one was about Lady Anne, who lived on our creepy landing by day and in our haunted cellar by night.

A horse pulling an open cart went by with steam rising from the contents. I thought it was on fire, but when I asked Tommy he told me it was just hops from the brewery, and would I ever grow up. Then he started to remind me of the embarrassing position I had put him in when he had taken me to the pictures in the Tivoli Cinema. Flash Gordon had fallen out of his spaceship in the previous episode, to the great concern of Tommy and his pals. It had been my first time to see a follyinupper, so I said, 'Can he not swim?' After a moment's silence, four voices blended to tell me how dopey I was and that Flash was up in space, not in the water, and what age was I anyway? I was even more upset when one of the boys said I should have more sense. They did not seem to know that I was already big and sensible, and that if I stood on the toilet seat I could reach up and pull the chain.

Mammy's voice behind us was saying, 'Seán, get away from that window and go out and play with Tommy. I want to sweep the floor so don't go too far because I have to take you somewhere.'

I said, 'All right, Mammy.' I knew that her real name was Nell, and that she hated being called Nellie because she said it was a horse's name. Even so, once when I called her Nell, she stopped smiling and told me not to be so bold. I didn't think it was fair because I had to answer to three names. Mammy and Daddy called me Seán and Tommy called me Shonny, while my sisters called me SeánOliver. This was just about all right, but I did not like the way my two big brothers, Tommy and Billy, addressed me as 'Snotty Oliver' if I annoyed them.

Tommy and I left the front room and started down the ghostly staircase. We could hear Nannie coughing in her bedroom. I began to tell Tommy again about Lady Anne, the woman I had seen on the landing, but he just said that there were no ghosts, and that I was only saying it because Eileen had told me the story. The staircase in our home was very, very old and gave me the shivers. There was an ancient wardrobe on the long landing with a yellow mirror on its door, reflecting the sun's rays from the lantern light on the flat roof. I had told Mammy, too, about Lady Anne, but she just said, 'Shush,' and that she would speak to Eileen and Joe about frightening me with ghost stories.

None of them understood that sometimes, going upstairs on my own when it was getting dark, she appeared to me. Her face was white and she wore a white dress. Her lips were red and she slowly brushed her long yellow hair in the mirror. She never spoke but her eyes followed mine and, although she had a little smile on her face, I was afraid.

Tommy was usually very kind to me. He told me not to mind when Mammy said I was always crying, and we both knew that she liked our big brother Billy more than us. He also taught me how to swallow air and belch if someone annoyed me and then say it was an accident. Mammy had told him before that he was to tell me stories to keep me quiet because I was always asking questions. The first one he ever told me was about Murder in the Blue Room and the first words he explained were 'walleyier' and 'golleyier'. One was a big stone of the sort that could be thrown to smash the empty bottles in our backyard and the other was the word for a spit.

I loved to play games with Tommy. He took me down to play hide-and-go-seek with his pals in St Patrick's Park one day. He was onit, and the rest of us hid. I ran down behind the drinking fountain at the other end of the park so he couldn't find me. Tommy went home without me, but I was able to tell the gardener. He asked me if I had no mother or father and where did I live and was just about to take me home when I saw Mammy coming along with Tommy. When I ran behind the shed to hide again, Mammy just said, 'Will you stop your alligations' and made me hold Tommy's hand.

The gardener was giving out to Mammy, but she said he was just another plaster saint that would go to Hell without sin, and not to pick her up before she fell. I knew then that I would have to mind her on the way home. When we got there, Mammy told Aunt Molly what had happened, and I heard her say, 'Good God tonight, is he at it again?'

As we came to the bottom of the haunted staircase, Tommy said he had to go down to the cellar to chop sticks for the fire. The cellar was pitch black except for the rickety door to the backyard, so he wanted me for company as he was afraid of the dark and he knew I was too. That was because Lady Anne spent each night there. He started to catch bluebottles that were landing on the rotting pig bones lying on the floor, ready to be buried in the grassyard. Then he was throwing the bluebottles into the spiders' giant webs that were all around the walls and ceiling joists of the cellar, and shouting with delight when the spiders came to take them away.

'Look at this fella,' he exclaimed, 'wrapping the bluebottle up in a ball for his next dinner,' then added, 'Take him to the laboratory,' in the voice of Ming the Merciless, the great enemy of Flash Gordon. The gastronomic customs of the spider left me uneasy. I preferred to look out the back window in the mornings to hear the birds singing from the grassyard or from Stanley's farm in Lamb Alley.

When Tommy got bored with his entertainment, he decided that we should have a look at Johnny Rea's fish. Mr Rea owned the ice-cream shop next door and had built himself a big concrete water tank on the roof of one of his outhouses, beside our wall. It was open to the weather and stocked with goldfish. But first we had to collect food for them. We searched under the wet sacks and in the loose mortar of the old stone walls of the cellar where centipedes, earwigs and clocks flourished. Some of these we put into an Andrews Liver Salts tin.

Next was a visit to the spot in the grassyard where Joe buried the old meat from the shop. This should have been taken to O'Keefes, the knackers in Newmarket, but every so often he buried it quietly in order to save himself a journey with a smelly sack of meat over his shoulder. Tommy called out to me, 'Last eats the barrel of rats,' but he had to help me scramble over the crumbling wall at the end of our backyard, dislodging bits of brick as we went. From there we could get into the grassyard, which was now an overgrown plot slowly reverting to nature.

A pigeon carcass lay on the ground. It was walking alive with chandlers, and bluebottles buzzed around enjoying the last of the feast. Perfect for our needs! Tommy shouted, 'Open, Sesame,' as he dug with a stick. The rotting bones were near the surface and had drawn plenty of worms so we topped up our Andrews tin with them. When the fish saw our shadow, they swam towards us. Tommy threw in a long worm and a few chandlers. One of the worms was sniffed at by some of the larger fish, and sampled, but spat out disdainfully after a moment. Having second thoughts, the same fish tried again, but the victim had been taken away by another. The worm was torn to pieces in the following fishfight, but Billy had told us once that these fragments would grow back to life again.

I could see Luigi Rea, Johnny's son, in his backyard from where I sat on the side of the tank, and I could hear pigs grunting and budgies chortling from Stanley's farm. I knew it well because Tommy took me there every few weeks with a chip of greenmouldy bread heels for the pigs. This was no ordinary bread because Joe loved Vienna rolls but never ate the tapered ends. They were worth a few pence to my brother, who valued the proceeds for spending on sweets in Minnie Whelans or Meenans in Francis Street.

When we went back upstairs Mammy was standing with her coat on, ready to take me out. Joe was in the shop, wrapping up pigs' feet for Mrs Fox, the nice dealer who had given me a free slice of melon. He told her that they were short trotters from the front legs of the pig, which was all he would eat himself. Then he explained that when the pig was hung up by the legs after slaughter, the hooks spoiled the taste of the back feet. When he tried to interest her in backbones or a cheek, she replied that she had a party coming up and the pigs' feet would do grand, with a coddle for later on. Then she said, in a slow emphatic way, 'And what parties we have.' I was impressed with this hint of the forbidden unknown and wondered what delights were planned.

I thought backbones were lovely myself, the way the red meat fell away in chunks when Mammy cooked them for us every Thursday. Once, I tried to chew the white cord, but it had no taste. My second favourite was rabbit, and I often asked Mammy to bring me down the steps into the fish and poultry section of the Iveagh Market to see Mr Honer taking off the fur in one piece.

Just as we were saying goodbye to Molly, there was a sudden shout from the parlour behind the kitchen. It was Paddy and he was complaining about the cats again. There were a few of them in the house. They refused to go upstairs or into the cellar, and would leave the house only through the front door. I carried one upstairs once but his hair stood on end and he flew back to the kitchen when I put him down. The problem this time was that a cat had laid her kittens behind a sideboard where they could not be reached. Molly said to leave them alone for the moment, but Paddy replied that, as God was his judge, he believed Molly thought the cats were human, and that all they hadn't got was a knife and fork.

This was because she put down our plates on the floor every day after dinner so that the cats could eat what was left over. Paddy was in a bad humour because Joe had seen him the night before, sleepwalking in his pyjamas under the influence of the full moon, and had had to rescue him from his perch when he sat out on the back window ledge to stare at the sky. That would not have mattered, but Joe had told Mammy and Molly about it and they could not resist making fun of Paddy as a result.

As we were leaving, Joe was telling Mammy that he was going up to Harry Mushatt's chemist shop to buy saltpetre to make the barrel of brine for steeping the cuts of pork. Mammy asked him to bring her back some opening medicine and whatever Mushatts had for the oirick on Tommy's hands. We left when Eileen started to empty the slatted crate of meat from McCarrens of Cavan. Molly was calling out the number of pigs' tails, feet and heads on the list, and Eileen was checking them off.

It turned out that we were going for my baptism certificate for my new school. Mammy let me walk beside her as she pushed the pram down Francis Street to St Nicholas of Myra Church. The street was busy as ever, and she told me to hold on to the pram and we would be there in no time. I loved it when she said that because it was like being carried in her arms, and I knew everything would be all right.

She asked if I knew any little song that would pass the time, so I sang one that I had learned from the boys playing cards on the steps of the market:

> *Fourteen flays, got fourteen days,*
> *For hopping on a German's back.*
> *The German swore*
> *If he caught them any more,*
> *That he'd break every bone in their back.*

'That's not very nice,' she said. 'Sing a nicer one.' Then I started into another song that I had picked up:

> *Come back to Éireann, you baldy-headed German …*

'Don't sing that either,' she said, before I could finish, 'you shouldn't be making up songs about the Germans,' and she had a frightened look on her face for a second.

Mammy seemed to know everyone we met. The men touched their caps and strolled on, but the women sometimes stopped the pram to have a look at the baby, and one of them told me I was a real O'Neill, with that nose. Another asked about Nannie and told Mammy that her husband was a Knight of the Shrine in John's Lane Chapel, and that she would get them to say a prayer for such a lovely old lady to grant her a speedy recovery or a happy death.

When we got to the presbytery of Francis Street Chapel I asked Mammy about the coloured picture on the cover of a book there. It showed a man nearly naked, with light shining on his body, and people all around him. 'That's poor Jesus being taken down from the Cross,' Mammy said. I was surprised to hear this: the last time I had seen Baby Jesus He was in the crib, and now here He was, a man already. I knew that He could not have grown up so quickly. When

I asked Mammy about this she stopped smiling again, and told me that I would soon be starting school and then I would understand.

She asked the clerk for my baptism certificate, saying, 'His name is Seán Oliver O'Connor, born on the eleventh of July 1938, the feast day of Blessed Oliver, and baptised on the fifteenth.' The clerk had a look at the register and then said there was no Seán Oliver baptised that day, although there was a Joannes Oliver O'Connor, which was probably him.

'No,' said Mam, 'his Aunt Lucy was standing for him. I distinctly told her to have him christened Seán and that's what we call him. Can I have a look at the book?' He would not agree to that, saying that there were special reasons why she could not see it, and that her baby was only one of fifteen baptisms that morning. 'Joannes,' she said. 'Sure that's not a name at all. Whoever heard of it, and I hope there was no such mistake made with my other five.' When we left, she continued to examine the certificate suspiciously, leaving me to slindge along behind her.

When we got home, Joe was talking to Eileen as if he was telling her something. She kept nodding. I heard him say, 'It's all true anyway,' but he stopped when he saw me. After a few minutes she asked me if I'd like her to tell me the ghost story about Lady Anne again, and she promised to put on a voice like Kitty the Hare, the country storyteller. Eileen knew I loved this tale, even though I was always afraid when she came to the end because it left Lady Anne haunting our staircase and cellar. But today turned out to be different. We sat together in the parlour, she in Nannie's red velvet rocking chair and me at her feet, lying on the worn brown carpet and she began.

Now the story I'll be after telling you tonight is one of the tales given to me by your Uncle Joe, may God bless him. Once upon a time hundreds of years ago, wasn't there a poor farmer named Peter. He lived in a thatched cottage in a clearing in the forest with his wife and their baby son Will and their dog Venus. Although they had very little, they were happy together because they loved each other, thanks be to God.

Will loved their home in the country, but weren't the family so poor that they only had one cow and two calves, so when he was eighteen years of age he told his parents that he wanted to go out into the world to seek his fortune in Dublin. They were very upset, but his daddy sold a calf, and gave Will some of the money and so he said goodbye. Then they kissed him and gave him their blessing. When he came to a hill overlooking the cottage he looked back sadly, knowing that he would never return, God between us and all harm.

Faith, didn't he work hard and he saved up all his money to build a house at 15 Francis Street in the Liberties, exactly where we live today. It was a lovely tall house of four storeys and a cellar, and Will sold clothes in the shop downstairs. Poor Will was lonely until he met a beautiful girl named Anne and in no time they were pure crackt alive about each other. He called her Lady Anne for a pet name. Soon they got married and lived happily in this house. God blessed them with a little daughter and they called her Martha.

Some years later, didn't a terrible thing happen. Lady Anne died in this very house when Martha was only fifteen years of age. And now I am coming to the strangest part of my story. Before Lady Anne died, she promised Will that she would stay in this house to keep himself and Martha company, and would never leave until another baby named Martha was born here.

Martha was very sad because her mammy was dead and she had no brothers or sisters to play with. Will's heart was broken at being left on his own, but Lady Anne kept her promise, glory be to God. And so, although she could not be seen, she lived on the landing of the staircase by day and slept in the cellar by night.

Not too long after, when Martha was twenty-one years of age, didn't she meet a nice young man, and didn't they fall in love. They got married and went to live in Marks Alley where they were very happy together, God bless them. But still Lady Anne spent each day brushing her beautiful long yellow hair in the mirror on the landing and sleeping each night in the cellar because she had promised to stay until another baby named Martha was born in this house.

Then what happened was this. Didn't Will meet another girl and they got married and went to live in England. Lady Anne was glad that Will was happy again, but she could not leave this house because of her promise to stay until another baby named Martha was born here. Hundreds of years passed and many other families came to live here in 15 Francis Street:

the Maguires and the Stephens and the Loughlins and more. They all had children, but none of them called their baby girl Martha, so Lady Anne could not leave. More time passed, and slowly the house got tired and started to fall down, the Lord save us. First it was the roof, but Lady Anne still waited on the landing by day and slept in the cellar by night. Then it was a floor, but still Lady Anne waited on the landing by day and slept in the cellar by night, not wanting to leave until a baby named Martha was born here. Then one day Nannie O'Neill came to live in this house. She had it all repaired and painted, but there were two places that were never changed. The first was the staircase, because a little voice had told her that Lady Anne lived there by day, and the second was the pitch-black cellar, because the same little voice told her that Lady Anne slept there by night.

Then Nannie invited your mammy and daddy to live with her here. God blessed your mammy with little babies. First there was Billy and then there was Nell; then there was Peggy and then there was Tommy, but no Martha. Lady Anne still waited on the landing by day and slept in the cellar by night, hoping for another Martha to be born. Then one day, in the lovely spring month of April, your mammy had a little baby girl and they named her Martha, aililiú!, just two years before you were born yourself.

Lady Anne was very happy when that happened because now she could leave the landing and the cellar in peace and go to sleep for ever, thanks be

*to God. She sang a little song for your sister Martha
and it was heard in Heaven. Nothing was ever seen
of Lady Anne afterwards, but the old staircase and
the dark cellar in this house were never changed to
remind us of how faithful she was to her promise.*

*So there's no need to be afraid any more of Lady
Anne because she's gone home for ever, praise be to
God. And as for your sister Martha, she was given the
gift of being able to talk to ghosts, and so it is to this day
and will be always. Now that's my story for you today,
Seán, and it's on my way I must be to visit our relations,
the O'Connors, beside the library, in 21 Thomas Street.*

When she was finished I knew that I would never see Lady
Anne again, although sometimes when I went down to open
the back door I felt something brush my hair in the pitch-
black cellar. Mammy said it was only cobwebs, but when I
got older I was not surprised to notice that my sister Martha
indeed had the gift of being able to talk to ghosts and spirits.

Later on in life Martha bought an old house in London.
She lived alone, but planned to use it as a guesthouse. It had
been locked up and was virtually derelict. The neighbours
were all aware of poltergeist activity there, particularly in
the sealed cellar where a gang of noisy ghosts had taken over.
Martha thought they would be great fun, so she renovated
the cellar and made it into a bedroom for her guests. The
building work was finished, despite the mysterious noises
and relocation of physical objects, but when it got out of
hand she became annoyed and lectured the ghosts on their
behaviour. After her harangue she felt sorry for them and

wished God's blessing on them. In that way she made friends with the ghosts, and they sometimes reminded her of their presence by leaving a handprint on her bed.

In my own case, I was not long forgetting Eileen's story in the dread and excitement of going to school. Mammy had explained to me what it would be like and Peggy had sometimes taken me into her class in Francis Street Girls' School to mind me, so I knew a little already. But I had never spent a day away from home on my own before. The school chosen was the Presentation Convent Warrenmount, at the other end of the parish, in Black Pitts. Mammy had gone there herself and some of her teachers were still in action.

We left the house early as Mammy said it was a good walk to the school. I held on to the pram tightly as we headed down Francis Street in the direction of the Coombe, passing by familiar places. I became more anxious with each milestone. Soon we had passed the Iveagh Market and Francis Street Chapel. Mammy let me stop for a minute to look at the stray cats in the ruins on the corner of Hanover Lane, and said that there was once a cloth shop on that spot named The King of Denmark, and it was owned by the man who had built Nannie's house. A boy from Tommy's class was coming out of Cummins shop in the lane with a bag of winkles and offered me one while he fished with a pin in the shell, but Mammy told me not to take it.

Then we passed the house where my cousins, the Copleys, lived, beside the Catholic Repository. A lorry filled with sheep went by and Mammy said they were on the way to Kehoes. The pram started to roll down the hill at the end of Francis Street and I was told to hang on tight. It was great fun. We called into Smith's sweet shop on the corner and that was the last outpost before we crossed the forbidding border of the Coombe, and ventured into the unexplored territory of New Row. I looked around, fearing the worst from unknown forces, but Mammy's manner consoled me. She told me that her family, the O'Neills, had lived in this area for hundreds of years, and showed me where their old home at number thirty-four had been, so that I felt happier walking past the houses and the high stone walls of the mill buildings.

When we turned the corner into Black Pitts we walked into a smelly mist coming from a factory chimney. Mammy said it was only O'Keefes the knackers melting bones to make manure and this was where Joe took the old meat from the shop. When I told another boy about this he said the right name for the place was Keevesenackers. As we passed Fumbally Lane we joined the parade of prams on the last part of our journey. Mammy told me to be a soldier and not to be like the little one who was crying his eyes out on the far side of the street, clinging to his mother's legs. The stern convent buildings could be seen when we crossed Warrenmount Place. There was a high wall at the end of the terrace. 'That's the convent wall,' Mammy said. 'The nuns are never allowed to leave.' I felt sorry for them and made up my mind to try and get them out if I could: Daddy had told me to think about other people besides myself sometimes.

The wide gates under the archway into the school were open and Mammy told me to give her a hand to push the pram up the slope. There were plenty of women with their children to keep us company. When we passed the big wall of the playground Mammy stopped to chat to another woman with a child who was crying. I saw her dip into her handbag and take out a piece of chocolate. 'Give him this,' she said. 'It always works.' I looked away so that she would not realise that I was now armed with secret information.

At the top of the slope there was a little yard between the school buildings where the parents and children were gathering and waiting to be called into the parlour for interview. A crow was drinking from a pool of water at a leaking tap on the wall. I noticed that after he drank he held up his head to let it go down his throat before he took some more, and I knew then that birds had no swallow.

Mammy was told that the High Babies' class had started the previous week and today was for Low Babies only. I was a Low Baby so there was no problem. There were two nuns waiting for us in the parlour. The first was Sister Bonaventure, who was to be one of my teachers, and the other was the head nun, Mother Agnes. I had seen nuns before but being close to them was different. Their hair was invisible with the headdress they were wearing, and for that matter, I could hardly see them as belonging to the world I knew. Their dresses made their bodies shapeless and covered them from head to foot. A belt wound around their waist and dropped almost to the floor. Only the sound of their conversation connected them to anything I knew about people, but their voices were kind and put me at ease.

There were holy pictures of the Infant Jesus on the wall of the parlour. A huge picture of the beads making up the five decades of the Rosary was stretched out on a frame, and images of little black children, as well as elephants and giraffes, filled the blank spaces. Mammy told me what it was for as we waited. 'The nuns are collecting money to save the souls of the little black babies in Africa. It says here that, when a person gives a penny, it will help to bring them to Jesus and they won't die as pagans. When you give a penny you are allowed to stick a pin into one bead.' Some of the Rosary had been pierced already and I found it hard to understand that people would give their money away and get nothing back.

I knew what the Rosary was, because we used to recite it every night before Daddy went to work in England, and I had the words off by heart. He would say, 'Thou, O Lord, will open my lips,' and we would all answer, 'And my tongue shall announce Thy praise.' Then, 'Incline unto our aid, O God,' and we said, 'O Lord, make haste to help us.' I suddenly missed Daddy and I hoped he would be home again soon. Mammy had told us that he had been knocked off work in Jordans as a wood machinist and had had to go away until something else turned up in Dublin. It came to our turn, and I saw Mammy giving Sister Bonaventure the bar of chocolate. Daddy had told me to be a good boy while he was away so I had no intention of being bold.

My attention settled on a nature cabinet in the corner of the room. Among the acorns and dried flowers was a little bush with artificial leaves. In the cleft of a branch was a nest with four speckled eggs in it. Standing nearby, staring at the eggs, was a little brown bird. Higher up the foliage was a red-breasted robin with his beak open as if singing, and daring anyone to trespass. Just looking at it gave me a warm feeling of security that reminded me of our happy home.

A nice young teacher came over to me when she saw my interest and told me her name was Miss Kavanagh and that she lived in Cork Street. I asked her if she knew Barber's shop and she replied that her house was next door to it and, in fact, Ken Barber would be in my class. I was glad, because Barbers, at the Coombe end of Cork Street, was a secure beacon in this new sea.

The classroom was set out with little tables allowing two children to sit side by side at each one. Sister Bonaventure told us to be good boys for the sake of Jesus, who was always good for His mammy. She also told us that we would be chastised if we were bold or cheeky. Complaints were entertained daily from mothers of boys who were unkindly treated by their classmates, and retribution would then be swift but not very terrible.

Sister Bonaventure would take the left hand of the troublemaker in her own left hand, then half pirouette so that her back was to him and his arm was extended, ready for slapping. She would then reach for her belt of soft leather with her right hand, and her arm flailed up and down in a frenzy of harmless slaps for a short minute, until the devil of boldness had been exorcised. It never hurt and its purpose seemed to be a general warning about behaviour and the consequences if you did not conform.

Miss Kavanagh handed out a workbook of grey paper for drawing class. With it came a stick of white chalk and another of blue. I drew mountains as I had seen them in the pictures, just huge overlapping semicircles, and when that was done I put a few spots of white here and there. When Miss Kavanagh saw this she said, 'That's lovely, but what are the white dots?' I explained that they were sheep, but when she laughed and asked me if I had ever seen sheep on a mountain before, I had to admit that I had only seen them on their way to Kehoes. She seemed to be pleased anyway, and when it came to the holidays she gave me a banana as a prize.

She also taught us to write the letters of the alphabet in a copybook with red and blue lines. 'Barely touch the blue lines for the small letters and touch the red lines for the capitals,' she would say, as she got us to make the sound of each letter. It seemed to be no time until we could read. 'Fionn's Little Harper' was my favourite story in our English book. In this tale Fionn M'Coole is trying to persuade a little leprechaun harper to leave his employer, the High King, and go to work for him. Negotiations are in progress and Fionn asks the Little Harper what his requirements might be to tempt him to change employers. The Harper replies that 'A suit of green cloth twice a year and a glass of mead every day' would suffice. Fionn confirms the arrangement with words I shall never forget: 'All these and more you shall have if you come with me.'

I realised a few years later that the story had touched a latent instinct of mine and that it was the beginning of my understanding of money and its cousin, power. I already knew its value as a means of buying nice things, but it was the first time I noticed its wider use. In that way I came to have an early inkling of the benefits of money and this seeded my desire to own some of it myself one day.

One sunny morning in the following year the door of the classroom opened and Mother Agnes swished in. Our teacher, Sister Bonaventure, was busy dealing with a complaint from Mrs Clery about her child having being struck by a classmate, so I was keeping my head down. It was true that there had been a fight, but Clery had given me a ferocious kick on the knee to begin with. The arrival of the head nun ended the possible inquisition, and the woman left when she saw that there was some urgency in Mother Agnes's manner.

We were told to continue to read to ourselves from the poem we had been learning, and the two nuns huddled together in conversation. It was a welcome relief from schoolwork and it was not long until the whispering started between us curious children, so we were ordered again to go on reading quietly. I was sitting alone at a table on the end of a row in the classroom, and I did my best to listen to what was being said at the same time as I silently repeated the poem:

> *Apples red apples, so high on the tree,*
> *Far too high for Billy and me,*
> *When the wind blows the apples will fall,*
> *Billy and I will gather them all.*

Above the verse was a happy picture of the scene. The tree was laden with apples of green and red. Under it stood a little boy and girl, smiling, well dressed and dainty, both pointing at the fruit. The door opened again a few minutes later and we were amazed. In came a policeman with his arm outstretched as far as it would reach. He was holding the hand of a haggard little boy. All eyes turned on the intruders as they stood for a moment at the door. Mother Agnes called the man forward, leaving the boy marooned near me.

I stared at him in wonder. He was standing with his head bowed slightly, wiping his nose with the back of his hand, impassive and shivering. I could see he was about my size and dressed in raggy trousers and a dirty white shirt that was too big for him. His gaunt face was dirty too, and his hair was matted. The scruffy shoes he had on were worn out and loose on his feet. His socks drooped at his ankles. His demeanour was tormented and an air of sadness enveloped him. He looked like a little boy deserted and forlorn and in need of pity, so I gave him all of mine with the zeal of childhood.

The policeman was talking to the nuns in a low voice and I could only hear bits of what was said. 'On his own ... neighbours.' The problem was clear, even to us. Mother Agnes and the policeman left then, paying no heed to our visitor, and Sister Bonaventure addressed us without calling the boy up to her. 'One of you move over and let Stephen sit with you. He won't be here long.' I was nearest to him so I made room. Then I could properly see just what state he was in. We looked at each other with all the interest on my side, and when I asked him where he lived, he replied, 'Fumbally Lane.'

'Are you not going to school?' I said, but he put his knuckles to his trembling lips and whispered that his daddy was dead. I was shaken and tried to imagine how I'd feel if that had happened to me, but it was too terrible to grasp. I could not visualise a life without my own daddy.

'Stop talking,' a voice said, 'and look at your book.'

I moved closer to him to share the page. He was sitting on my left-hand side with his right hand to his cheek, and leaning over to see my book, while I did the same in reverse.

A boy was commanded to read, and a hesitant voice started into 'Apples red apples'. Stephen's hand moved from his cheek to fumble in his hair. Our faces were nearly touching when a huge louse fell from his head and landed upside down on the bright picture. We looked at each other and took in this experience without embarrassment. Head lice were nothing new, but the speed and size of this specimen impressed the two of us and made us forget everything else for the moment. I rolled it over on to its legs with the point of my pencil, leaving it racing over the branches of the apple tree.

We were interrupted by Sister Bonaventure calling us to attention. My new friend was suddenly animated and killed the louse with a single fluent stroke of his thumbnail with imaginable sound and colour effects. I had to admire his technique, being an expert in such matters, but then his face grew sad again. The diversion was over.

The door suddenly opened. The policeman came in and went up to Sister Bonaventure. Stephen reached across our table and held on to the back of it with one hand. His other hand lay beside mine on the book. His hand touched mine. They spoke quite openly. The policeman said, 'Have to go … can't find her …'

The nun advanced towards Stephen. His hand pressed down on mine. He turned his face to me. The agony of his suffering and terror etched my mind. The policeman took his hand at arm's length again. We gaped as they left in dreadful quiet. In the stunning silence of the aftermath, Sister Bonaventure told a boy to continue reading the poem and normal routine resumed. I told Mammy about it later and she said that Stephen would be all right, but I could not forget him.

I imagined that I might have been able to take him home to our house, but there would be no room. So, instead, I asked Lady Anne to mind him in her home in Heaven, and if she did, then he would not be so lonely without his mammy and daddy.

3. A RARE THING TO PRAY FOR

Sister Bonaventure was in serious mood. 'Come up the aisle one after the other to the altar rails with your hands joined in front of you, and kneel down. When Father Byrne is giving Communion to the boy beside you, hold your head back slightly and put out your tongue. And, oh,' she commanded, 'close your eyes when the priest stands in front of you.'

She was preparing the High Babies' class in Warrenmount School for their First Communion. We were in the oratory behind the main building, practising for the big day. She inspected and corrected the deportment of each boy and, when she was satisfied, walked along the line, touching each tongue with the cap of her fountain pen. As she did so, she told Clarges to put his face in his hands for a moment afterwards, like the rest of us. She was always picking on him. When the exercise was over, we were asked to sit in the pews again.

'And now,' she added sternly, 'I am going to give you some of the questions we were learning in class. Robert Clarges, how are we to prepare for Communion?'

Clarges started to stumble over the answer. Whispered hints broke out all around him. 'We must be in the state of grace, and we must have a lively faith, a firm hope and an ardent charity.'

'Very good, an ardent charity,' she confirmed, 'and you, Seán O'Connor, can anyone come out of Hell?'

'No one can come out of Hell for out of Hell there is no redemption,' I answered, without adding the Liberties ending: 'When you get there, you get a pension, tuppence a week for working hard, chasing the divils around the yard.'

When Sister Bonaventure asked Doyle to give her one of the things we must do at Confession I began to worry again. I knew the complete answer to this question and repeated it to myself as Doyle responded: 'One of them is that "We must accuse ourselves of our sins".' I was feeling low with the burden I carried and this did not help.

She told us to examine our conscience but, for the avoidance of doubt, she gave us examples of sins to be confessed. Not doing what your mam told you, not saying your morning and night prayers, and giving her back-answers were all on the list. We knew these would have to be confessed before we were forgiven. I had the dilemma of not knowing what to do about my own sins because I rated them in an appalling category of wickedness.

On the way back through the convent grounds to the school, Clarges and I compared our misdeeds. We had certainly erred in the matter of the sins Sister Bonaventure mentioned, but he had a few of his own that were causing doubt. He asked me if writing *Kilroy Was Here* on the school wall might be a sin and, if so, what sort, and if we didn't know how many times we had fallen, would we really be forgiven? Then he admitted saying to his sister, 'You think you're the cheese, but you're only the cow on the paper.' He was having remorse of conscience over that one. After a little discussion we agreed that what you might say to your sister could never be a sin as *she* would most probably have started the argument in the first place.

As well, Sister Bonaventure must have meant to count the sins of the last few days only, as otherwise the list would be as long as your arm. Clarges thoughtfully repeated, straight out of the Small Catechism, that, after all, 'God knows all things, even our most secret thoughts and actions and all things are naked to His eyes.' I shuddered again. I had two secrets troubling my conscience. The first one was known only to me, the second known to me and my family. I was too ashamed to mention either of them to my pals.

My fearful state of mind was not helped by my sister Nell alarming me with her vivid description of eternity, where people who died in mortal sin spent for ever in the fiery agony of Hell. This was made even worse by my brother Billy assuring me that your legs were held in a vice, so that you could not escape even for a moment to get a drink of water and you were bound to be very thirsty there.

When the day for First Confession arrived, Miss Kavanagh came into our class to take us to the parish church in Francis Street where they were to be heard. I knew that I had to endure the shame of confessing the matters that were troubling me as a necessary preamble to making my First Communion. Skerritt clutched the teacher's hand because we would be passing by his house in Black Pitts on the way and his mam would be looking out for him. I walked along behind the teacher, too preoccupied to join the gang of boys who ran on ahead down the slope to the front gate, yelling and shrilling as we always did on that short sprint.

We had a good look up the road to make sure that the big boys from Black Pitts Primary School were safely in their classrooms and that the trail to Francis Street was clear. Some of Skerritt's pals gave a loud hurrah when they saw his mam standing outside their little house opposite Fumbally Lane and, after he had waved goodbye to her, he pointed out where Tom 'Bang-Bang' Dudley lived behind the knackers' yard in Mill Street. By the time I had walked down New Row and pushed up Francis Street, my worry had turned to dread and, when we turned into the chapel yard, I was certain the priest would be furious with me and perhaps would attempt an exorcism.

The blue stone floor of the porch to the side entrance of the chapel was pitted and hollowed from wear. We could see the staircase curving towards the old bell tower and O'Brien ventured up the steps to have a look at the platform where the bell ringer stood to pull the rope. A massive holy-water font stood on each side of the front door. The granite floor in the front porches was scabbled from use. The lovely church was so much in need of decoration that it reminded me of home, drably brown and a bit shabby. Little books on religious subjects were displayed for sale on a table. Someone had taken down one entitled *May I Keep Company?*

and, presumably affected by whatever it had to say, had left it open on a folded page.

I thought of Uncle Joe when I saw the collection plates on the table near the shrine at the back of the church. I had often heard him mention the time before the war when he had only a half-crown and a penny to his name on the way to Mass there one Sunday morning. He threw a coin on the plate without looking. The collector called after him and Joe thought he was being smart over his penny, but he had actually given in his half-crown, worth thirty pennies, by mistake. There was no going back after Mass, regardless of need. Pride was widespread in the Liberties and Joe had to suffer the consequences.

Miss Kavanagh explained that the lamp over the altar was permanently lit to indicate the presence of God. She demonstrated how to genuflect and bless ourselves at the same time. As for me, I could see only the gigantic painting of a human eye just above the statue of the Virgin Mary holding Jesus like a baby. It looked like the picture postcard on the wall at home with the words *Michelangelo's Pietà* printed under it. When I asked the teacher what the eye meant, she said that it was the window to the soul. Its purpose was to remind us that He can see everything. *What was I to do?*

Miss Kavanagh showed us the inside of a confession box. There was a kneeler for the penitent and a shelf to lean on, with a little crucifix to kiss if you liked. In the partition between the confessional and the priest's box was a wire grille with a little wooden door over it, just big enough to frame a human face. When we had taken it all in, she ushered us into the pew in front of the confessional where the pastor was already in occupation. She said that the priest on duty was lovely, and we would be seeing him often when we started in Francis Street Christian Brothers' School after the summer holidays. I read out his name over the door, *Fr J. Byrne CC*, then knelt down, covering my face with my hands. The number of times I had committed venial sins kept slipping my mind, but I had no trouble remembering my major wrongdoings.

The queue got smaller and my heart raced faster. Then, suddenly, inexorably, horribly, it was my turn. The curtain on the door of the confession box moved as Masterson made his exit. He was like an angel and held the door open for me. He might as well have been wielding an axe. Miss Kavanagh peered in through the door and made sure I was kneeling in the right place. I knew that Father Byrne was hearing Graham's confession on the other side of the box because I had seen him go in, and my time was coming. A finger of light shone on the wall and distracted me, but I quickly reverted to the dilemma of my wickedness.

I heard the sound of the door to the wire grille being opened. Father Byrne's profile came into view. I started off as we had been taught: 'Bless me, Father, for I have sinned, this is my First Confession. Father, I told lies about four times and did not say my morning and night prayers about five times. I was bold in school twice and I gave cheek to Sister Bonaventure once because I was upset when she told me that I had seven pins in my clothes and she called it "The Liberties Zip".'

A kindly voice said, 'I'm sure you told your mammy when you went home. Wouldn't she make it better for you?'

'Yes, Father. Mam said that Sister Bonaventure had never changed and that she must have said *several* pins, but there were never seven.'

'I see,' said Father Byrne, seriously, and I noticed his hand near the grille although I had not even started to unburden myself.

'Anything else, child?'

My face was hot and sweaty with keeping the most grievous sins for last.

'Yes, Father.' Here goes. I took a deep breath. 'I broke my fast when Sister Bonaventure told us to practise for First Communion at home. I didn't have any breakfast but I was biting my nails and I bit off a piece by accident.'

'Indeed, child, that's no harm,' the gentle priest said.

I was so relieved that I could have gnawed my way through the latticed grille to kiss the very hem of his garment. But now, the big one. I earnestly hoped that the Deity might be feeling well disposed as I launched myself, through Father Byrne, on His infinite mercy. 'I said a bad word,' I confessed.

'How many times, child?' asked Father Byrne.

'Just the once,' I replied. 'I was in the kitchen at home standing under the bulb where the flies land. One of them went by just over my head. Mam and Dad and all the family were there with me and they were getting ready to go to Mass and Communion for the First Friday. I was putting on the pullover Mrs Byrne knitted for me so I threw it up at the fly and shouted at the same time, "Come down, yeh hoor yeh." They all stopped talking and I didn't know why.'

There followed a silence you would have to describe as tense. Then the voice asked, 'And what did your mammy say?'

'Mam said, "It's all right, he doesn't know what it means," but I knew *then* that it was a bad word.'

'That's not a sin either,' said Father Byrne. 'Is there anything else?'

I said there was nothing else and awaited my fate. 'For your penance say three Hail Marys and a prayer for me and the poor suffering souls in Purgatory. Now, a good Act of Contrition.'

I said the prayer with feeling. *O my God, I am heartily sorry for having offended Thee and I detest my sins above every other evil* ... When I was finished I blessed myself and went out to kneel in the pew. I swore allegiance to God and his saints and to St Nicholas of Myra in particular, and told him that I would give him some of the money I might collect from my relations for getting me out of trouble.

My appearance was transformed on my First Communion Day. My usual suit of brown corduroy trousers and zipped top was laid aside and replaced with a new outfit with everything to match, right down to the cap in the colours of my new school. I walked around stiffly, as if my body was matching the newness of my clothing. Joe showed me the old family photograph with him sitting as a little boy wearing the same sort of cap as I had. Aunt Molly said what a great lad I was to fast for so long and that there would be a nice fry for breakfast when I got back from Mass.

Mam came with me and smiled and patted me on the head when I went to the front pews of the church to join my classmates. I thought myself lucky that Father Byrne did not seem to know me when he was giving out Communion. When I caught a glimpse of the white dove over the *Pietà*, I felt as if

I had joined the legion of the saints myself. None of my family was omitted from my prayers and I said a special one for the kindness of all of the relations I would be visiting that day. I hoped the Almighty would encourage their generosity.

When the priest had spoken and the Mass was over, I had a feeling that my baby days were finished, but I didn't mind. I met my pals from Warrenmount School in the big chapel yard. This was a last goodbye to some of them because their families were moving out of the Liberties to the new suburbs and they would not be going on to Francis Street Christian Brothers' School as I was. Mam had told us that we would be moving too because we had been allocated a nice house on Keeper Road in Crumlin. I was not too concerned about that as she explained that I could stay and live with Nannie until I was finished my schooldays. In the meantime, she would see me every weekday because the family ration books were with Nortons in Francis Street and Boland's bread shop in Meath Street. None of that was to change, and I was free to go home at weekends if I wanted to. I was quite happy to stay because all my pals lived in the Liberties anyway. The class photograph was taken at the front porch of the church and then it was home to Nannie's with Mam. I set about devouring breakfast in the kitchen while I thought about my visiting arrangements. I could hear voices in the parlour and went in there as soon as I could.

We had some visitors. Molly was talking to her husband Jack Hilliard and her son John. Uncle Jack was on his way to Brittains in Dawson Street to pay the rent on his wireless set. I knew that in his position he was good for a contribution to my big day. Genial Jack Hilliard was famous in our family for having two pensions from the British Army. It seemed he had spent the First World War in France and was not too long returned from a desk job in Belfast where he had sat out the second. He was given the respect due to his position of being a foreman in Guinness's and had developed the gravitas of a man who was in a safe job for life. Consequently, he spoke seriously on every subject. I liked him because he was full of stories and told them whether or not children were in the company.

Cousin Eileen said, 'Hello, Shonny, love,' when she saw me. Then she smiled at me as if I was a baby in a pram, patting my cheek. Joe said I was a real Mickey Dazzler and told me he was going to give me a rise in my pocket money, even as he was handing me a sixpenny piece for myself. Uncle Paddy reached for his pocket and I leaned forward in anticipation, but he just said, 'Watch this kid. He loves the money,' before giving me a penny. I told Tommy what had happened and he said that Paddy would put two pound notes in a cage to breed, but I knew that my uncle was only joking.

Jack Hilliard started into an update of a saga that had been his favourite subject for the previous few months. Reportedly, a man named Fottrell had died in America leaving a lot of money. There were Fottrells in the Hilliards' ancestry and Jack and his son had answered an advertisement calling on possible descendants of the deceased millionaire to contact the lawyers.

No decision had yet been made in respect of their claim, but that did not stop the Hilliards from making plans for a dreamy future. Jack was reclining in an armchair. He said, in the faraway voice of a venture capitalist sensing major opportunity, 'If this comes through I imagine I'd go into pigs.' He began to describe modern methods of pig breeding, sharing with us the intimate details of the way slatted floors could control the slurry and the smells. Mam said she could only imagine what it was like.

His son John, who was also looking forward to a bright life from the same source, said, 'I might open a book. There's money in gambling.'

'Now, John,' said Mam, with Molly nodding her approval, 'remember what happened to your poor Uncle William.' It became apparent that another O'Neill family secret was about to slip out.

William had been an on-course bookie who opened a turf accountant's shop at the end of Francis Street on the corner of the Coombe. He had taken big bets on a horse called Tipperary Tim for the Aintree Grand National in 1928 and hadn't bothered to lay them off, as the odds against him winning were one hundred to one. Paddy took up the story. 'Forty-one of the forty-two horses in the race fell at the fences, leaving only Tipperary Tim on his feet. William lost his shirt on that race and barely managed to survive. He didn't learn much from that experience, though, because he did the very same thing ten years later with a horse called Battleship. This was an American horse that no one thought could win, but win it did, at forty to one. This time, William couldn't pay his gambling debts and his licence was withdrawn.'

That's the way it was with Mam's family, the O'Neills. They were guarded with their secrets and I could only pick up their stories in their own time, but I promised myself when I was older to ask directly about some of the things that were hinted at. The O'Connors, by comparison, never seemed to stop talking about the past. However, even I could recognise the land of dreams, although what might happen in the future seldom came to be a matter of discussion, given the preoccupations of the present. As it turned out, the Hilliards' plans were based on a hypothesis that ended in failure, but Uncle Jack remained his likeable self and turned his attention to the possibility that another son, Jimmy, might one day become a winning jockey.

I was sent up to Nannie in her little windowless room overlooking the staircase. She was sitting up in bed, coughing and clearing her throat, but lay back when I came in. 'Let me look at you,' she said. 'You have the O'Neill fringe, like my own, and nobody would ever mistake you for anyone else.' Then she rooted in her purse and gave me a briny-green thrupenny bit. When I told Billy about it he advised me not to spend it all in the one shop. Tommy was nominated to take me around to some of our relations to give them a chance to admire me and demonstrate their fabled generosity. The weather was grand, but Mam had known in advance that it would be so, because she had left a statue of the Child of 'Praigue', with the fingers broken off, on the windowsill overnight to entreat a good day.

We skipped across the busy street to see Granny and Granddad O'Connor first. Uncle Bartle whistled when he saw me and said, 'Who's a smart boy today?' Then he introduced a friend of his named Jack Tutty who was home on holidays from Australia, saying he was a distant cousin of ours. That was easy to believe because the visitor was quite like Bartle in appearance. We were told that Granny had gone up to the Mayo Stores to get something for the tea and would be back in a minute. Granddad was cleaning his bent-shank pipe and said that I could call him 'Father' now that I was such a big boy, and continued to show the visitor some old pictures hanging on the wall. He liked all his grandchildren to call him 'Father', because that had been the practice when he was a small boy.

Mr Tutty took down a little framed picture and read aloud: '"Government of the Irish Republic. Five per cent Registered Bond Certificates (1919), received from William O'Connor of 142 Francis Street, the sum of ten shillings, signed: Michael Collins, Minister of Finance".' He laughed and said, 'Up the rebels!'

Granddad answered, 'Sure your family were rebels when it was dangerous,' but Mr Tutty was already studying the second picture.

'Ah,' Granddad said, 'that goes back a long time. It's the baptism certificate of Patrick O'Connor in our direct line. God knows poor Patrick and his wife didn't have it easy. A mixed marriage, you know, in those days.' He drew on his pipe and the smell of Velvan Plug filled the air as Mr Tutty handed me the picture. I knew what it was because I had often seen it before, and I read out: '"Church of St Nicholas of Myra, Parish of Francis Street. This certifies that according to the Register of Baptisms kept in this parish, Patrick O'Connor was born on the eighteenth of February 1771 and was baptised according to the Rites of the Catholic Church on the eighteenth of February. Parents, James O'Connor and Margaret Kavanagh."'

Granddad began to tell Mr Tutty the story. A Protestant couple, William and Hanna Cole, had come to live in the Liberties from the parish of Kilcormick in County Wexford just before their daughter Dorothy was born. When they grew up, Patrick O'Connor and Dorothy Cole met as neighbours and they fell in love. Patrick was a Catholic and Dorothy's family were Church of Ireland, so both sides were against any marriage. 'That's Patrick's baptism certificate you're looking at there,' he said, and then went on: 'Well, the couple defied their families, and since they couldn't get married, they simply lived together in a love match. That made things worse. You can imagine what people said about them in those times, and the families were no help, especially when they produced two children. Dorothy became pregnant again and the pressure was too much to bear. On the fifth of April, 1805, Dorothy did two things which are remembered to this day. In the first place, she became a Catholic and was baptised in St Catherine's Church in Meath Street. The second thing was that the couple got married on the same day, and in the same church.'

Granddad continued, 'Dorothy had her third baby, a boy, exactly a month later, and they called him James after the grandfather. It's a funny thing about the O'Connors. They never strayed from the Liberties, but often married women from the country who came to live here. Sure that's how the Tuttys became part of our family as well.'

Mr Tutty looked at him and said, 'That's a long story,' and was about to go on, but Granddad had gone over to the bookshelf above the fireplace.

He took down an old volume and handed it to the visitor. 'That's more of it,' he said, 'potted history, and no mistake. You can borrow that for a few days but don't forget to let me have it back. It's an old family diary.' I had seen it before and Granddad had already promised to let me read it when I got bigger.

Tommy had gone down to meet Granny, and after a while Bartle and Mr Tutty went out to Madigans on the corner of Francis Street for a drink. I remained with Granddad, waiting for him to tell me something important as usual. Almost immediately he started to talk to me in the way that I loved, as if I was a grown-up. 'I must take you on my walk to Lucan with me one of these Sundays, now that you're getting bigger,' he said confidentially. This was an honour for me. Granny's family were old McDonnell stock from Lucan. We all knew how Granddad sometimes walked the Strawberry Beds road to meet her brothers in the Spa Hotel. The story was that he took a Baby Power with him on the journey: half of it for drinking and the rest of it for rubbing into his feet.

But this day I was restless, intent on moving on after getting his present. I said goodbye and ran around the corner into Thomas Street, getting ready to jump across the break in the footpath at the entrance to Madden's Court at Rosie Flynn's chandler's shop. I had been trying to leap that gap since I was first let out to play on the street, but on my First Communion Day I cleared it with ease. Granny was coming out of the Mayo Stores with Tommy when I saw them and we said our goodbyes.

From there we planned to walk the short distance up Thomas Street to Aunt Lily's flat over Dunfords, the hairdressers. As we passed the fire brigade station, Murray caught up with us. He kept white tumbler pigeons for show. Now he started immediately to tell me the best way to make the non-return doors to a pigeon loft, and how he hated cats, commoners and hawks. Then it was all about squabs and squealers, and the trick in ringing them without breaking the claw. 'Use Vaseline to stick the feet together,' he said. 'The claw will bend easy when they're very small.' I liked his pigeons because they made a great show, tumbling and rolling in the air as they flew.

I was not gone on him because he had canted the ball on to the roof of the Iveagh Market the last time we were playing football in Lamb Alley, and he hadn't even offered to climb up for it. Now he was on his way to Guinness's hoping to trap one of his pigeons that had fallen in with bad company on Echlin Street. His intention was to snare his own bird, but if a commoner happened to stray into the twine noose, he would break its neck immediately. He asked me if I knew a boy named Clive Mew, who had a great collection of birds' eggs, and if I ever met him to tell him that he would give him some pigeon eggs if he liked. I did not know him, but I kept his name in mind and Murray said he lived in Chapelizod. We left him entering the Blanchardstown Mills, where the big wooden doors nearly closed on his hand when he took too long to say goodbye.

We arrived at Lily's house via an inspection of the monumental headstone being carved by old Mr Courtney in the adjoining yard. He was a quiet man who didn't mind the locals looking over his shoulder as he fashioned the latest stone for the recently departed who could afford it. We could hear Aunt Lily singing as we were going up the stairs to her flat. The building vibrated with the sound. The melody of the song was beautiful, a slow air of yearning and love. We stopped to listen to her deep voice until she was finished. When we knocked and went in at her bidding, she was alone with her husband, Tim Copley. Tim was a soldier, and his face was a mass of roughened flesh, healing under a layer of ointment, from an accident when a grenade had accidentally exploded near him a short while before.

'Here, boys,' Lily said, 'have this lemonade and a biscuit. You're a lovely boy today, Seán. You can see a real family likeness. And a new school in September, your daddy was telling me. That'll be grand. The same school as all your family before you.' She opened her purse and said, 'Here's a little something for yourself,' and hanselled me nicely. The music of the song Aunt Lily had been singing lay on the table and I picked it up. It read 'Softly Awakes My Heart' from the opera *Samson and Delilah* by Camille Saint-Saëns.

> *Softly awakes my heart,*
> *As the flowers awaken*
> *To Aurora's gentle zephyr,*
> *But, say you, dear beloved,*
> *No more I'll be forsaken:*
> *Speak again, oh, speak for ever!*

'And where are you going next?' Lily asked, after a little chat. 'Bill and Eva would be nearest.' We agreed, and went on our way. Uncle Bill was Dad's brother, and Eva was his gentle wife. Everyone in the family said she had a lovely nature, and I knew this from my own experience because she never said a bad word about anyone. They lived at the end of James's Street in Mount Brown and, although they had no more than most other people, they were renowned for the warmth of the welcome they gave to their visitors. Granddad said that when

Shakespeare had written 'Small cheer and great welcome makes a merry feast', he'd had people like them in mind.

When we arrived at their house, Bill was delighted. 'Seán, Tommy,' he exclaimed, 'come in. Eva, look who's here. Isn't it great?' Eva welcomed us, and told me how nice it was to see me on my First Communion Day. In no time we were enjoying chunky cheese sandwiches and more lemonade. Bill was out of work, which happened often in the woodworking trade, and I was well used to this from Dad's experience. He started relating his exploits in staying up late during the war to hear about the progress the Allies were making and told us once again about Lord Haw-Haw as he imitated his voice. Then he gave us his Churchill speech, which I absolutely loved. It reminded me of the strength of mind of some of the Liberties people I knew:

> *We shall not flag or fail. We shall go on to the end. We shall fight in France, we shall fight on the seas and oceans, we shall fight with growing confidence and growing strength in the air, we shall defend our island, whatever the cost may be, we shall fight on the beaches, we shall fight on the landing grounds, we shall fight in the fields and in the streets, we shall fight in the hills; we shall never surrender.*

Bill said it sounded like Thomas Street on a bad Saturday night. Then he told us again how he had met Eva on a mystery train excursion to Tramore organised by his union. 'That was the end of me,' said Bill. 'Any man who walks up the hill to Mount Brown never escapes,' but he smiled as he said it. Eva added that Bill's idea of a date was to take her for a walk by the stone beds in the Back-of-the-Pipes. He was an extrovert who loved life, but we all knew that, although he was endearing, he was a bit feckless. When he went on a drinking bout it could last for a few weeks, but Eva was very forgiving. Once, when Dad remonstrated with him, I heard her say, 'Sure I married a child that hasn't grown up and that's the only way he knows how to behave,' and made the most of her blessings.

Bill and my cousin Rory went with us part of the way back to Francis Street as they wanted to show us the carving of Daniel O'Connell, the Liberator, on the stone arch over the entrance to St James's Church. When I asked Bill who was the second figure at the other side of the arch, he said it was the local parish priest of the time who had decided to have himself commemorated in good company. After that, we crossed the road and, as was the custom, we walked three times around the fountain outside the Church of Ireland cemetery for good luck. This was where Catholics from the locality were allowed to be buried in the old days. Bill said that the custom was to carry the coffin at any Catholic funeral three times around the fountain before burial, giving time for a last prayer, it being a matter of courtesy not to extend your welcome in a Protestant graveyard. 'In fact,' Bill said, 'one extremist C of I archbishop had forbidden Catholic prayers in Protestant graveyards altogether at the time of Catholic Emancipation and created such a commotion that a new cemetery for Catholics was opened at Goldenbridge.'

A young man passed us by heading in the Francis Street direction. His hands were covering his face and he was crying bitterly and calling out, 'No one remembers me.' We looked at him in sympathy and Bill said there was a terrible call, like a spell, on anyone who was born in the Liberties so that they could never forget where they came from, no matter how far they might travel. I understood this myself, because I knew that when the time came for me to leave I would be the same, and I felt sorry for the man who had left it too long to return to his birthplace.

We decided to go to see Aunt Tillie. She was partly a mystery woman who lived in a room on her own in a tenement house in front of St Audoen's Church on the forty steps in High Street. We always called her 'Aunt Tillie', although she didn't actually seem to be related to us. However, Mam was very fond of her and made sure that she was visited on such days as First Communion. Furthermore, we could always depend on an appropriate financial recognition of the big day, which made her popular with us.

Tillie was in when we called. 'You're a big boy now and you'll be able to take care of your mammy,' she said. 'Remember me to her, and tell her I said she's always welcome.' She gave me some money and sent us on our way. We walked over to Cobaloes in Cuffe Street. This was where we were taken for a special treat as the homemade ice cream there was delicious. Our agenda was to take stock of my financial situation. I knew that I would have to hand over all the money I had collected when I went home. In fact, it was a moment of pride when one or other of us presented our takings to Mam on our First Communion or Confirmation Day because the proceeds were very useful in offsetting the costs.

On the other hand, I reasoned, the money was really mine and would not be there at all only for my big day and, furthermore, it was *my* First Communion. So I dwelled on this idea and aired the ethical problem with Tommy. The compromise we arrived at was to order two Knickerbocker Glories brimming with canned fruit and ice cream and topped with cordial, along with a bottle of Coca-Cola each. Tommy was going to order the newly arrived drink, Pepsi-Cola, but he overheard the conversation of two boys in the shop who were studying an advertisement for the product, which was hanging on the wall. It showed a bottle of the brew floating on a green, icy seascape, ideal for slaking a thirst. One of the boys said to the other, 'I told you that Pepsi was made out of seawater.'

Tommy thought he might be right so we settled for Coke and cried, 'Down the red lane,' as we clinked bottles together in a brotherly toast.

I realised after a few years that to be a benefactor, as I was on my First Communion Day, you had to look after yourself first of all so that you could share in comfort. Discomfort arising from generosity was self-defeating, as the whole idea of money was to bring calm and reassurance to the owner in the first place. So I became an early patron on that basis, and since it was a mutually happy experience, I later adopted it as a life theory. It was different if you were in the bunts with another boy in playing cards for buttons. That relationship meant a solemn covenant to divide all profit and loss equally. I learned the difference between friendship, which depended on love, and partnership, which depended on principle, while playing Don on the three steps of the Iveagh Market.

Anyway, Mam was delighted both for herself and for me when I gave her the money. She said she would buy flowers for the May altar in school when the time came. My big day was coming to a close. I had the warm inner glow of virtue and I felt secure in the little round of our busy household, being nourished by my elders and having an overview on the younger ones. Mam gave me a towel to put across my knee when I was having my tea, and told me to change into my old clothes when I was finished. That left me ready for instant action in the many ways of pleasure available, such as teasing the cats, playing jackstones with Tommy or running races on the street. My day had ended on a high plane, with justice being done in the manner of the distribution of my wealth, and the prospect of starting my new adventure in Francis Street Christian Brothers' School.

Not long afterwards, Tommy came home in a great state of excitement. Francis Street had won the Primary Schools' Gaelic Football Cup and there was to be a parade around our block, up Thomas Street, down Meath Street and back by the Coombe, before returning to the chapel yard at the school. On the day of the march past, I stood on the top step of the Iveagh Market in the crowd with Mam, up on my tiptoes for a good view. In the distance we could see the flags and banners leading the pageant and we could hear the band playing martial music, before the leading float came into view, draped in the green and white school colours.

The captain, Martin Harnett, tall and dark, stood on a height, holding the cup aloft. The rest of the team were jumping up and down on the float, their voices drowned by the band. They were followed by a group of enthusiasts from the school, pupils, teachers and parents, making such a stir that people stopped and clapped, and the traffic pulled in to let the cavalcade pass uninterrupted. Shops closed their doors for a few minutes and the population came out to support the heroes. It was the most exciting sporting moment in my young life. I heard Tommy say to Patsy Moody that Franner always won the cup when Shamrock Rovers won the soccer league, because they both wore green and white hooped jerseys and so had the same luck.

The band was playing away as they approached us, but just before they got to Matt Moore's shop on the corner of Swift's Alley, they stopped, and the only sound to be heard was the marching rhythm of the side drums. Suddenly the boys on the float took up a chant on the beat, the old anthems that I had often heard before:

> *Folly them up, folly them up,*
> *That's the way to win the cup,*
> *Up the field, up the field,*
> *That's the way to win the shield.*

Then to an air,

> *Before the match was over, before the whistle blew,*
> *Harnett got the ball, and up the wing he flew,*
> *And he passed it over to Rooney,*
> *And Rooney put it through,*
> *And that was a goal for Francis Street*
> *Before the whistle blew.*

And rollicking on,

> *It's a rare old thing to pray for,*
> *It's a rare old thing to know,*
> *For all we know, there's going to be a row,*
> *It's enough to make my heart grow saaaad,*
> *We don't care whether we win or lose or draw,*
> *For all the heck we care,*
> *For all we know, there's going to be a row,*
> *And it's good old Franner will be there.*

My mother smiled but her face went serious. She said to Tommy, 'Those songs were sung by our boys in the trenches of Belgium and France. The poor Dublin Fusiliers were massacred in their hundreds. They sang their songs from home to keep their spirits up. So many of them were killed that the black bunting hung from house to house along the Coombe.' I could see the boys from the Liberties then, making ready to fight in the trenches, singing the songs of home to keep up their courage, and dying in faraway fields. They were always spoken of with respect. The poor half-crazy ones who came back damaged by shell-shock and mustard gas were adopted as characters and their eccentricities were laughed off by the locals.

I was curious about the feats of the Royal Dublin Fusiliers and I had often heard the names of the places where they died, but it was only when I met Georgie Smith's dad a few years later that I realised the scale of their misfortune. He told me that he was one of the Old Contemptibles of the Dublin Fusiliers, a name that had been given to them by the

German Kaiser at the start of the First World War. Mr Smith knew all the men who kept us amused by their odd behaviour around the Liberties. Mad Jembo, who kept a lark in a cage and spent the day roaring at passers-by over the half-door of his house in Garden Lane, was reputed to be a survivor of the dreadful nightmare at Gallipoli in 1915. The Fusiliers had been among the first to disembark from the landing ship in Turkey and were slaughtered by machine-gun emplacements on higher ground. Those who were left after Gallipoli were sent into action again and again. At the Somme, they fought hand to hand in the trenches of mud, suffering horrendous losses. Mr Smith was bedridden himself, and said plaintively, 'The Somme was in June 1916, just two months after the Easter Rising. You can't win.' I admired the courage of our local boys who had gone through so much, and I hoped that I could be like them when I grew up.

I started primary school that September. It was a short walk, just a few hundred yards to Francis Street Christian Brothers' School. The school abutted St Nicholas of Myra Church and I could hear the noise of boys having fun in the play yard when I walked past the new buildings in Thomas Davis Street.

The sound gave me a happy, homely impression, and I knew that my brothers, uncles and generations of O'Connors and O'Neills had attended there. It was exciting to think that I was about to have that same experience. I was seven years of age, and serene.

4. FRANNER

It was a damp September day. The chapel yard at the side entrance to Francis Street School was crackling with the excitement of boys back after their holidays. The quieter ones, like me, were slightly overwhelmed by the thought of starting in a new school. 'New boys, go to the top floor, classroom number eight,' a voice was intoning at the door. I stood on the threshold, fingering the crumbling brown brickwork around the doorway behind me and surveying the teeming action inside before taking my first step into this historic place.

Airy dust glinted in a ray of light penetrating the hall and I sniffed twice to confirm the familiar smell of Mansion Polish on buffed linoleum. I could see a distinct sag in the flight of stairs in front of me. The timber panelling on the walls was overwritten with countless names, mostly illegible, etched and inked. Above that, the paintwork had faded to a mottled pale green. I had already visited the little toilet block standing on its own in the play yard, but the smell of Jeyes Fluid and the look of the long urinal wall, recently painted with tar, were not inviting and neither were the dry toilets.

I said to myself that, after all, the school was very old, and I remembered how my brother Tommy and the rest of the boys had been given a day off for its hundredth anniversary celebration some years before. I took a few tentative steps into the hall and held my ground in the jostling horde. On my right I could see into a big classroom. A Christian Brother with a Northern accent was selling school supplies from a tall cupboard that ran the length of the wall, telling the boys not to buy new schoolbooks until they saw the second-hand ones later. A boy beside me started to chant, 'Ham, jam, anything you want, ma'am,' but a teacher gave him a dirty look and told him not to let Brother Devitt hear him. Another brother was stirring black powder into a bowl of water and began to fill the inkwell on each desk with the mixture as I watched.

I recognised a few boys from my old class in Warrenmount School but I wanted to make a new start, so I ignored them. A lad named Seán Ralph, who lived in Marks Alley, said hello, and I knew we would be friends. He had often seen Tommy and me trying to sell bottles to Mr Boland, the junk man in the old Stuart yard. The voice declaimed again that new boys were to go to the top floor, classroom number eight. I dawdled up the stairs under the watchful eye of some bigger pupils, who stood like sentries on the landings, and I had a look into other classrooms as I went. They were all equally run-down, but the boys assembling there filled the place with exuberant life, calling to each other, with one in particular shouting about some dunce who was being kept back in the same class.

I was only one of a group converging on the top floor, and we had to walk through two other classrooms to get to ours. I thought it was a nice secluded nest. All of my primary schooldays were to be spent in that room with just one teacher. This Christian Brother was already in the classroom, standing at his desk and talking to the early arrivals. He looked very young and his pleasant voice was clear and musical, but his accent was unlike any that I had ever heard before.

The man had a round, cheerful face and his hair was doing its best to curl, despite a severe haircut. He exuded vitality, and gave life to his speech with energetic hand gestures. His bright features were decorated with little spectacles, which he removed often and rubbed vigorously with his handkerchief. The shoes were Nugget Black shiny and his galoshes lay in the corner behind him with his umbrella and briefcase. Although he smiled a lot, I could see that his jovial manner did not invite mirth in his audience and there was a certain steel in the way he pursed his lips before he began to speak. In fact, he looked like the manager of Findlaters, the big grocery shop in Thomas Street, inclined to smile and well spoken, but quite conscious of his dignity and the inherent power in his position.

When he thought we had all arrived, he gathered us around the classroom and began to speak: 'Morning, boys, and welcome to Franner. I'm Brother Thomas Devane, your teacher. First, let's have the Morning Offering.' He blessed himself with his left hand, in the way some teachers do, so that his movements mirrored ours. 'O Jesus, through the most pure heart of Mary, I offer to Thee all the prayers, works and sufferings of this day for all the intentions of Thy Sacred Heart, Amen.' I knew the Morning Offering, but I never liked the reference to sufferings very much. In the context of school, I liked it even less.

He resumed speaking, still smiling amicably, but shushing the whisperers by pointing at them without change of tempo. 'I have to tell you a few things. Your morning hours are half nine to half twelve. After dinner it will be two o'clock to four o'clock. If you're staying in school at dinner hour you can have a free bottle of milk and a sandwich from Lawlors of Naas each day, one for each boy. You are not to run or jump on the stairs and no writing with biros because they'll only destroy your handwriting. Now, about your school books. If you want new books, go down to Brother Devitt at the school press during the break – he's the head brother by the way – and if you want second-hand books you can buy them from last year's class. They'll be here today at half twelve. You can make your own bargain and bring in the money tomorrow.'

That's how I met Dan Curran. He was a quiet chap, a couple of years older than me, and we said almost nothing as he showed me his books. The new boy beside me was saying in a loud voice that he was not going to buy a pig in a 'poe', and wanted to see every page of every book he was being offered. Dan's books looked almost pristine and we soon struck a bargain. The occasional margin notes on his English reader were like a useful set of footprints. One of them read vertically, 'ballon baloon, balloon', and a note on the cover of his *Forty Specimen Essays* said: 'See you at Meenans after school.'

This reference to Meenans I could understand. Mrs Meenan's shop in Francis Street was the social centre for those of us who liked a varied culture. She sold sweets and second-hand comics and kept a few slot machines, so that all tastes were catered for. These three items were integrated in a way that any business could usefully copy. If you sold her a second-hand comic for a penny, you could buy sweets or, better for business, lose it on the slots. If you entered with money, you could buy sweets or a comic or both, or try the slots. Nobody had much to spend, but the true merits of this local school of economics arose when you had a little pocket money.

For instance, my uncles Joe and Paddy gave me a penny each as my Saturday money most weeks, but it cost fourpence to get into the Tivoli Cinema. These two pence thus became the object of intense financial speculation and analysis. You could get Cleeves Toffees at a halfpenny each square in Meenans and your tuppence spent on four Cleeves equalled hours of blissful slobbering while trying to pull your jaws apart. On the other hand, if you tried the roulette slot on a two-to-one chance, you might win and increase your store to three pence. With thruppence, Mam would lend another penny to make fourpence, which was what was needed for the Tivoli, but a penny was her limit. If you lost, then you still had a penny, and that would buy sweets in Meenans or possibly a sticky apple in Jack Harold's shop around the corner in Carman's Hall.

Decisions, always decisions! I took the way of danger, usually forsaking the sweets and going straight for the slots. When I lost, I consoled myself with a fizz sherbet or a lucky bag with the remaining penny. But when I won, leaving me with thruppence, the world was mine. I could choose between sweets, comic or the slots again, or maybe borrow that penny to go to the pictures. The combination of choice and risk was very exciting. I never lost that feeling.

When we resumed class in the afternoon, Devane set about organising us, counting heads and comparing numbers with those he had on a list. There were sixty-three boys in all. While we were standing around he noticed that four or five of them, who had grouped together, were barefooted. 'And where are your boots?' he asked.

One boy spoke for them all: 'We haven't got any, sir.' Devane looked surprised but said nothing. I had never seen a child without shoes in Francis Street, except in the height of summer, so these boys were unusual and invited a few stares. After a minute, Devane called one over and told him to stay back when the bell went and I noticed that, within a few days, the bare feet had disappeared from view within sturdy black brogues, which were distinctly uniform in appearance.

'I have to fill in the roll,' Devane said, 'so sit down in alphabetical order. Agree between yourselves and I'll call you up one by one while I'm checking your names on my list. It's all right to speak to the boy next to you when I'm doing this, but keep your voice down.' It meant that we new boys, who were mostly strangers to each other, had to socialise from the beginning, and it also explains how Austin O'Brien, whose pet name was Olly, and Tom O'Neill became two of my friends in the class and how I began a lifelong camaraderie with Seán McQuillan. It was no surprise either that Devane knew all our names by the end of the first week.

Each boy called out, '*Anseo*,' when he heard his name, and went up to the desk at the front of the room. There he had to give his address and previous school for the record while at the same time the whole class could share in this information. Georgie Graham gave an address in Meat Street, using the local pronunciation. 'Do you mean Meath Street?' asked Devane mildly.

'Yes, sir, Meat Street,' replied Georgie.

Another boy said he was from Breffers Street and the puzzled teacher asked him about the name. 'Braithwaite,' he spelled out, which the class knew already.

Devane seemed to have a word of conversation for us all, asking Aloysius Jordan which saint he was named after, and wondering through what event in history might Majoram have become a local name. Halpin was complimented on his head of white curls, and the attention of the class was brought on Alfie Walsh for the quality of the patches darned on the elbows of his short coat, which Devane said was a certain sign that he came from a good home. Other boys, like John McNamara and Francis McPhillips, were already living in the suburban parish of Drimnagh, but most of our group lived within a short walk of the school.

When it came to me, Devane pointed at the back of my hands, smiling a concerned question. My skin was red and cracked from washing too many empty sauce bottles in cold water for selling to the junk man. 'That's oirick,' I said. 'You get it from not drying your hands properly.'

He became animated and jumped to his feet. 'That's the Gaelic word for "chapped",' he said, 'I haven't heard it used in a long time. I used to get that myself sometimes when I went fishing with my father.' He stood up, and wrote on the blackboard: *oighreach = chapped or chafed.* 'It's amazing that the word is still in use here. Irish hasn't been spoken in Dublin for a hundred and fifty years.' I told him that it was the word we used at home to describe skin roughened by dampness and that Mushatt's chemist shop sold the ointment for it.

When he had finished the roll and the class was settled in, Devane said, 'We're going to have twenty minutes of mental arithmetic each day, so be on the *qui vive.* There will be a paper on it in the Primary Exam and I want you all to be very good at this.' I knew from the emphatic way he spoke that I had better concentrate on the subject as I did not want to be the first to test his patience. Anyway, I liked mental arithmetic and I often jousted with Mam at home because she was adept at doing sums in her head from her shop experience. He jumped up, all action, and started off, 'What's seventimesthirteen? Saywhenyouhaveit.' This was going to be great. Competition already, I thought, as some hands flew up along with my own.

When we had our new books with us on the following day, he took the measure of the class at English language, giving each boy a few paragraphs to read, passing quickly over those who were proficient and allowing others more time. Within a few more days, everyone in the class had been tested in English and Irish, their familiarity or otherwise with arithmetic tables had been revealed and our knowledge of the Precepts of the Church had been given a full airing.

But it wasn't all work. To our initial amazement, Devane spontaneously broke into song once in a while and invited us to join him. '*Gaudeamus*,' he would cry, looking for volunteers to sing or tell a story. He often led the way himself with this cheerful folk shanty about a mermaid:

> *On Friday morn as we set sail,*
> *And our ship not far from the land;*
> *We there did spy a pretty, pretty maid,*
> *With a comb and a glass in her hand, her hand,*
> *   her hand,*
> *With a comb and a glass in her hand.*

Then it was every boy for himself in the chorus!

> *For the raging seas did roar, did roar,*
> *And the stormy winds did blow,*
> *And we jolly sailor boys were up, up aloft,*
> *And the landlubbers lying down below, below,*
> *   below,*
> *And the landlubbers lying down below.*

And so it was that our class settled down into a happy routine of learning and a little lighthearted fun, while the first term and the first years slipped by without notice under the temperate control of Brother Thomas Devane, once known as Timothy Devane, of Station Row, Dingle, County Kerry. In the words of the Psalmist, the boundary lines had fallen for me in pleasant places and a delightful inheritance was mine, so there was no thought of the morrow.

As time passed, I realised that there was an indefinable quality of reserve in the way Devane treated us. He understood us as a group but, as individuals, the relationship was superficial, and he declined to identify with us beyond the field of learning. He was our advocate, willing to pass on his knowledge in proportion to our capacity to absorb it during school hours, and shaping our morality by his example, but he made no attempt to be a surrogate parent, despite his warmth, and I came to regret this.

When I had just gone eleven years of age I had an attack of unsightly and sore boils on my neck, combined with a chest infection. 'Boils are caused by a bacterium known as Staph getting through a break in the skin and then into a hair follicle,' said Dr Fitzpatrick, adding that they would take two weeks to heal. No number of hot poultices and Vick applications on the chest made any difference and I was pleased to languish for a fortnight until I improved. I could have gone back to school then, but the summer holiday was just on us so Mam decided that I might as well be completely rid of the problem and allowed me to take the rest of the week off.

When we came back to class after the holiday, Devane was talking to a stranger at his desk and addressing him in a serious way as 'Mr McCarthy'. The two of them leaned over the attendance roll, examining it intently and murmuring together. When they stood up, Devane pointed quickly in my direction and peered at me. I stared back, beginning to fear what might be happening. Mr McCarthy looked at me coldly and I quaked. I guessed he was a school attendance officer, and what I knew about them I did not like. When the stranger had gone, Devane called me up to him and calmly told me that I might be sent away to an Industrial School as I had been absent for three weeks.

I was demoralised by his cool acceptance of that possibility and it was obvious to me that he had said little in my defence. I tried to hide my tears. Devane kept his distance and did not attempt to lessen my anxiety, and I was surprised at his acquiescence in my possible banishment. I had heard of Artane Industrial School and I had played football against their boys in the Primary School League, feeling sorry for them. And now it was my turn! I went home in a terrible state thinking about my little friend Stephen in Warrenmount School and hoping they would not take me away.

Mam told me not to worry and Dad said it was a funny old school where they could read out your English composition in class one week and threaten the State on you in the next, while at the same time the whole school had closed down for the teachers' strike without thought for the children. He took time off work to see Devane and the subject never came up for discussion again.

On the other hand, in matters of shaping our ethics, Devane had a style of his own. It was not just a matter of our being told what was moral, but he had the Kerry gift of weaving it into a story. One day Father Byrne came into our class on a pastoral visit to say his usual few words, this time on the importance of not being late for Mass. When he was gone, Devane continued the lecture with a little homily of his own on the same subject. 'For example, boys, you will sometimes see a person, usually a young girl in high heels and lipstick, going up for Communion, deliberately being a little late so as to make herself the centre of attention. That is very poor behaviour.'

We knew what he meant. When Communion was being given out, a queue would form. When the people had received, the priest would look intently down the aisle to see if there were any latecomers before returning the ciborium of wafers to the tabernacle. Sometimes there *were* such people, and their lone progress towards the altar would certainly become the centre of attention for many. Of course we had all seen that kind of shameful carry-on and we sighed and nodded our pious agreement with Devane's insight. He started to write on the blackboard but, after a few minutes, turned to us again, saying, 'Boys, I was thinking about what I said just now. I was being uncharitable when I spoke that way about the girl and I shouldn't have said it. She might have had a sick mother to look after and she might have made a special effort to get to Mass, and being late was not her fault. No, I was not being very charitable. I'm sorry about that.'

The class was silent and I was astonished. We, who had been decrying the girl's behaviour in the first place, now had to admit that what he said was possible and, coming from him, it had the power of impeccable logic. That was his subtle way of impressing the virtue of charity on the whole group. What he said had a lasting effect on me and I understood with enduring clarity that initial impressions were not always correct. When I thought about it afterwards, I realised that Devane's apology was the first I had ever heard from an adult directed towards a child. I wondered if he had set out deliberately to tell the story in the way he had.

After the episode of the school attendance officer, I settled down in the class with a resolve not to miss school and to work hard, but grief came again from a different source. During the summer, Uncle Joe had taken Nannie, Eileen and me on a motor-car outing to Enniskerry. Nannie had not been very well on the trip and her respiratory condition had worsened after that, and she became bedridden.

Joe was sombre those days. Aunt Molly and Eileen were always in attendance on poor Nannie. Mam visited every day as usual, but despite all the medical care and family efforts, Nannie sank lower each day. Finally, when I ran home from school as usual one dinner hour, I was met by Joe. He was very upset and told me that Nannie had passed away. I was sad myself, and sat alone on the chopping block in the cellar to come to terms with her loss.

I thought about her kindness and how she was so often the centre of conversation in the house, although out of sight in her bedroom. Life would be so different without her. I remembered the time that Mam had let me go to the Spring Show in Ballsbridge one year and I had enlisted myself in the St John Ambulance Brigade of Ireland as a trainee cadet in first aid. When I told Mam what I had done she had smiled and said there was something fizzing inside me and she did not know what it was. She was not so pleased when she heard that I needed a uniform.

Nannie declared that she would pay for my uniform, provided Mam did not mind my going into the city headquarters of the Brigade in Strand Street every

Wednesday night on my own for my classes in first aid. As a result, I was soon fitted out in the smart black and grey uniform of a cadet in St Patrick's Division. How I flaunted that streamered black beret, worn over the left eye, per the rules, and there never was a silver buckle more burnished than the one on my belt! I laughed to myself when I remembered how I had been allowed to go on duty by Dr Rock to the football matches in Parnell Park under the supervision of Corporal Savage, a good-natured redheaded Dubliner who could tie a reef knot in a St John's sling with his eyes closed. There, rival football teams and spectators provided a steady demand for first aid, although my own contribution was confined to administering sal volatile, smelling salts, as directed by my superior officer in the field. Nannie had even paid for my brown sandals to be dyed black in Lynch's shoe-repair shop. She was really lovely and I would miss her.

When I came up from the cellar, Joe told me in a purposeful way that I could go to the funeral with him. Nannie was buried two days later in Glasnevin Cemetery. Every member of the family mourned in their own way, because we all knew that changes after her death were inevitable. Joe had given up his job as a radio operator in the Merchant Navy many years before to look after the shop when his father died. Her passing made it possible for him to consider furthering his career in political activity. Molly and Eileen continued to come in from the Northside every day to help in the shop, but the heart of 15 Francis Street had been stilled, and I knew from their demeanour that things would never be the same.

The funeral party stopped off for a drink on the way home and, after a while, Joe started to talk fondly about his mother. 'She was a Howlett from New Row and when she married Daddy he set her up in a little provisions shop of her own in Francis Street. When the present house with its butcher's shop came up for sale in 1913, she bought it herself. D'ye know? She paid two hundred and thirty pounds for it in those days, and the deposit was just one pound as between Mr Meredith and her being neighbours.'

As Joe told it, just at the very time that Nannie had bought the house, the Liberties was in turmoil because of the lockout of workers by the employers. In Cornmarket, many men from our locality had attacked the trams, throwing stones and bottles, and blocked the tracks in protest at strikebreaking. Baton charges were made in Francis Street and Christchurch and, indeed, all across Dublin. Policemen and civilians were injured, and in one infamous incident in O'Connell Street, two men had died as a result of police overreaction. Mam told me the rest later on.

There was no one to represent general operatives, who had no trade, except the new Irish Transport and General Workers' Union founded by Jim Larkin. Numerous employers were determined to crush its development and some big companies, like Jacob's Biscuits, locked out their workers if they joined. The strikers and their families had six months of terrible hardship before the men and women were left with no alternative but to go back to work.

Nannie sympathised with them and was outraged by the behaviour of the employers, so much so that she made up her mind that her new butcher's shop would cater for the poor by stocking the cheaper cuts of pork and by giving the locals as much credit as possible.

She made no real distinction between the poor and the working classes. To her, the poor were the widowed, the unemployed and the sick, and the working classes were families where the man had employment but was always at risk of losing his job anyway. In that way the two categories were almost interchangeable. The shopkeepers and the property owners were all well able to take care of themselves. During the strike, the workers and their families suffered very badly, and she did what she could for her neighbours.

After Nannie's death, Joe got more involved in his work for Fianna Fáil and in due course became its national organiser. In fact, he was made a senator in later life. He always seemed to have dozens of letters for me to post and spent most nights on voluntary work or down the country on by-election business. One day when I came home from school, he told me about the India Mutiny and asked me to take a flag box around the neighbouring shops in a collection for the survivors.

Seventy men of the Connaught Rangers in the British Army in India had mutinied in 1920 because of the activities of the Black and Tans in Ireland. They had replaced the Union Flag with the Irish Tricolour in their barracks and refused to obey orders. Their leader, Private James Daly, who was only twenty-two years old, was executed and the others were imprisoned after two soldiers were shot dead in defending the armoury. I had to report to Joe how each shop had supported the collection, which went very well, although I was told to get out of Norton's grocery, where young Mr Norton said he didn't support such a cause.

Joe took a note of those who had and hadn't bought a flag. When I asked him what the information was for, he said it would be useful to know where support might come from in the next election, as his party was Republican and those who had supported the flag day were likely to vote for them. He impressed on me to take notice of what went on around me in the Liberties, saying I could learn lessons for life there. I thought I knew what he meant.

I was on the way up to the shop one day after school when I stopped to have a look at the boys playing Pontoon for buttons on the steps of the Iveagh Market. Pontoon, or Ponner, was a favourite card game, and gave an extra thrill because it was a quick gamble, like playing the slots. You could play Ponner recklessly or craftily but, no matter what your approach, it was still a game of chance, and you could make or lose a fortune in buttons very quickly. I was scunched myself, having lost my all on the previous day's play.

Billy Delamere had the advantage of being the banker and, since each person on box made his own rules on betting limits, he had stipulated that there was to be no limit to a bet on aces, which was very daring, because the odds favoured the holder of an ace. In fact, Pat O'Grady had been dealt two aces in the same game, and had split them to make two separate hands, both of which had Pontoon, so that only the banker's Pontoon could beat him. With those cards, Pat was nearly invincible. There were twenty buttons at stake on each hand. Delamere, on box, faced ruin if he lost, and began to chant his mantra to the gods in a singsong voice, 'Moaney oh, macravey oh, that you make me lucky oh.' When he turned his first card over, it was an ace, and when he dealt himself the second card, it was the Jack of Diamonds.

This gave him the call of Ponner, which he promptly shouted, as nothing could beat those cards. He swept the board, including the buttons piled on both of Pat O'Grady's hands, but Pat took it manfully. It was said about him that recently he had adopted a cool approach to playing whether he won or lost. His attitude now was proof of this, even if his heart was breaking. It was not always that way. Only a few months before I had seen him crying after losing. There was silent contempt for him among the players at the time, although Pat was very young. Now here he was, dealing with losses without a word.

He made such an impression on me that I remembered Uncle John quoting that the Battle of Waterloo was won on the playing fields of Eton. I compared this to our school in the Liberties. Nobody knew or cared about it except those who went there, and yet it had ways of teaching boys how to bear up to present loss in preparation for future hardship. In this way, it was just as effective as any English academy.

Life went on after Nannie died. Relations and friends called in to pay their respects to Joe for months afterwards. I was there one dinner hour when Uncle John called in. He had taken over the chimney-contracting business when Granddad died and had developed it into a successful enterprise. He never dirtied his hands himself, but had good contacts with the local council and the Board of Works, and he certainly enjoyed the profits of his business. He was a great lover of the sporting outdoor life and today he had brought in some snipe he had shot on Silseán Mountain as a present for Eileen. They were wrapped in bloody brown paper, which he opened to show off his bag. Inside, there were two bedraggled little creatures, stiff and cold, their plumage still gleaming. Eileen took one look and politely declined the present, so John said he would give them to his dogs.

Later I told Uncle Bartle about what happened and he said that you could get worse than that. 'There's a man in America who's world famous for his paintings of birds. His name is Audubon. Do you know what he does?' I had to say no, so Bartle replied triumphantly, 'He shoots the birds, and then paints them, and after that he eats them, the savage. That man would eat any bird going, be it crows, sparrows or robins, anything.' Bartle was still indignant when we settled down to admire his own painting of parrots and lovebirds, executed with real style on a timber fire screen, although he had to explain the joke to me when he smiled and said, 'Now this is the real macaw.'

On the following day, Uncle Rory called into the shop with a beautiful girl. Her name was Marie Harte and she was the brightest person I had ever seen in 15 Francis Street. Her suit was blue to match her eyes, while her mouth was a smashing red. I gazed at her, fascinated by the way her youth made the dull kitchen brighter. She was Rory's fiancée and was being introduced into the family before the wedding. It reminded me of my Communion Day, the way she was shown off, but she was like a Christmas decoration in that house, which was becoming more threadbare with every passing year. Mam was keeping her distance from

Rory because of something he had said on his last visit. Then he had mentioned that while he was in St Patrick's Park he had seen a girl let her big dog off the lead. When Rory told her that the dog shouldn't be on the loose, the girl apparently said that she would put *him* on a lead if he wasn't careful. I thought it was a real threat at the time, but Rory was laughing, almost as if he'd enjoy it.

One Saturday morning, having time to spare, I went across to see if I could do any messages for my O'Connor grandparents and to listen to Granddad's wisdom, which he freely imparted. 'Now, if anyone asks you a question, answer them at your discretion and then ask them the same question and see how they like it. They won't be long shutting up.' He had an opinion on most things and I revered his views.

Today his wants were few. 'Will you go over to Bertie O'Connor for my tobacco and on down to Caulfield's nurseries in Dame Street for a pint of canary seed for the bird,' he said. 'And on your way can you call into High Street with that coat and have it mended.' This mending was done by two old ladies who did needlework behind the counter of their little shop opposite St Audoen's Protestant Church. They seemed to be sisters and were such gentle creatures. The last time I'd seen them I had noticed that one of them was on crutches with her leg in plaster of Paris and I wondered how long more they could keep going. However, when I got there, the same lady was making a collar for a shirt from the cannibalised tail of the same garment. She took the coat and gave instant advice on what needed to be done. I was sent back to tell Granddad that the only way they could mend the rip invisibly was to darn it, then turn the coat altogether. On the way to Caulfields I saw my sister Peggy in Gannon's fruit shop, trying to scrounge some of the lengths of rope they used to hold the crates of oranges together so that she could use them to make a swing on the lamppost for herself and Mary Durney.

While coming back down Francis Street I met Michael Keating, whose family owned the Hazelhatch Dairy. He was emerging from Johnny Fox's barbershop, but when I was sent up there for a haircut a few weeks later, the shop was closed for good. I could hear the dealers outside Madigans pub calling to each other about the noise of the new bells of the Catholic church in Meath Street. These had been set to peal out the Lourdes hymn 'The Bells of the Angelus' every quarter of an hour, but this was changed before very long. When I left in the bird seed, Granddad was busy cleaning his stand of six pipes, but I still had things to do anyway. I had to run down to Poutch's workshop in Bonham Street to leave in Dad's broken bandsaw to be brazed, set and sharpened for a start.

Joe wanted a few postcards from Barrys in Meath Street so the easiest way back from there was down Engine Alley and around by Matt Moore's shop. I joined a crowd looking at a marvellous mosaic, designed in coloured tiles, which was coming to life under his shop window. It showed cows' heads and country scenes far from Francis Street, and some people said that it was just to bring Mr Moore notice because he was going up for the elections. Joe said that the mosaic was Matt's personal Valley of the Kings, and it was as good as anything in Egypt. Indeed, that mosaic was still there forty years after the shop had become a ruin but disappeared quite recently in the face of some developer's ambition.

By now it was July 1950. I had just turned twelve years old and school was about to break up for the summer holidays. When we returned in September it would be the beginning of our last year in primary school, as Francis Street Christian Brothers' School only went to School Certificate level. Ahead of us lay a year of hard study, mock examinations and, finally, the Primary Certificate Examination. The result of this would influence, if not decide, the direction of our future lives and careers.

But at this moment, that was a year – a whole lifetime – away and the only immediate concern was to fill the delightful weeks of freedom that lay ahead. For now, the future could take care of itself.

PART 2:

Interludes

Life for this Liberties schoolboy wasn't all school. There were random diversions and activities that brought their own sweetness and fulfilment to an impressionable boy and left unforgettable memories. It is from them that these Interludes are drawn, concerning Holidays, Sport, Music and Nature in the Liberties, followed by Family Voices.

5. SOUTH OF FRANCE-CIS STREET

'Now, boys,' Brother Devane was saying to our class, 'you're off on holidays from school today, and I'll be on the train for Kerry tomorrow, thanks be to God! But remember to read something every day during the break. I don't care what you read, comics or otherwise, but read you must.' As he spoke, his face shone on us with benevolence and he was well aware that most of us would not be travelling far.

'And don't forget your prayers,' he went on. 'Pray to the Virgin Mary in all temptation, and pray for the beatification of Pope Pius the Tenth, who came from a poor family himself, and I'll see you all in September.' How he loved that pope; he talked about him so often that I thought they must be related. Just then, the bell rang for four o'clock. Devane reached for his galoshes, asked us where he had left his gamp, and got ready to walk back to the Christian Brothers' Residence in Synge Street, where he lived.

The rest of us made a rush to dig out our damp coats from the whiffy pile hanging at the back of the classroom. Once Devane was gone, some of the classroom Michelangelos perfected their initials on the patinated wall panelling, but there was a general stampede to get away as fast as we could.

When summer holiday time came to the Liberties I had no notion of travelling anywhere, and neither did my parents. The fact was that, unlike some of my classmates, all of my uncles and aunts lived in Dublin. I knew this for certain because I had already asked the question at home. Of course, I did have relations in Canada and Australia, and I often bragged of how well they were doing, with farms as big as the Phoenix Park, and hinted at the magnificent holiday we might one day enjoy on their lands.

So I swallowed my jealousy when McNamara and O'Neill, in school, talked delightedly about things like the sweet smell of hay on the uncle's farm in Kerry, or spoke knowledgeably about the behaviour of bulls and cows. I convinced myself that such agricultural activity was not as enjoyable as rambling anywhere I chose in the Liberties, or as exciting as the adventures *I* could have, using our little domain as a base. However, the real truth was that holiday decisions were easy for us denizens of Francis Street, because the subject simply did not arise.

My pal Olly dismissed country holidays with bravado, claiming that the city ended at the South Dublin Union, otherwise known as Number One James Street, and anywhere beyond that was 'The Bog of Allen'. I was more influenced by Granddad, whose view was that the whole country was only four hundred miles long, and that the Irish were all one tribe, even if we ourselves were privileged to live in the independent republic of Francis Street. To me, that philosophy of innate tolerance was an integral part of our tradition.

Soon after, we had one of those periods of sunny weather that fill childhood summer memories. I was running everywhere in bare feet, taking the leap across Madden's Court in one jump, or racing Olly down the forty steps in High Street. St Audoen's Park, opposite the entrance to the church, was haunted by the Green Lady, so we stood under a tree and called on her to show herself. 'Green Lady, Green Lady, come down to us, appear to us if you're here.' The birds stopped singing, and the leaves on the trees shivered, and so did we because we could feel her presence.

The swing boats in the little grassy play space in Pimlico were great fun, but hard to get going on, as the children from the immediate neighbourhood were very clannish. St Patrick's Park was better. From there we could see the Bayno and it was only a few steps to the bird market on a Sunday morning. We could sail paper boats in the fountain, make daisy chains on the grass, or roll down the weedy slope to the cathedral railings. The barman in Ruttledge's pub, the only house on Canon Street, would always oblige with a drink of water, and a sticky apple made a delightful picnic. Uncle Joe told me that Canon Street was the shortest street in Dublin, and that the rest of it had disappeared when the magnificently named Lousy Acre was demolished and became the site of St Patrick's Park.

Olly had a bike, but cycling was a dangerous sport on Thomas Street, because the tram tracks were just the right width for trapping a bicycle wheel, and a toss was certain when that happened. That did not stop him giving me a crossbar up to the Grand Canal Harbour at James's Street to see the turf being unloaded from the canal boats arriving from the midlands. We stayed to admire the little railway carriages darting out of the arched doorways of the Guinness Brewery on to the street, like the ghost train at a carnival, carrying materials from building to building.

I convinced myself that this was better than any farm in Kerry, but I sometimes thought wistfully about Mam's stories of when she was a child going on family holidays to a rented house in Skerries for the month of August. I knew there was no chance of that happening with us. When I said that to my brother Billy, he laughed sarcastically and told me not to forget that we were all off on holiday to the South of France-cis Street on the 'first of Septober' and to quit moaning. I made up my mind that I was well off as things were, and I soon stopped making gloomy comparisons.

Not long after that, Martha told me that the whole family was going to Sandymount Strand the next day, as Mam said she was feeling the heat and would love a little break. Martha and I were great pals. She was next to me in age, and let me read her poetry books from school. I had rarely been to the seaside and a glimpse of the ocean was not an everyday event, so going to Sandymount Strand was a bit like going to a Tarzan film, truly exotic and exciting to imagine. Martha explained the fine points about the tides and the cockles that marked their own location on the sand. However, there were essential preparations to be made.

Early on the morning of the expedition, Tommy and

I volunteered to make sand-shovels in the manner of the Liberties. We got a stock of empty tin cans, and chopped some sticks off the longest log we could find in the cellar. Then down to the nearest bus stop on the Coombe. The stick was placed in the can and wedged under the back wheel of the first bus to stop. When the bus rolled forward it flattened the can. Behold! Our disposable shovels.

Mam was wrapping the jam sandwiches when we got in, and I saw that she had used the awful cornflour butter that Granny O'Connor had shown her how to make as a spread. Nell would be going off on a hike to the Hellfire Club with her pal, Nora Kinsella. Billy, as usual, was set for spending the day with his Alice. Tommy had clicked with Maura Meates, and was busy typing out the words of the song 'I Know Why, And So Do You' for her. The old Underwood was a present from Uncle Joe, which was surplus to his admin needs and had been very useful in preparing my eldest sister Nell for her first office job. The ribbon was worn through, and so the script was a study in black and red, which gave a lurid undertone to his overtures.

Peggy was engrossed in finishing the embroidery on a headscarf to a design that had to be ironed on to the fabric. It was a study of a pastoral scene, a thatched cottage and accompanying garden in kaleidoscope colouring, the splendour of which only existed in the artist's imagination. That left six of us and the baby, plus Mam and Dad, so I roughly divided the number of sandwiches on the table by eight, and found it satisfactory. Martha would fetch along her books to read, and Dad would take the *Reader's Digest*, as he was intent on increasing his word power. I proposed to learn the words of the song 'I'm My Own Grandpa', which I had got in a lucky bag in Meenans, as a party piece. The words fascinated me as they showed conclusively that it was possible for a man to be his own grandpa when a son marries a widow and his father marries the widow's daughter.

Martha sat beside me on the bus, laughing as usual. I showed her the Liberties way of wiping your snotty nose in decent company without benefit of handkerchief. First, you had to remember the words, 'There's a soldier over there', followed by 'with stripes down there'. On pointing at the soldier 'over there', you wiped your nose with the back of the hand in passing, and when describing where the stripes were, on the side of the leg, you deposited the result on your trousers. Martha did not get it at first, but I persisted until she had learned the choreography. Of course, nothing would please her then but to compare the hankies we had been given for the day. They were both of very fine material, pale blue in colour, roughly cut from the same garment, with an inch of elastic still caught in a hem on Martha's. I told her it was some fine snot rag.

As we set out through town, Mam pointed out Lucky Coady in College Street, where they sold tickets for the Irish Hospitals Sweepstake with great success. She started to say something about it, but stopped when Dad looked at her. She told us later that it reminded her of when they had been in Montréal and thought she had won a Sweepstake prize. We got off the bus at Trinity College, and as we walked across O'Connell Bridge the tide was out, leaving a few little streams running on the black bed of the River Liffey. Martha said it smelt like the stink bombs the boys made by setting fire to rolls of film, and Dad said it was about time the mills in Clondalkin and Crumlin Valley did their bit to clean up the filthy water left behind after paper-making before discharging it into the rivers.

On O'Connell Bridge, beggars huddled from the wind at the solid sections of the parapet wall. Little children were throwing papers into the Liffey, laughing and shouting. One of them was selling newspapers, calling out, '*Herally Mail*,' although he had only the *Irish Press* to sell. His face was gaunt, and he was as thin as could be, but he was laughing too. I found it hard to understand what they were saying because they spoke so fast, and I saw them pointing at a drunken man and calling him 'Gobee the wall' and 'Froggy' because of his croaking voice. A street photographer had set up his tripod camera on the bridge and he was assuring a young couple that all they had to do was to take their photograph home and run it under the tap to bring up the colour.

Dad pointed out the clock at a big store, and told us that it was one of the best-known landmarks in Ireland. This was where country people arranged to meet for dates. They would say, 'Under the clock at Clerys,' and no further directions were needed. Right enough, it was approaching the top of the hour, and a few men and women were gathered there, looking up and down the street as if waiting for a bus. Martha and I were curious about the bullet hole in the breasts of two of the winged ladies on the O'Connell statue but had not got the nerve to ask what had happened to them.

We stood at the stop outside Clerys until the number 2 bus bound for Sandymount Strand screeched slowly to a halt. The hold under the stairs was already full and the conductor stood back as we tried to crowd on. 'Four standing,' he said, but when we all hesitated, he spoke the magic words I had often heard before. 'Are all these kids yours?' When he heard the answer, he stood back in awe as he waved us aboard, allowing Mam to leave the go-car on the platform. I knew that Mam used family numbers to advantage, whether it was in the Iveagh Market bargaining with Hughie Matthews on the price of meat, or organising credit in a shop. I heard her say more than once that she would not be running away with a Highlander with her big family, giving the correct impression that the large clan was good security for her borrowings.

Everyone seemed to be happy. Four young men taking up the front seats of the bus started to sing in harmony about having to get out and get under their automobile, and then one of them turned around and asked for a song. A man with two kids on his knee obliged with 'Ireland, Mother Ireland'. Martha and I thought he was great, and fit for the Queen's Theatre. Dad was his usual watchful self, keeping an eye on everything and all of us, to make sure there was no messing. A woman sang a song about tiptoeing through the tulips, and a man without a note in his head insisted on singing although his wife commanded him loudly not to.

The conductor called out the names of the stops as we got closer, and at Sandymount Green we were poised for exit. As we turned the corner on to the coast road, the busload of us saw the sea at the same time and gave a huge roar of approval. The tide was out, and the glorious vista of the sandy beach stretched to the horizon. Mam sent Martha and me ahead to stake a claim on a site near the exit, as it seemed that the crowds could be like prospectors at a gold mine. By walking on the wide boundary wall we were able to skip past the throngs at the Martello Tower. By the time the rest of the family had come down the few narrow steps on to the strand we were pacing our claim.

We settled for a site not too far from the sea wall, as Dad said that the tide could sneak in around by the Bull Wall and get in behind us if we went out too far on the strand. Mam told us to offer up a prayer for the Prizeman family, neighbours in Francis Street, whose little boy Patrick had disappeared in a second on this beach and whose body was recovered a few days later at Dún Laoghaire pier. Stones were put on the sand to mark the corners of our boundary and we all crowded on to this patch. Mam laid out a blanket for comfort, and we set up camp. The sun shone as hoped. The baby was put down on the blanket between two pillows with an umbrella to keep him in the shade. Soon it was time for a swim, which was a euphemism for a paddle in a warm pool as the tide was still out, but we practised skimming flat rocks on the water, which was great fun.

It was obvious that many an underwear drawer had been raided for the occasion, their contents doing duty as bathing togs. Afterwards, we made sandcastles with our shovels or dug for cockles under Martha's direction where the telltale grooves and depressions marked where they had burrowed into the sand. Soon after, it was time to eat. The big numbers of people must have given notice to the battalions of flies and wasps in the vicinity. We were making more jam sandwiches, so we were in the front line. Wasps dropped in on us and the sticky pot was covered with them.

Even the sandwiches had to be inspected before every bite.

Hordes of flies and bluebottles shared the party. There was sand everywhere, but we did not mind the gritty taste, as nothing could interfere with the delight of being there. I could not remember if I had ever been taken anywhere with both my parents before, although they gave us great freedom to go places on our own.

Dealers had set up their tents at the sea wall by the Tower just beside us. They were selling boiling water, so that you could make your own tea. Dad went off for a while to have a bottle of stout, but Mam said he was very good and would be back in a few minutes.

We were much quieter on the way home, and the baby fell asleep. The woman next to us said the rest would be the crowning of the babby, and asked about the blue stain of gentian violet on his lips. Mam told her that it was an old cure for thrush.

Going to bed that night, we asked Mam to sing our favourite bedtime song before we fell asleep. It was 'This Little Piggy Went To Market', with a special ending she had learned from her own mother in the Liberties:

> How I recall my dear old mother,
> Putting me to bed,
> Go to sleep she said,
> You're my own little curly head,
> But this little piggy was a bad little piggy
> And he cried all the way home,
> That's the part that I'll recall, wherever I roam,
> And I hope and pray, some day I'll say,

To a cute little girlie of my own,
That this little piggy was a bad little piggy,
And he cried all the way home.

God bless her way of making happy memories from so little.

The month of July came, and I found myself on a train on the way to the Conamara Gaeltacht to improve my Irish, courtesy of a scholarship from Dad's union. We were met at the railway station in Galway and taken by bus to Spiddal where Pádraic Costello from the host family collected three of us on his pony and trap. Two men were making conversation over the half-door of a house beside a pub called Tí Tim Johnny in the main street. Pádraic explained that the one who lived there was Martin Thornton, and he had been a great boxer in his time. 'The Connemara Crusher,' he said with a smile. 'He beat Freddie Mills for the European title.' All I saw was just another unkempt, boozy man who looked in need of help, like other poor victims I had sometimes seen in the Liberties.

We travelled the few miles to Pádraic's house at quite a canter. We had been assigned to the home of Máire Ní Choisdealbha, or Máire Costello, his mother. That led to my first introduction to Baile na mBrabhach, named Ballinabrough in English, a tiny hamlet two miles up a boreen off the coast road in Inverin. Máire was a lovely lady, with silver hair and a gentle voice, whose husband had died some years before.

I was one of hundreds of children staying in the Gaeltacht, including some I recognised from the Liberties, but I found straight away that I seemed to have a natural rapport with the Costellos. The family had a frugal way of living, and a happy character that reminded me of home, and I loved my conversations with Máire, the *Bean a' tí*, or housewife. Her husband had died leaving her with ten children, 'A boy and a girl repeated five times,' as she remarked. Some of the family were living at home and others in Boston, but she just got on with life in an uncomplaining way, and I soon grew fond of her. She explained things to me rather like Granddad O'Connor did, ignoring my age.

Pádraic showed me their glasshouse, which was part of a government scheme to promote the growing of tomatoes as a crop in the Gaeltacht. Unfortunately, the produce all ripened at the same time, causing a glut on the market. It seemed that Pádraic would have made just as much money from selling the lorry loads of turf that he had used in keeping the glasshouse boiler going during the winter.

Máire was amused by my interest in the way they lived. She allowed me to eat with her children rather than with the other boys, who were given a more balanced diet than the Costellos themselves had. The family dinner was usually a mound of potatoes spread in the middle of the table, with liver or a river fish for company. Sometimes she would fondly call me Seán Dubh, or dark-haired Seán. She reminded me of my own mother in the way she would occasionally touch my hair as she passed me while clearing the table.

I asked Máire one day, in a slightly condescending way, if she had ever been to Dublin. She said crisply that she hadn't, but before I had time to imagine how such a catastrophe could happen, she asked me if I had ever been to America. I was trumped, and no mistake, but that was not all. 'Oh, yes,' she said, 'I go down to Shannon every spring and fly to Boston to see the Yanks, and that's why I never get to Dublin.' I laughed to myself for starting this.

'Now,' she said, 'have you ever seen central heating in a home? It's wonderful in Boston. All the equipment is kept in the basement, a big boiler, and pipes going everywhere.' I had never seen central heating anywhere, and I thought of our open fires with the wet logs, smoky coal and the newspapers stretched across the fireplace to make a draught. 'And,' she says, 'they have tuna in cans. Have you ever seen that?' No, I had not, and indeed did not know what a tuna was. She teased me a bit more until she was certain that I had learned manners, and after that we got on even better.

One day I had a letter from Cousin Eileen, with important news. The main thing was that she enclosed a postal order for half a crown, but it also contained information about a baby girl, newly born. I was delighted for Eileen and Jack Nesbitt, her husband. I saw Eileen every day in the shop, and I loved her vivacity. In fact, I thought for an envious moment what a great life this only baby would have but then, after all, I had my brothers and sisters and I would not have swapped them for anything.

The couple had longed for children, so this information about the baby was great news, and I knew it would bring Eileen joy. I wrote to say how pleased I was for her, and asked what was she going to call the little girl, and who would stand for her at the baptism. I got no reply, and just got on with my holiday.

I helped to cut the hay by hand with a sickle while Pádraic used the scythe, and I enjoyed the wild honey when they found a hive in the clover. They had tiny rock-filled fields, none of them abutting each other. Ballinabrough had neither electricity nor running water. It was candles and oil lamps for light, and Joe Donohue's well for the sweetest *uisce*. Máire cooked and made bread for the household on a huge open turf fire, but the food for the visiting children was prepared on a little bottled-gas stove.

It seemed very like home in the sense that there was little recognition of deprivation, and a great will to just carry on. It was a way of life, and I never heard complaints, which again gave me the feeling of having things in common with the Costellos. The boys from Dublin talked about the fun at the *céilí* and such things as a first kiss, but I was far too shy to get involved in amorous adventures. In any event Devane had warned us so often that there were more people in Hell for sins of impurity than any other sin that I was afraid to even contemplate such behaviour.

When I got home at the end of the month there was a pram behind our kitchen door. A lovely little baby girl lay in it, and she gripped my finger when I offered mine. 'Say hello to your little sister,' Mam said, to my amazement, as I had been given no notice of this event. I realised then that the baby Eileen had written about was actually my sister, Mam's thirteenth child. She was to be called Elizabeth Carmel, or Eily for short, after the Colleen Bawn, the heroine of the opera *The Lily of Killarney*. My brother Joe said the three of us were special pals because there was exactly six days between each of our birthdays, all in July.

Well, that was true, but Eily and I never had a conversation until she was seven years of age. We often smiled benignly at each other and recognised our mutual existence, but she was nearly thirteen years younger than me, and with five other children dividing us, conversation just didn't happen. When she was seven, she asked me a simple question about whether Mam was in or out, and that moment of our first exchange is still rooted in my psyche. Mam was forty-seven years of age when Eily was born. Any time I meet Eily now, I remember the dear friends of mine in Conamara who took a little boy from the Liberties to their hearts, and how lovely it was, and still is, to visit Baile na mBrabhach where Máire's children's grandchildren live to this day in the same house as I first stayed.

A little while after that, word got around that Lambs Jams were looking for fruit-pickers on their farm beyond Rathfarnham in Dublin. It sounded wonderful to me, with my picture-house experience of seeing happy workers in the cotton fields, and it gave me a warm feeling to think that I might be able to bring in some money to help at home. Mam had said anyway that she was going to get a new square of lino for the bathroom, so I made up my mind that I would try to pay for that. My brother Tommy told me that he had earned two shillings in a day's picking the previous year, and it happened that the lino was to cost ten shillings.

How neat: all I needed was a week's work. The problem would be to get on the picking gang. The cognoscenti said that you had to be known to the overseer in order to have a chance. I was not daunted by this, as I already knew that some people had the mystifying habit of giving up before they tried. I simply did not understand meek acceptance, or how these individuals were so easily discouraged.

Mam gave me permission to go to the picking fields with a neighbour, Mrs Byrne, and this was arranged for the next Monday. Sleep was uneasy the night before. In my dreams I saw fields of bushes drooped with black berries.

In the morning my sister Nell gave me the bus fare and made me a sandwich. I was in the packed crowd on the first number 17 bus bound for the terminus at Rathfarnham Village. After a little walk we came to the Yellow House pub, and it was truly an oasis from where the lone and level fruit fields stretched far away, to misquote 'Ozymandias'. From there, we got directions from a milkman. It was down country lanes surrounded by meadows of ripe fruit, blackcurrants and strawberries, with the hills of furze rolling away towards the mountains in the opposite direction. Unfortunately, there were crowds of children and adults with the same idea in mind as I had, all bent on a grand day out and with high hopes of being selected.

There was great banter about which was the easiest fruit to pick, and how demanding the overseers were. It seemed a particular misfortune if you were told to strip a field of the last of its fruit where the main crop had been already cleared, and did you know that if you were chosen today, it meant you were good for a week's work? The big test was to come. To be allowed into the area where field hands were given specific jobs to do, you first of all had to be chosen as a picker by the overseer.

There was no chance of outwitting the system, as each lucky person was given a docket and this was the passport to being put on a picking team. In any event, we were soon ushered into a fenced corral, and the crowd made a shameless rush towards the front platform where the overseer stood. I was dismayed at this behaviour, and stayed at the back, sullen and perplexed. Mrs Byrne left me on my own, having told me how to get home.

The overseer was a squat lady in her forties by the name of Peggy. She had the hauteur of a Pharaoh despite her turned-down wellingtons. As she stood on the platform at the front of the corral, she gazed without emotion at the quality on offer. My heart sank when I saw her. She acted as if she was blind and deaf, and I surmised from her face that her hobby was disappointing people. The mob continued to push for space as the choosing began.

Most of the adults at the front of the crowd held up their hands or called out for notice, and the children jumped up and down and shouted. The critical finger pointed, seemingly at random, to individuals here and there at the front of the crowd, and murmurs of disappointment were heard from those standing next to them. As the chosen were indicated, an aura of quiet responsibility descended on them as they were allowed through the guarded gates. Once that far, they would be handed either a bucket for strawberry picking or a chip for blackcurrants, and allocated a field. I was standing on the boundary dyke at the back of the corral, scowling, when this lovely lady on the platform, growing more beautiful, pointed in my direction, ignoring the crowd up front for the moment.

I glanced quickly to each side and then pointed at myself, with *that* quizzical look on my face, goldfishing for breath in pleasure. She nodded once, and I smiled my thanks. I think I saw her smile as well. I wondered for a moment why I had been chosen. It was another lesson for the future: that calm when surrounded by bedlam was the best policy, and gave happier results than trying to outshout the herd.

I moved fast and got behind her and into the picking gang at a speed that Steinbeck conveys in *The Grapes of Wrath*, the classic story of migrant fruit-pickers heading for California. The rest of the day was wonderful. I was put on the blackcurrants. The bushes were laden with plump bunches of fruit, ready for easy picking, just as I had dreamed. The overseer was reasonable, and merely pointed out where I had left some berries behind, rather than getting into a rage over it.

There were bullfinches everywhere, attracted by the orchards. Yellowhammers and buntings, which I had never seen in the bird market, entertained us with song. I slowly filled my basket. Lunch was a short break, with the pickers comparing notes on the merits of being asked to pick strawberries as against blackcurrants. Tall stories were told about the time the guy was caught adding a stone to the berry bucket for extra weight.

At the end of the day there was the great weigh-in. A queue was formed for each different fruit, with one man on the scales and another logging the weight and calling out the wages earned. It was an amazing thrill to be there, next in the queue, your chip overflowing with blackcurrants after a full day's labour. I handed mine in. When it was weighed the man called out, 'Half a crown.' Wonderful! And I had been chosen for the week, which meant that if I could do as well every day, I could give Mam the money for that lino and, ahem, maybe keep a little for myself.

When I got home I handed over the money, all of it. Mam took it and smiled, and told me I was a great little worker, to the atmospheric approval of the rest of the family. Dad just looked straight into my face, almost surprised, and then he nodded as well. It reinforced my budding belief that money was a commodity central to comfort and, while Divine Providence was great, the capacity to earn cash was not to be belittled. I realised, too, that I had a personal latent anger at not being better off, and I felt for people like us, an average family in the Liberties. It's a feeling I've never lost.

I remember too, in the last few years of Nannie's life, Joe would sometimes take her out for a drive in the summertime. By then poor Nannie was almost constantly confined to bed in her airless little room. Her breathing had become heavy, and when she was giving me my pocket money on Sunday mornings, she would no longer rub the halfpenny to make sure it was not a shilling discoloured by brine, but would just tell me to take it from her purse.

Every now and then she would spit up into a small bowl on her locker. She often asked me to say a prayer for Granddad and would point to his memorial, a big picture on the wall, and get me to read it out. *In loving memory of John O'Neill, 15 Francis Street, Dublin, who died on the 27th February 1927, aged 50 years, dearly loved and deeply mourned, on whose soul, Sweet Jesus, have mercy.* I had never met Granddad and sometimes wondered how it was that his presence was still in the house and he was mentioned so often and so kindly in conversation.

One August day Joe arranged a jaunt into the country to give Nannie some fresh air. He hired a Model T Ford and parked it outside the shop, and it was the first time I saw a private car in anyone's possession in Francis Street. The personnel for travelling were carefully chosen. I was allowed to sit in the front with Joe as a reward for services rendered in running messages, lighting fires and doing special jobs, like collecting lodgement slips for him from the Hibernian Bank in Thomas Street.

Nannie sat in the back with Cousin Eileen, who was fond of mentioning how she had been a finalist in the Dawn Beauty Competition won by Maureen O'Hara, who went on to become a great film actress. Eileen often slept in Nannie's bed during the winter to keep her warm. This was the cause of the occasional distinctive smell in the bedroom of Vick Vapour Rub and face powder combined. Today Eileen had to make sure that the blanket around Nannie was in place, and to keep her comfortable on the trip.

We set off in great form, heading for Dundrum and the road to the Wicklow countryside. Nannie was silent in the back, except for her wheezing cough and spluttering mucus. Eileen was very attentive to her as they sat close together. Joe started to talk about the way things were with him, for the sake of conversation, but Eileen, smiling, said, 'Little pigs have big ears,' without looking at me.

Joe rambled on anyway, quoting some people as saying that the initials FF, as in Fianna Fáil, might stand for Faith and Fatherland, and how he must buy the sweep tickets for his cousin in America. Then it was about the letter from his brother Jim in Montréal that was overdue for an answer. When Nannie heard Jim's name she cleared her throat and tried to say something. These topics were hard for her, I knew, because her eldest son, William, had fought in the British Army in the First World War thinking that it would be good for Ireland, whereas Jim had been a member of the Irish Republican Army in the War of Independence. I heard Mam say once that Joe had taken the middle road when he chose politics and it was great that Fianna Fáil had kept us out of the war.

I was more interested in Joe's career as a Marconi wireless operator, as I had found out about his travels when I discovered a piece of coral he kept in the china cabinet. When I mentioned it this time, he started to tell us the details of his great journey to Argentina in the year 1926, on the steamer *Darro* under Captain Matthews, when he was only eighteen years of age.

I listened like a radio antenna myself. Brazil, the River Plate, rounding the Horn: he made it all come to life, and I thought Joe was the best uncle I had, what with loving his mother more than a life on the ships, and taking me with them today. I promised myself that I would try to be like him, and not be causing trouble at home.

The road drifted by, and Joe had just started into a story about two brave Irishmen who died for Ireland on an English gibbet, when we came across the Scalp, a spectacular rock cliff by the wayside. Huge boulders were balanced in equilibrium, making it look as if the whole mountain would collapse at any moment. Joe stood out of the car, staring at this magnificence, and as I followed him, he said in wonder, 'God made the world.'

I replied, *sotto voce*, 'But I helped to carry the bricks,' which was the Francis Street boys' way of explaining the story of creation. I was glad when we moved on, as I imagined I could see movement in the cliff face, and the pile of huge boulders and scree on the ground gave me no comfort.

As we left the Scalp, I noticed that some of the houses had timber sheds or awnings attached, with big signs reading *Tea and Scones* in the front gardens. Eileen told me that the people around there made extra money by catering for visitors like us, and she suggested to Joe that we have a cup of tea. We sat outside under an awning. The sun shone fitfully but Nannie did not complain. Eileen was telling her that the nice smell she had noticed in the car was her Odorono, which she was trying out at the suggestion of Mrs Rickerby, the chemist across the road from us in Francis Street.

Nannie never said much any more, but she did tell us again how she missed Granddad on days like this, even if it was more than twenty years since he had died, and that she was sorry in a way that the two of them had been in business separately, as it meant they had had less time together. 'He was a lovely man,' she said, 'so kind and decent. He had his mother's nature.'

I had heard before about Granddad's mother. Her name was Catherine Deveraux and she once lived in New Row, across the Coombe. In the family, she was renowned for her capable strength, and in her time had brought up six children, four of her own and two stepchildren. I knew she must have had a heart of gold.

Eileen told me the story again. Both my great-grandparents were married twice. William O'Neill married Bridget Kelly in the Liberties in 1863 and had two children, but poor Bridget died a few years later. A man caring for children could not work, so the family introduced him to Catherine Deveraux, and they married – her first marriage and his second – in 1875, in Francis Street Chapel. After another few years, William himself died of a fever in Cork Street Hospital, leaving Catherine with two stepchildren and three of her own, one of them being my grandfather.

'You know the way it is in the Liberties,' Eileen said, 'there's no place for giving up, and you have to go on living, so they went looking for another mate for Catherine.' This time they made a match with Christopher Downes, a widower, and in 1881 they married, again in Francis Street Chapel.

They, in turn, had one child, leaving Catherine to mother all six, four of her own from two marriages, and two stepchildren of the earlier marriage of William O'Neill. 'I hope you can follow that,' Joe said, and I barely could. Eileen told us that the children of Bridget Kelly and Christopher Downes were half-blood relations to us, but we were not in touch with them any more and they are still lost to us. I thought how nice it would be if we found them again, but that did not happen.

As we were having our tea and scones, there was a sudden movement on the table where we sat, as we were joined by a chaffinch. He was in brilliant array, and quite fearless. I had never seen a wild chaffinch so tame. Joe said he was a little gourmet, who must be local to that neighbourhood, and had learned the way to an easy feed. Then he reached for his Baby Brownie, and took snaps of us all for his album before we set off again.

As we rounded a turn near our destination, Joe leaned forward and murmured, 'This is Enniskerry. Some people say that it's the prettiest village in Ireland.' I can still hear Joe's voice in my head, exactly as he said it, and I could pick out the bend in the road where it was said, even today. I loved these superlatives even if Joe had the habit of attributing any opinion he had to a third party, and so could easily disown that view when it suited. However, anything that was biggest or prettiest was well worth hearing about, and even if Joe did not commit himself to agreeing with the people he mentioned, I thought it a most remarkable observation, full of insight.

We all got out of the car, except Nannie, and had a good look at the Clock Tower in the centre of Enniskerry and admired the shamrock shape of the surrounding wall to the monument. The atmosphere was gentle, peaceful and slow, unlike our life in the Liberties, but I could not understand how the locals tolerated living at this leisurely pace all the time. I remembered Granddad O'Connor reciting a favourite poem of his by Donagh MacDonagh,

> *Dublin made me, and no little town*
> *With the country closing in on its streets*
> *The cattle walking proudly on its pavements*
> *The jobbers, the gombeenmen and the cheats...*

> *I disclaim all fertile meadows, all tilled land*
> *The evil that grows from it and the good,*
> *But the Dublin of old statutes, this arrogant city*
> *Stirs proudly and secretly in my blood.*

and I felt the full impact and attraction of the noisy streets of home.

It was overcast as we started on our way back. When we got to Francis Street, Nannie had fallen asleep and Joe carried her up to bed. I did not know it then, but there was never to be another such outing, as poor Nannie was fast approaching the end.

6. BOXING AT SHADOWS

I came across Paddy Merry on the rickety landing of the school stairs. He was eating an apple and giving out to young Brady for trying to travel a complete flight in one jump. 'I'm going to report you,' he was saying. 'You can run, creep or walk when you get out of here, but on the stairs you can only mooch. You were warned not to jump. You'll get it when we come back on Monday.' Paddy was a 'policeman', one of those anointed by the Head to make sure that the boys negotiated the stairs quietly, because the plaster was already spalling off the wall under the landings of the old school.

'Bad cess to yeh,' the little boy called up from the ground floor. 'Your sister is a rossie!' Then, after a pause, 'Does your trousers cut under the arms?'

Merry shouted, 'You imprint little get,' and faked a lunge in his direction, but Brady fled out the side door, almost bumping into the caretaker who was rodding the school drains. The taunt had been made because Merry was dressed in a black suit that had been visibly altered to fit him, however badly. His dad knew someone who worked in Polikoffs the tailors, and every now and then a bargain would come along. Merry had told me himself that the suit had been ordered by a man who had died before he could take delivery and it was let go cheaply. No one wanted a dead man's outfit. Paddy's sister worked in the Buttoner so he was never short of the wherewithal to play cards. Because of this I often went into the bunts with him, although we were pals anyway.

I asked him for butts on the apple he was eating but he just said, 'No nagoes,' and continued to chew the apple in my face, but then he relented. 'All right, Seán,' he said. 'Take a bite, but will you do me a favour?'

These words triggered my Liberties instincts and the saying 'Fair exchange is no robbery' came to mind, so I bit off twice as much apple as I normally would, in prepayment for services yet to be rendered. 'Go ahead,' I sputtered. 'For you, anything.'

'Well, it's about the comp we have to do on Monday. Devane says we have to practise writing in a different way about ordinary things, and to spend some time on the opening.'

Right enough, I had heard Devane ask meaningfully the previous week if a group in the class had got together to write their English compositions, because there was noticeable repetition which, he said, would have to stop. Merry went on, 'We have to write about "A Visit to the Dentist" on Monday, so what about giving me a hint?' This boy was well up in a class of sixty-three pupils, which contained a representative spread of every level of intelligence, but he was not richly endowed in the sphere of imagination.

'Say you were playing cricket and the bowler sent down a full toss, or that you were playing in the silly mid-on position and the ball hit you in the face,' I said, in a moment of mischief. Now, a pal of mine, John Kenny from Winetavern Street, was cricket mad. He insisted on getting us to play a Liberties version of cricket in the local park. He had all the jargon, and could name the English team, and I was somewhat familiar with the terms as a result. 'Better still,' I suggested, 'why don't you read about it in the library?'

As I said this to Merry, I was aware that there was a ban on playing cricket for boys such as him, who were picked for the school Gaelic football team. This was because the GAA called cricket a 'garrison game'; in other words, it had been played by the British Army over centuries of occupation. Indulging in any such sport was supposed to be an undermining of nationalist principles. I was sure that Devane would have an interesting reaction to the use of a cricketing incident as a reason for visiting the dentist. My own purpose for such a visit was going to be that my teeth had been damaged falling off the back of a Guinness dray when the driver had lashed his whip at me. I reckoned that the duality of the offence of scutting being met with appropriate punishment would appeal to Devane's code of ethics.

On Monday, we were all in racing form at our desks in classroom number eight. Casimer Kane was idly enjoying the view of St Patrick's Cathedral, while asking Skerritt if the steel rods he could see in the battlements might be old embedded swords. Brereton was talking things over with his cousin Brierton, probably about the different spelling of their names. Alfie Walsh took off his sports jacket with the leather elbow patches that were so admired, and prepared himself mentally by reading a comic. I could see that Merry, who was sitting beside me, was concentrating on a page in his jotter. When I tried to speak to him, he just shook his head and waved me away.

As Devane appeared, Dessie Hamill handed him a cloth duster that his mother had made for the blackboard. Dessie's mother had a clothes shop in Francis Street and the duster was a token of her support for the teacher. However, Devane hardly ever noticed this type of gift as he was generally too engrossed in trying to improve the work habits of the feckless idlers. He said, 'Right, boys, I want originality, and no cogging. You have forty-five minutes. The subject is "A Visit to the Dentist", and pay special attention to the reasons why you had to go there.'

Amid the symphony of sighs, Merry swivelled his head towards me as much as would not be noticed, then rolled his eyes sideways to complete the rotation needed to look at me. 'Thanks, Seán, you're a pal,' he said, in a way that showed he meant it. I started to regret what I had told him.

The following morning in class Devane reviewed our efforts. He often read out the best composition, and sometimes it was mine. I was looking forward to basking in the sunshine of his appreciation. Not today, however! In front of all the class he said he did not approve of scutting. 'You, O'Connor, have you not been told often enough about the dangers? What's the use of talking to you?'

Now, I thought, here was a man who had once described sinning as like a person walking on ice and that you could slip without meaning to. Where was his understanding?

However, in such a school as ours, you were free to think what you liked, but that was the extent of intellectual freedom available if you valued a quiet life. I was annoyed, but that turned to anxiety when I thought about what he might say to Merry for playing cricket. I feared for us both.

I need not have worried. Devane was quite excited. He announced the arrival of a new talent in the class and said that Paddy Merry's composition was original and well researched. He complimented him on the way he had introduced the terminology of cricket into it and said that he was now going to read out the highlights to us, and Paddy would explain the cricketing terms. This was indeed surprising news to us all and I sat there in self-abasement, wondering how could I have been so stupid as to give Merry my best idea. I looked at him, and he smiled – but did I see a smirk around the lips? Devane started to read. The Sermon on the Mount could not have had a more fascinated audience.

> *I joined a cricket club last summer and after a few weeks I was selected for their rabbit team in a match against the older members of the local sports club. A fine fresh sunny morning it was after a night of rain and the pitch played well and true. Our selectors knew that I had no experience as a fielder, and that I was a stodger as a batsman as I had just taken up the game. As a result, I was picked at tenth man, the death watch, being the last batsman to go in during our innings, and the captain told me with a smile that I was to play at square leg when the other team got in to bat.*

When I asked where square leg was, I was told it was very close to the batsman. Another player told me it was called Boot Hill, because it was such a dangerous place to be when bat met ball. We won the toss, and went in to bat first. The other team mostly depended on one bowler and someone said that he sometimes aimed straight at the batsman's body and not at the wicket.

His first ball was a long hop to a bad length, which gave our batsman plenty of time so that he canted it into the terracing for a six. I was hoping that the bowler would be as kind to me. For the next ball, he came steaming in and our batsman swung at the ball, which passed the fielder at square leg, where I was to play, very close to his head at terrible speed. Our team seemed to be afraid of him and our opening batsmen were out in no time, leaving our middle order to face this bowler, but without much success. It was not too long until I was told to get ready.

I went in at tenth man as planned. The bowler began his run and threw down a full toss to try me out, but I stuck out my bat and managed a glancing shot just past the hands of silly mid off. The bowler stared at me and muttered to himself, and then sprinted up again and threw down another ball, this time aimed at my body. I met this with a wild swing, missing the ball completely, and it flew past the wicket keeper. Next time, he ran at full speed and threw up a sun ball in the air. This started to drop out of the sky and with the glare in my eyes I could not see it. As I looked up,

> *the ball suddenly came back into view and hit me on*
> *the mouth, breaking one of my teeth, and that is how*
> *I had to pay a visit to the dentist.*

'Excellent,' said Devane, to my intense vexation. 'You have tried to be original. Boys, it's no use being in the middle of the pond. You have to go to the edge and break the ice if you're going to get anywhere in life.' I frowned to myself at the consequences of intermeddling in the mysterious world of adults. It was a lesson for me in several ways. First, it was clear that trying to write a composition in a unique way was important, but I already knew that. Next, it made sense to keep my novel ideas for myself, but how was I to know in advance if these were any good, since that depended on the reaction of other people? I had given myself a conundrum to which I had no solution. Either I would have to write in my own way and take my chances or lose myself in trying to write essays to please the teacher.

Later in the day, McQuillan whispered to me in class that Louis Jordan had a blonde girlfriend, and was in the habit of meeting her after school at the bus stop outside St Patrick's Park. I was amused by this, and jealous, although I had no real interest in girls, having been warned off by Devane and being a bit bashful anyway. It did not matter that I had six sisters. The presence of a real girl made me tongue-tied.

I decided that this news from McQuillan required my immediate creative attention, and made up my mind to write a poem about Louis and his paramour. I had little time to spare, so I adapted a humorous rhyme written by Billy Bennett, an old music-hall performer, who billed himself as being 'almost a gentleman'. The piece in question was a saucy number called 'The Drummer Boy', which I had memorised from a book of monologues at home. I composed the first four lines of the planxty myself, in order to personalise it, then adapted it to feature a schoolboy, rather than a drummer boy, with the following result:

> *Louis Jordan had a blonde,*
> *Of whom he was very fond.*
> *Every day, he said 'I must*
> *Go down to meet her at the bus.'*
> *He said to that girl, who was taller than him,*
> *'The way schoolboys love I will teach you,'*
> *Sez she, 'You're too small', sez he, 'Not at all,*
> *If I stand on a wall I can reach you.'*

I gave the scrap of paper to McQuillan, who happily passed it on to Louis. I was chuckling privately at the joke when I received an unexpected blow on the arm, a full-force deadener, at the point halfway between the shoulder and the elbow. It was Louis, and he was not amused. That punch was a challenge and a warning that there was to be a fight at four o'clock in Chapel Lane when school ended. This did not bother me at all, as every boy in the class knew where he stood in respect of his chances of standing out successfully with every other pupil.

We were all experienced gladiators, except for the meek. I had never fought Jordan before, but I knew I could put up a show after two years of survival at infant school in Warrenmount and a few more in Francis Street Christian

Brothers' School. When the bell rang at four o'clock, those in the know gathered in the yard outside the side door of the school in the shadow of St Nicholas of Myra Church. A circle of onlookers was formed. Jordan and I started to fight at once. He was determined to avenge the insult to his budding manhood and I was just in the humour for a scrap. Jordan was about my height but heavier and, being in the same class, we had an automatic agreement that neither would go for the face but concentrate on body punches only.

We were swinging away wildly at each other, both landing smacks to the arms and chest, but after a few minutes the growing crowd of boys scattered. 'Devane is coming,' someone shouted and, just as we heard the warning, he appeared out of the vanishing horde. When he saw who had been fighting he gave us a terrible glare and turned red with annoyance. 'Aloysius Jordan and O'Connor, see me in the morning,' he snapped, as we made our way out of the arena. I had a bad night's sleep and dreaded what might happen the following day, but the next morning Devane said nothing, which was worse. I stayed behind in class when lunch hour came and the rest of the boys, including Jordan, had left the room. Devane asked me what I wanted as if he had forgotten what happened. When he saw I was nervous, he just gave me a telling off and told me I should join a boxing club if I wanted to fight. I went on my way, rejoicing, and saying to myself what a good idea a boxing club might be.

I had been expecting to be biffed with six of the best, although I had only once seen Devane carry out this punishment. It was a misnomer for six of the hardest slaps a Christian Brother could give with a leather strap, an implement of torture that was part of the teaching equipment. The troublemaker had to hold out his hand, while the teacher wound himself up by leaning backwards to exert maximum leverage for greatest pain. On some occasions the slap with the leather would be a mere tap, such as the day Devane once read out my composition for its excellence, then biffed me because he was slapping for bad writing that day. Oral tradition in the school was that it was best to accept the punishment as delivered, because if you pulled your hand away and made the teacher look ridiculous, the reaction could be fierce. No wonder I was happy to escape!

The outcome of my clash with Louis was that I decided to take Devane's advice. After all, Uncle Bartle had been an amateur champion in the old days and maybe it was in the blood. A couple of my pals were in Terenure Boxing Club, so I became a member there. They trained in a mews gym in the Tenters, off the South Circular Road, and I got a warm welcome from the trainer, Christy Carroll. There was a small boxing ring at one end of the gym. The smell of embrocation and sweat gave an atmosphere of serious training. On my first night, there were two boys sparring in the ring and one of them was an obvious talent. Seamus Cowen told me that this lad's name was Larry Martin. He was the son of a club official who lived in the Moracrete Cottages on the Crumlin Road.

Mr Martin was always in Larry's corner when he sparred. There was a demand for use of the ring, but Larry seemed to have easy access most nights. He was a pleasure to watch as he moved with fluency and grace even when he was just shadow boxing. Mr Martin would cry, 'Jab, cross, hook and move out,' and Larry would glide like a dancer. I was put throwing shapes in front of a full-length mirror and soon learned to grunt and exhale aloud through my nose during these exertions. I was told that it was best to breathe that way because when you took a blow to the mouth it was advisable to have it shut: you were less likely to have your jaw broken. Such advice made me think.

My weight was light and I was just a beginner, so the trainer did not involve me in any ring activity. Nevertheless, he put my name down for the schoolboy Dublin Amateur Boxing League in the National Stadium on the South Circular Road, 'to give you experience', as he put it. That was fine with me. I thought it would be great to fight in the same ring as Jimmy Ingle and Harry Perry. After all, the boxers in my league would be novices like me.

I went on training as usual, boxing at shadows and puffing mightily at the punch bag. I even hung up a sack filled with sawdust from the ceiling joists in the cellar in Francis Street for a few days, but Uncle Joe heard the groaning of the timbers upstairs. He came down and told me to give that up before I knocked down what remained of the house, and would I get him a tin of Rito for the leak in the flat roof. I realised then that no one was taking my first fight seriously. But I kept going. At least Mam tried to understand. She got me a white vest and dyed it the daffodil yellow of Terenure Boxing Club and I arranged to borrow a pair of trunks and boxing boots. When the draw was made, I felt apprehensive. I had been matched in my first fight against none other than Larry Martin, who knew everything about boxing. I had hoped his father would be in my corner, but there was no chance of that now. It led to moments of soul searching and, may I say, fear of the unknown, and brought me face to face with the real me, which I found was no consolation. On the other hand, I could not back out of it now as it would lead to denigration and slagging. My pals assured me I was going to get done and that I was just another step in Larry's unstoppable climb to greatness.

On the night of the fight I was nervous. I had never even sparred in a ring before and here I was facing a lovely stylist. We were in the same colours, so the referee tied an appropriate white handkerchief to the back of my singlet so they could tell which of us was which. Mr Martin was in Larry's corner. A man I had never seen before, a gent who volunteered from the small audience, was in mine. He must have known Larry. 'Keep your eye on him and keep your jaw down,' he said, giving me the first bit of advice I had received for the fight. He told me to keep moving when I got in range and make myself a hard target to hit. Hmm.

When the bell went I advanced cautiously towards the centre of the ring in classic posture with my chin down and my shoulders up to protect my jaw, basically hiding behind my enormous gloves. Before I got there I was met by a whirlwind of leather around my head. I could hardly see the perpetrator as I immediately started to sweat profusely. I heard Tom Byrne shouting at me, 'Move right, Shonny,' and I did. That got me behind the referee, who was not too impressed. A sibilant, slightly funereal voice was coming from Larry's corner: 'Left jab, right cross, hook and out.' I knew the advice was not for me, as I was a southpaw, leading with my right.

Larry was grandstanding, more like a matador than a boxer, showing off his exquisite footwork before planting another one in my face. 'Jab, cross combination and out,' called the voice, as I tried desperately to counter, but Larry upped the gears into autopilot. He was bobbing, weaving, and throwing leather to a ballet conducted from his corner, running through his punch drills and body-mobility exercises at will. At the end of the first round the corner man asked if I wanted to go on as I was completely out of my league. I said, 'Yes.' At that point I was unwilling to give in.

We came out for the second round and Larry lost all caution. His four fists threw a hailstorm of soft leather over me as I tried vainly to land a good one on him. The monotonous voice of kismet resounded from the corner. I tried the comeback techniques of the great boxing films I had seen, like Kirk Douglas in *Champion*, but had to admit that it was easier for him.

Larry's hands were flying in and out like snakebites and the thwack of leather on skin was audible. It was as well that the gloves were as big as shoe boxes, because I was outclassed and discouraged. My wits were clear, but I was getting nowhere, and that was the way it turned out. Larry was very gentlemanly about it and his dad shook my hand, but it was the night my boxing career ended. When I got back to the dressing room I met a reporter from the Dublin *Evening Mail*. Our fight had made him curious, and he asked me questions about how on earth I had arrived in such a tight spot, what was my name and where was I from. He had a photographer with him, and told him to take a shot of Larry and myself.

I had my moment of glory the following evening, and it was another 'far fierce hour and sweet', as Chesterton said about a different donkey. There on the sports page of the *Evening Mail* was a nice picture of Larry and me. This was a big happening in my society. It was almost like being famous, even if it was for the wrong reason. Most boys in school seemed to have seen the photo and I realised that in moments like this it did not really matter how you performed: just having your picture in the paper was enough to gain respect. I had been thinking of not going out to play for a while, but now that I had arrived on the scene, I went about as normal. My pals said, 'Better luck next time,' and spoke in an incredulous way about being put in with the trainer's son in my first fight. As for me, I took the glare of publicity quite well and better understood what impresses people, but I also did my best to put the experience out of my mind for good.

On a Saturday morning not long after that, Aunt Molly sent me to Honers in the Iveagh Market for a grazier rabbit, and on the way back I met my sister Peggy and my cousin Betty Hilliard at the washhouse talking to Mr Grogan, the market overseer. Everyone called him Daddy Aiken behind his back, which was the nickname of his predecessor Mr Blake. Peggy wanted me to turn the rope for skipping, as she and Betty were tired of swinging on the lamppost. I did not mind obliging because we were all planning to go to the follyinupper at the Tivoli Cinema in a group of cousins who went there most Saturday afternoons. Seeing Betty reminded me of when I used to collect scraps. I had kept a scrapbook when I was younger, and she let me play with her friends, as it was a hobby supposed to be for girls only. I saw nothing wrong then in spending my pocket money on coloured pictures of butterflies and flowers and I liked putting them into my scrapbook. There they would stay until I would swap them for other scraps showing pictures of animals and birds.

In fact, my scrapbook days ended when I gave it to Betty in exchange for a kaleidoscope she had made from a Toblerone box. Coloured sweet papers were pushed through little holes in the body and the triangular ends. The result was a dazzling rainbow when you held it to your eye. It was well worth the swap, but I never went back to scraps. Now I was prepared to render service for old times' sake, at least for a few minutes until some other girl came along. However, first I had to get rid of the grazier, which was beginning to seep through the wrapping paper, so I ran and left it in to Molly in the shop before I took over the rope. Betty got ready to jump in, and I sang the skipping song with Peggy, who was holding the other end:

> *Wallflowers, wallflowers, growing up so high,*
> *They're all pretty, fair pretty, do not like to die,*
> *Especially Betty Hilliard, she is the youngest child,*
> *Oh, fie! For shame, oh, fie! For shame,*
> *Turn your back against the game.*
> *Turn your back to saucy Jack,*
> *And say no more to me,*
> *For if you do, I'll chop you up in two,*
> *And that will be the end of you.*

Then we followed on with another slow air from the
Liberties:

> *Mammy, Mammy, take me home, from this*
> *   convalescent home,*
> *I've been here a week or two, now I want to be with*
> *   you,*
> *Goodbye all the doctors, goodbye all the nurses,*
> *   Goodbye all the nurses, and Dr Corrigan too.*

I was beginning to get fed up with these sad songs, and one
of the hard chaws playing Don on the steps of the market had
started to jeer me, so I told Betty that this was the last one.
Then the mood changed:

> *My girl Betty, my girl Betty,*
> *She can wash and she can scrub,*
> *And she's her daddy's little love,*
> *And if you want to know her name,*
> *Her name is Betty Hilliard.*

'Play a different game,' I said. 'Everybody's looking at me.'
Sinéad de Burca had just come along. She was very brainy,
and her parents spoke Irish at home.

   'Let's do riddles,' she said, in a voice that meant we were
about to do riddles. 'I'll start. Now listen to this,' and she
chanted:

> *In the garden, there's a lake, in the lake there's a*
> *   boat,*

> *In the boat there's a lady with a green petticoat,*
> *Eve you don't know her name – then you have*
> *   yourself to blame,*
> *Because I told you in the middle of the riddle.*

'Now,' she said, 'what's the name of the woman in the boat? I gave it to you already.' I had no idea, so Sinéad sang it out again. Still silence. 'It's Eve,' said Sinéad. '*Eve* you don't know her name. Remember?' She had to explain once more before we understood.

I said, 'Did you hear this one? A man writes a letter to his boss and says: "Dear Mr Florin, Meet me at The Crown Hotel. Make no delay. Yours truly, Bob Tanner." What amount of money is mentioned in the letter?'

Sinéad started straightaway, 'Well, a florin is two shillings and a crown is five shillings, so that makes seven, and a bob is a shilling and that makes eight, and a tanner is sixpence, so it all amounts to eight shillings and sixpence.'

'Wrong,' I said, with some pleasure. 'It's eight and sixpence halfpenny, because a "make" is a halfpenny.'

Our game was interrupted by a call of 'Mamma's pet and Dada's love' from the card school, so I left the girls to it and went over to the boys. I could not play cards myself as I was scunched, but they were talking about the school sports. I had nice memories of the last sports day. Every boy in the school had to take part, and whites were compulsory. Long white trousers, white shirt and green tie, topped off with a new school cap, or skull basher, showing the insignia of the school in gold, and this had to be bought in McGoverns of Aungier Street. White runners completed the ensemble, as the Head was determined that we would be a grand sight when we took to the field in Harold's Cross Greyhound Stadium that Sunday afternoon.

I had entered for the bicycle race and the sack race. I was on Peggy's bicycle, an all-steel Raleigh, with the basket still on the handlebars. I was doing well when the chain came off and the peloton flew past with a taunt. After a while, the starters were called on the Tannoy for the sack race and this was my only chance. 'I'm as fit as Jesse Owens and I can hop like a rabbit,' I said to myself, and I really wanted to win something. We lined up for the start. 'On your marks, set, go!' and we were off. Brierton left us standing but McQuillan was at my elbow. Martin Doyle, phenomenal competition from the Iveagh Buildings, was on my other side, as we fought it out. Jordan jumped the gun but was not noticed because he immediately fell on the ground crying out and nursing his leg.

Suddenly, there was a move away from the pack. Halpin passed us all as if we had stopped, moving in defiance of the laws of dynamics by running in the sack. I did not think it was possible to do what he was doing, so I concentrated on my own orthodox efforts. I shook off Brierton and Kane, and McQuillan fell awkwardly in a noisy heap in my path. I got around him and then there was only Halpin to beat, but we were nearing the tape and he was well in front. The roaring was incredible from the boys standing by. Two teachers held the white finishing ribbon and were ready to judge the outcome. I tried my best, but there was little hope. Yet Fate took a hand, in the way it sometimes does for a Liberties boy.

Halpin looked around and saw me hopping madly behind him, so he accelerated again, still performing his little turkey trot inside the sack. Just as he came to the tape, he tripped in a way that took him over the finish line, but under the tape, and I saw my opportunity. While he was vainly reaching his hand up to the tape, I took off in a swan dive from a distance, beating him to it. It did not matter, as it turned out, because my sack-running friend was disqualified anyway. There was a right old row, but the judges were adamant that I had won, and I was presented with a fountain pen at the awards ceremony. It was a baby step in my athletics career.

In the following year on a winter's day, I was in the Phoenix Park, walking on the grassy plain near the Army Grounds, when I saw a young man running towards me. I had slipped into the Iveagh Grounds on Crumlin Road in July to see the famous sprint called the Guinness Hundred and had marvelled at the spectacle to such an extent that it had strengthened my ambition to join a club. This man was flowing along with easy elegance, moving fast, but still managing to look relaxed. His style was impressive, so I smiled and held up my hand, seeing my opportunity. As he came nearer to me, I could see the decency in his rugged, good-natured face and that encouraged me. He was dressed in a black singlet and green shorts with running shoes to match and he was as neat and trim as any athlete I had seen at the Guinness Sports in the Iveagh Grounds.

He stopped when he saw me and I asked him about joining. 'Yes,' he said with enthusiasm. 'Come up to the Army Grounds at eleven o'clock on Sunday morning and I'll see you there.' He told me he was in the St Augustine Athletic Club, and that it was for workers in the printing houses, but in my case that would not matter as I was so young. His name was Harry Gorman. That name became familiar over the decades to Irish athletes as the embodiment of sportsmanship in competition and the man who won fifteen national championships at every distance from two miles to the marathon.

So, the following Sunday morning I joined up. I loved it, and it was a growing-up process as well. A number of clubs trained there, and the talk was lively. 'Did you see the final of the hundred yards that year? The guy on the inside lane was so nervous that he called out to his coach to say so. The coach roars back at him that it was his own fault, because he never trained anyway.' The showers were cold, but the athletes negotiated with Tom, the old army caretaker, to light the boiler. In the meantime they walked around in the nude, heedless of the temperature, or indeed of any schoolboy who might not have seen all this before.

I had been in the club for just a few weeks when Charlie, our organiser and coach, told me that the four-mile club handicap was to be held on the following Saturday. He said that the best runners would be off scratch and everyone else would be given a start based on how good they were. It was to be a race confined to members of our club except for a few really good outside athletes who were invited to run as guests. The course was to be four times around the one-mile cross-country circuit in the Phoenix Park.

When Saturday came I stood at the starting line having a good look at the runners. Big names like Willie Brennan and Terry O'Connor, Tommy Markey and Harry Gorman were all there, warming up for a fast race.

Charlie had decided that the youngest and the oldest runners would be given a ten-minute start in order to get maximum effort from the scratch men. That's how I met Austin, who was about sixty years of age. 'On your marks, set, go,' cried the starter, and we were off. Now the one-mile cross-country route in the Phoenix Park takes you over wooden planks fording a stream, and we were told to watch out for that point. Austin ordered me to follow him as we set off together. We were on a worn track when my companion repeated sternly that I was to stay right behind him, which was what I was doing anyway. I soon found myself up to my ankles in water, which I had not been told to expect, and a few minutes later we were back at the start again. The scratch men were still there, as our ten-minute handicap had not yet elapsed, which meant that they were now expected to give us more than a mile start in a four-mile race.

There were groans and stares, but Austin commanded me to ignore them as we went into the second lap. This time the course we ran was slightly different, and I found myself running across some wooden planks further up from where we had been wading before. When it came to the last lap, Austin was tired and told me to run on, which I did. I looked behind me but there was no one in sight, so I galloped on to victory, witnessed only by Charlie. He told me to go to the pavilion and shower, and that was how I learned where the expression 'home and dry' came from. I was presented with first prize, which was a chit for a custom-made tracksuit in any colour I liked from the sports shop of a namesake, Seán O'Connor, in Talbot Street. He helped me to choose a classic fabric in maroon, and threw in a pair of defective running shoes, which fitted me perfectly.

This little victory was an encouragement to train, and in the passage of time I was entered in a race for boys under sixteen at the sports in Castlebellingham, more than forty miles from Dublin. My transport was a bicycle. I reasoned I could cycle there on the Saturday night before the sports, so as to be fresh for the race the following day. I was a member of An Óige, who ran cheap youth hostels, so I booked an overnight bunk in the nearest one to the venue.

My financial situation was not good, but Mam had given me an Irish fry that I could cook for breakfast at the hostel. After that I had two shillings, which was the cost of getting into the sports ground and included the entry fee for the race. I set off at five o'clock on the Saturday evening, heading up into the hills and meadows of County Meath, but I might as well have been on a German tank going through the Steppes of Russia. The land went on and on. By seven o'clock I was in quiet farming countryside and I was told by a local that I was in Grangegeeth. Around nine o'clock I heard the call of an owl near a hilly place named Smarmore, and I knew then that I would never get to the hostel, so I kept my eye out for a suitable free lodging for the night. After a while I came to a farm, which had one of those barns where the walls did not come all the way down to the ground but was well filled with baled straw.

The farmer got a surprise when he saw this boy from Dublin in shorts, pushing a bike with filled panniers in the middle of nowhere. He let me stay in the barn, and I made myself as comfortable as I could in my sleeping bag. By heaping the bales of hay to a suitable height, I kept myself out of the direct wind. In the morning, I was cold, hungry and lonely. It was very early when I started off and I had no idea where I was. After an hour I stopped a car and enquired. Castlebellingham was still a few miles away and I was nowhere near the hostel. I was in a dilemma, because all the food I had was for cooking, and there was no chance of that, and the two shillings I had was for entry, so I could not spend it on food. But I was determined to go on and see how I could manage. I already knew that one good athlete would be competing in my race. His name was Tony Murphy and he afterwards won the hundred-metres title in the Catholic Students' Games in Lisbon.

I was making my way towards the entrance to the sports ground when who did I meet but my old friend Harry Gorman. I did not have to explain anything. He paid in for both of us, leaving my two shillings free for a cup of tea and a sandwich. The track was a bit rough, but it was the same for everyone. There was a full line-up for the Under 16 Hundred Yards, and I was ready for it. The announcer called the race and, as I was rubbing my stiff leg muscles, he told the crowd that we were eight of the fastest boys in Ireland, which made us look at each other. I got a great start, but Murphy went in front with no trouble. I fought my hardest for a place and came second. Oh, delight! It was my first trophy in open competition.

My prize was a little cup made of EPNS silver and I immediately headed for the exit. My tiredness had gone and I was on my way home to tell about my adventure. When I mounted the bike I was energised, and did not get off it again until I asked for a drink of water in a pub in Santry. After that, it was straight home to show off my prize and to dwell on what I might achieve in the future. Lord, if I could only reconcile my plans for that future with what actually happened afterwards, I would better understand the paradox of life.

However, that was the basis of my teenage love affair with athletics, and I persevered until I had won the Irish Junior Quarter Mile title at the National Championships a few years later. In fact, after some more training, and a change of club to Phoenix Harriers, I managed to win the Guinness Hundred and the Senior Quarter Mile titles of Dublin and Leinster as well, before the call to study took over most of my spare time. From my reading of Charles Kickham's novel *Knocknagow*, I knew about Mat Donovan throwing the sledge for the credit of his little village. I, too, gave homage to the street that gave me birth and the school that formed my spirit.

7. WESTERING HOME AND A SONG IN THE AIR

When I was nearly seven I'd graduated from eating my dinner with a spoon to using a knife and fork. It was a rite of passage that Nell celebrated by telling me I could use her toothpaste, but not her toothbrush. She also said that she was going to take me to the opera one of these days, and allowed me to write a poem and send it to the *Sunday Independent* poetry competition with her own. This was her reward for my reciting from memory a poem I had learned in my High Babies' class in Warrenmount School:

> *When I eat my porridge,*
> *I often stop to see,*
> *If someone in my pudding spoon*
> *Is really, really me ...*

Learning poetry off by heart became a pleasant hobby for me, and in this I had great encouragement from my sister Martha.

I was in our kitchen one day, trying to memorise Tennyson's poem 'The Lady of Shalott', when the door behind me opened and a voice cried out, 'O listen, listen, ladies gay!' by way of saying hello. I knew it was her, and that her salutation was the opening of Scott's poem, 'Rosabelle'. I also knew that I was expected to respond with the next line, 'No haughty feat of arms I tell', which I did. How Martha loved her drama!

She then relapsed into prose to tell me to prepare for music that evening: it looked as if the kitchen would be free. I had to volunteer without rancour, for fear she would return the poetry book I was reading to her school library in Weaver's Square Convent.

And so it was that Martha took centre stage in our kitchen, and addressed the audience of one. 'Ladies and gentlemen, welcome! We are delighted to have with us tonight, as guest conductor, Sir John Barbirolli, who has graced us with his presence. Sir John will conduct the Santa Cecilia Orchestra in a programme of Rossini Overtures, beginning with *La Gazza Ladra*, better known as *The Thieving Magpie*.'

Martha was about to adopt the persona of the great conductor, and I was her willing assistant. She had reached this pinnacle of performance as a result of her activities as an impresario in her backyard theatre. This musical fantasy had begun when she had started organising concerts for the neighbours' children. Her auditions were strict, and many a nascent career did not survive her critical feedback. Only those who met certain standards were allowed to perform.

I was tolerated on the grounds that I was willing to go around the neighbours in the role of fairground barker, crying out, 'A pin or a button to see the show.' The event usually opened with the full company singing 'There's No Business Like Show Business', before introducing a solo by Dickie Richardson giving his a capella impression of Al Jolson singing 'By The Light Of The Silvery Moon'. Rita Kennedy did an Irish jig while skipping in the rope and the twin Larkins made music on the kazoo, a tissue-paper comb, with accompanying slate ralleyers for rhythm.

I was allowed to sing my party piece, 'I'm My Own Grandpa' and, as an encore, I followed with my ovation-inducing trick of touching my nose with my tongue.

Martha sang 'Any Umbrellas To Mend Today', with an ensemble of locals dressed in crêpe-paper costumes. From this modest beginning, she was encouraged towards greater goals. Her knowledge of the music of the Viennese classical period became profound, and when she played the first theme from the Beethoven bagatelle *Für Elise* on our old piano, we always gave her respectful silence during the performance. She had a practice of leaving the same record on our turntable, running incessantly, resulting in her choice of the day being engraved on my brain. This had consequences.

I was upstairs on a stuffy bus one day, idly whistling over and over the theme from a Hungarian Rhapsody by Franz Liszt, when an irate passenger walked the length of the bus to ask me to please stop whistling that music, for the love of God, and did I not know anything else? I blamed Martha for that. She was also responsible for an international incident on the Coombe. I had been listening to Jussi Björling singing the aria 'Cujus animam', from Rossini's *Stabat Mater*, with its incredible high D in the last phrase. Martha played it so often that I knew the complete melody, and it went round and round in my head until it wore a groove in my brain. I was walking along the Coombe, whistling this air when, behind me, the cultured voice of a woman interrupted: 'Do you know you are whistling a hymn? Please stop it at once.' I halted, and peered at her in disbelief. 'Yes,' she said sternly. 'That is sacred music. Do you know that?'

Now, I knew all about *Stabat Mater Dolorosa*, because Nell had told me the story. It seemed that many composers since the thirteenth century had taken this poem and set it to music, in honour of the Sorrowful Mother of God. So I said I *did* know, in my best accent, as I was not going to let the Liberties down if I could help it, but was otherwise silent. She walked beside me in a familiar way and said, 'Thank you for not losing your temper. I just could not stand the whistling. I suppose I should not have said anything. I hope you don't mind.' I told her that it was all the same to me, and she replied, 'You're a very mannerly boy, aren't you? Are you English?' With that, we said goodbye, as further conversation would only have spoiled her opinion of me.

One way or another, Martha had progressed to the stage where she now wanted to become the conductor of an orchestra, which was an unusual ambition for a girl whose musical education consisted of a few terms' piano instruction from Mr Fox on the Sundrive Road. On certain evenings, she would actually become Sir John Barbirolli, or so it seemed to me. This was one such occasion, and the welcome speech she made was followed by her transmuting into her hero. His distinguishing custom was to wear a large signet ring on the little finger of his left hand, and Martha had discovered that the stone was blue. As a result, the metamorphosis from

Martha to Sir John was accomplished by her putting on such a ring. In the absence of anything better, it was made from a blue-coloured sweet paper, with her little finger thrust through its centre. Furthermore, if she was to be a conductor, she needed an ensemble to conduct.

I was that orchestra, with backing from the Santa Cecilia playing away behind me. Of course, we had taken time out to rehearse. I had become quite accomplished in vocalising the solo side-drum rolls that introduce the overture, and my imitation of the trombone in the brass section was not bad either. After a little warming up, we settled down to perform, and it was all taken quite seriously.

This was an evening when we would have the kitchen to ourselves for a little while, and the performance was strictly for us alone. Having become Sir John, Martha stood ready to call the orchestra to order. In the meantime, I was gathering myself as, apart from the drum rolls and brass, I had to segue into the mime of playing the wind instruments, or strings, whichever had the melody at the time.

I had changed the needle on the arm of the record player, so all was ready on sound. Martha stood on a kitchen chair, prepared for action, and I sat poised on the shoe-polish stool in front of her, in a rising aroma of Nugget and Kiwi. Then I reached across, turned up the volume, and pressed *play*. Martha raised her hands and counted me in, *one and two and three*, on the downbeat, and I obliged with a couple of terrific shrilled rallies to imitate the drum rolls, then added my brass to the full orchestra playing the majestic martial air of the overture. Wind, brass, percussion, strings, and I played *tutti*. The dynamics were *fortissimo*, and astonishing.

Like Barbirolli, Martha eschewed the baton, but was full of awareness of the way I played, holding my attention, and keeping perfect time with one hand, while glancing down at her score now and then. This score was actually the record book of repayments on a piano that Nannie had bought in 1913. With her other hand Martha brought in the various sections of the orchestra, exactly on cue, indicating the great crescendos with an upward movement of her palm, and leaning away from me for the opposite effect, while the Santa Cecilia Orchestra, and I, responded to her every beckoning and finger stab. After the finale, she gracefully accepted the tumultuous applause of the audience, again played by me, and bowed a few times, then raised my hand, so that I could share in her triumph.

When that was over, I went in search of Tommy's hidden treasure. His contribution to literary activity was that he bought the *Wizard* and the *Hotspur* every week. These comics were full of tales loosely based on history, so that Johnny Appleseed and Bonnie Prince Charlie came to life again in our house. I saw Wilson, that fantastic athlete, break the four-minute mile when it was news, and having to survive being kidnapped and taken to Africa to compete against the Impi of the Antelope. Being white, he always had to win, but barely.

The trouble was that Tommy hid his comics until he had read them all twice over. I knew they might be under the mattress, but going through the horsehair filling lying on the bedsprings did not appeal. They were not in the china cabinet either, but I was elated when I found them in the pocket of his overalls.

These comics were good for vocabulary, and I loved to show off my new words, even if I could not pronounce them all properly. I was not alone in this. Only that morning, Higgins had told me that his father was biling-wall, that he could speak French and English as well. In my own case I had enjoyed diverse success in using my new words in school. We were writing a composition on the life of St Francis, and I borrowed from the *Messenger* to say that 'Francis was a holy man who renounced the wiles of Satan.' Now, Devane never used that word to describe the devil: he preferred Lucifer, and enunciated it with such delicious distaste that you could nearly smell the sulphur. As a result, I had never heard the word 'Satan' pronounced. He asked me who or what was that, pointing, and I confidently replied, 'Satin.' I knew from his face that I had got it wrong. He said nothing, but I was disappointed when Nell confirmed my mistake afterwards.

However, I did a little better a few weeks later. This time we were writing a composition on the life of Mary, Queen of Scots. There were some lovely phrases I had memorised from the *Wizard*, which included 'the wild skirling of bagpipes'. Down it went, and was noticed by Devane on his rounds. He asked me if 'skirling' was a word at all, and I explained that it was the sound made by bagpipe music. This time he walked away with a puzzled look on his face, staring back at me and raising his eyebrows.

Before that day was over, he told me that he had chosen Tom O'Neill and me to represent Francis Street Christian Brothers' School in an essay competition open to all primary schoolchildren in Dublin. The subject was to be the

St Patrick's Day Parade. Tom and I were among the best at English in school, and we considered ourselves honoured to have been chosen. His father owned the public house beside Winstanley's shoe factory in Cornmarket so he had more access to pocket money than I had. On the eve of the competition we went into Tyrell's stationery shop in High Street where he bought the necessary foolscap paper for the two of us, like the decent boy he was.

At home, Nell had been spending her money on a wide selection of appealing second-hand books and journals. It meant that I could memorise lines of Sean O'Faolain from *The Bell*, and read the poetry in the *Dublin Magazine* for inspiration. It also meant that I never had to read our school textbook, *Forty Specimen Essays*, which would encourage you to begin a composition with 'A fine fresh morning it was, after a night of rain.' I wanted more, and I wrote words that I would never use in conversation, such as 'The sun was rising in a blaze of glory behind the coppice of weeping willow.'

I was prepared for florid exposition but this essay title, 'The St Patrick's Day Parade', had been set by the National Agriculture and Industrial Development Association, no fosterers of young literati. I said it was a terrible subject, but the Head, Brother Devitt, who was from Belfast, explained things. He looked at me and asked what was the matter with me; if I did not want to represent the school to just say so. I reflected silently that he was not perfect himself, and that he had been seen by others in my class watching Shamrock Rovers playing soccer, which was against the rules of the GAA, and possibly a sin as well.

At the appointed hour we were put in his study to write our stories. I found it difficult to use my dainty palette of phrases in describing the parade, but the two of us went on until time was called. A few weeks later, Devane told us that we had both been Very Highly Commended in the competition, and that Francis Street Christian Brothers' School was the only school that had two pupils mentioned in the prize list.

I was disappointed that neither of us had won, but we turned up on a Saturday morning soon after at the Grafton Street office of the organisers. When the prizes were presented, Francis Street School was specially mentioned, and they gave each of us a copy of a book named *Columba*, the life story of the saint. It seemed to be written beautifully, but in the Irish language, and was too advanced for us, so we spent the walk back to Francis Street wondering what kind of a gobdaw had picked such a prize for an essay in English. But the outcome of the competition was further notice that a command of English was a useful asset for a boy from the Liberties, and I delighted in the fact that we had trounced most of the opposition from all over the city.

I made a point of telling Granddad O'Connor about the essay. He was charmed, and invited me to borrow from his impressive bookshelf, but to make sure to tell him if I did. He read from a volume of the works of Lord Byron, which was a family heirloom, and when he recited,

> *She walks in beauty, like the night*
> *Of cloudless climes and starry skies...*

I could see the moonlight on the face of the unknown woman, and I could nearly smell her perfume.

Not long after that, I was playing football on the street when Granddad and Granny passed me by on the way to visit us. I explained that Mam and Dad had gone for a little walk, and let them in to wait. I knew that they had lived in Scotland for a while, so I thought they were bound to have an interest in that country still, and I had an idea. I asked if they would like me to read for them and they said yes, without any sign of surprise. The sensuous poetry of Tennyson attracted me, although I did not understand why, but my idea was to read one of his poems in a Scottish accent.

I chose from 'Come into the Garden, Maud', where the unnamed hero has been waiting all night in the garden for his beloved to appear, while she is partying in the big house. When I put my plan into effect, I made a point of rolling the Rs, so it sounded like this:

> *She is coming, my own, my sweet;*
> *Werre it everr so airry a trread,*
> *My hearrt would hearr herr and beat,*
> *Werre it earrth in an earrthy bed;*
> *My dust would hearr herr and beat,*
> *Had I lain for a centurry dead;*
> *Would starrt and trremble under herr feet*
> *And blossom in purrple and rred.*

They loved it, and I was just about to give the same Caledonian treatment to 'The May Queen' when my parents arrived home, and I went out to play. Granddad waved goodbye to

me later on, but when Mam called me in for my tea, I had a
nice surprise. Granddad had left a message for me that, in
view of the way I had entertained them, they were going to
buy me a schoolbag for Christmas. When Christmas morning
came, the schoolbag was lying on my bed, and I thought to
myself what smashing grandparents they were that they had
remembered to keep their word and that I would try to do
the same whenever I made a promise.

Devane was a great lover of the spontaneous break.
'A little nonsense now and then is relished by the wisest
men,' he would say, and follow that with ten minutes of
non-curricular singing. He taught us his own favourites,
one of which was the 'Miya Sama' chorus from Gilbert and
Sullivan's *The Mikado*. Our sixty-three voices sang out in
joyful unison:

> *Miya sama, miya sama,*
> *On n'm-ma no mayé ni*
> *Pira-Pira suru no wa*
> *Nan gia na*
> *Toko tonyaré tonyaré na?*

Father Byrne from Francis Street Chapel called in one day to
explain that he needed two more altar boys, as there could
be almost forty Masses said in Church Festival weeks. The
problem was that they would have to learn the responses to
the Mass, and that would take time, particularly the Confiteor
in Latin. 'Leave that to me,' said Devane. 'My boys are gifted
intellectually.' There were already two volunteers for the
vacant altar boy positions, but the whole class was to learn

the responses to the Mass, from the beginning to the end. Since the big difficulty was the Confiteor, Devane's solution was to treat it as he would a song, and that meant learning it off by heart.

Learning by rote delivered certainty in remembering the material and any deeper search for understanding was left to the individual. After a few days of chanting the Confiteor from the Catechism, he told us one morning to put aside the words and say it from memory, which we did, and it was never forgotten afterwards:

Confiteor Deo omnipotenti, beatae Mariae semper
   Virgini,
beato Michaeli Archangelo, beato Ioanni Baptistae …

We were in the middle of perfecting the prayer a morning or two later, when Devitt came into the classroom with a stranger, who turned out to be a school inspector on a surprise visit. Devane explained what was happening, and the visitor seemed satisfied. When he was gone, our teacher told Devitt that we were probably the only primary class in town who knew the Latin responses to the Mass and could sing in Japanese. That was news to us, as we did not know that 'Miya Sama' was actually in the Japanese language. One or two of us thought it was Irish.

Devane was always on the lookout for new talent to audition. Olly O'Brien was his favourite singer, and 'The Rose of Tralee' got a great reception. There was one occasion after the summer break when he asked Ray McDonald to sing. Ray sang 'The Old House' like a thrush, to our great surprise, and it turned out that he had been sent to Dal McNulty, the blind chorus master of John's Lane Church, for lessons during the holidays. I envied the two of them, as I was fascinated by sheet music and would have loved to be able to read it. Devane would sometimes start the singing, and would join in when we sang his favourite, 'Sweet Marie', a Percy French song about a little mare:

> *I've a little racin' mare called Sweet Marie,*
> *And the temper of a bear has Sweet Marie ...*

He called on Rochford once to provide the entertainment. Rochford started into a Caribbean calypso, a beat quite unknown to Devane, swaying as he sang 'He's Stone Cold Dead in the Market', an opus about a husband being battered by an angry wife.

Devane listened attentively, looking as if his ears were deceiving him, and adopted the stance of an alarmed blackbird, head down, arms pointing straight towards the back of his ankles and ready to fly. Being a patient man, he allowed the next verse to continue. This turned out to be a light-hearted description of another assault on the husband by means of a kitchen pan.

It was too much. Devane darted at Rochford and seized him by the collar. 'Stop, stop at once! I spend my time trying to teach you boys some manners and you come out with this sort of rubbish! McDonald, sing your Irish song, "She Moved through the Fair".'

Soon after, a tough-looking educator called Brother Clancy joined the teaching staff. Devane had decided that the class should attempt the scholarship exams for secondary school and Clancy was to teach us history for that purpose. We rapidly found out that his sense of the past was founded on bitterness as to the multiple wrongs of the English colonists in Ireland, and that quotations from *Walton's 24 Patriotic Songs* were to be desired in anything we wrote for him.

Very early in his tenure he was imparting his views on what would have happened to Cromwell but for the scheming plot to poison the one man who would have saved the Irish, and he began to quote from the poem, 'Lament for the death of Eoghan Ruadh O'Neill', by Thomas Davis.

> *Did they dare, did they dare to slay Eoghan Ruadh*
> *   O'Neill?*
> *Yes ...*

He stopped there and asked, 'Does any boy know the next line?' *I* did, because I had memorised the poem from an anthology at home, as its madness was attractive.

> *Yes, they slew with poison him they feared to meet*
> *   with steel.*

'Excellent,' he said, 'now go on,' which I did, to his smiling approval.

> *May God wither up their hearts! May their blood*
> *   cease to flow,*
> *May they walk in living death, who poisoned*
> *   Eoghan Ruadh.*

The bloodthirsty nature of the poem drew no comment and he just said, 'Well done.' But music and poetry sometimes created their own problems, especially in the hands of the wrong person. One day, in sixth class, Devane introduced Mr O'Reilly, who was to teach us the words of a song for St Patrick's Day. O'Reilly taught the second sixth class, and their room was separated from ours by a windowed partition. The two teachers were swapping classes for the duration of this lesson. Based on the anguished yelps we heard from that classroom from time to time, we had formed an opinion that O'Reilly was a hard man and that it might be better to share a cell with Cardinal Mindszenty as a captive of Stalin than to risk being in his class.

O'Reilly was a small, balding man with a fairly low forehead, a moustache, an unsmiling expression, and dandruff on his sports coat. As he stood before us, I shared the experience of Goldsmith's boding tremblers in their village school in Auburn. Like them, I also could read the day's disasters in the teacher's morning face. O'Reilly told us to stand up, and that he was going to teach us the song, 'The Dear Little Shamrock Of Ireland'. He took out a tuning fork, struck it on the desk, put it to his ear, and listened. We all expected him to sing the note as usual, but instead, he began to whistle the air of the song.

Looking at him pucker his lips and whistle was a new experience, and we thought it was very funny, as it was so unexpected. Consequently, we all sniggered, which was a big mistake. Now, in our large class, there were a few who were particularly tall. One of them was Tom O'Neill, who was standing beside me. He enjoyed high social status as he always won the hurley stick for selling most books of tickets for helping the black babies, thanks to his father's pub.

When O'Reilly heard us laughing, he stared and went pale. We stopped very quickly, but he must have already noticed certain smiling faces, especially of the taller boys. Gibson was one of these, but was built like a rugby forward, and Kavanagh told us afterwards that he had wiped the grin off his face so fast that O'Reilly did not see it. However, he *did* see Tom O'Neill, and glared at him from the top of the classroom. Then he began a funeral march in his direction, exuding menace. Finally, he stood in front of Tom and snarled, 'Were you laughing at me?' I glanced sideways at Tom for a second.

He was white with apprehension, but said nothing. Without further warning, O'Reilly smacked him across the face with his open hand with savage force. I looked straight in front and hardly breathed. We were in the clutches of the brute, and silence was the only safeguard. Tom made no sound, and O'Reilly resumed his place, but the class did not go on. Devane suddenly returned, and after a few whispered words, O'Reilly went back to his own class, the song forgotten. That was the last experiment we had in having him as a teacher.

I was hoping there would be retribution, as Tom was a quiet boy who had done no worse than the rest of us. I really believed that, in view of the ranking he occupied in the school, there would be a row about the incident. The following morning, not a word was said, and there was no sign of Tom's dad to put manners on O'Reilly. It transpired that Tom had not told his parents what happened. I admired his brave stoicism.

That was the only unpleasant experience I had in school in the matter of music, and it was quickly put to one side. But there were compensations anyway, and one of them was the annual school concert. This was an evening of singing, drill display, and the usual laughable sketch, but for me, the highlight was the Humorous Recitation, delivered by our classmate, Paddy Brereton.

The school concert was staged in the Myra Hall, famous as being the foundation place of the Bayno and the Legion of Mary. Being in our last year, we had a full house, complete with dry reception before the event. I was sent around with a tray of Mi-Wadi cordial to little groups who were chatting and eating biscuits.

Shonny Maher's father was talking to another policeman about the latest stunt by Lugs Branigan, which involved him ordering a suspect to keep still, and then slowly closing the gap between the two until he could stand on the toes of the felon. Mr Maher said that Lugs's brother, Johnny, was only half his size but could put manners on Lugs any day. Billy Delamere, who had sung in a charity concert in Blackrock Town Hall the previous Sunday night, was telling Mrs O'Brien how he had brought the house down, and Kavanagh's sister was asking her pal if she was spin spout or black out, after a tiff they had had.

The school attendance officer was in conversation with the parish priest, and I heard the PP say how generous were the poor and working classes in the Liberties, and that only for them the new girls' school would never have been built. Gibson was slagging Kavanagh about going to the tall girls' dance in the Adelaide Hall. This did not surprise me, as Kavanagh already openly admitted that he had a girlfriend.

A shout went up at the door, so I went out to see the action. 'Bang-Bang' was on his way home after seeing a cowboy picture in the Tivoli Cinema. He never went to any other type of film, but the gunfights on the prairie always left him with pent-up emotions, as the ushers objected to him joining in. He was in a mean, if harmless, mood as a result, and ready for action. He brandished his trusty key in a careless fashion and, utilising his full vocabulary that we were aware of, kept repeating, 'Luvly day, luvly day, givvis a kiss,' to the girls, and saying nothing to the boys, just making mock attempts to pull their hair. I could not help noticing his long, slender fingers and I thought of music. Poor man. Then he went on his way to the Coombe, his favourite trail, where he would probably stand on the platform of the next 50B stagecoach, picking off the innocent and guilty at random, before making his getaway up New Row and home.

Some of the class went off after the choir had sung, but I waited for the Humorous Recitation. Paddy Brereton lived in Bride Street on the edge of the Liberties. He had the gift of an uncommonly pleasant speaking voice, which seemed to have been improved by elocution lessons. His monologue was always about some memorable event in the life of a schoolboy. This night, the boy was babysitting, and had to feed his little brother while his parents had an evening off.

When Paddy came out on stage, he epitomised the best of the Liberties boy. He was the smiling, confident and articulate artist, among his own people, and we all admired him for his sunny demeanour. The house was full of parents and noisy children, but when they saw him, there was a hush, and then a welcoming roar. He was given instant respect because he was dressed in the football colours of the school: green and white hooped jersey, white knicks, and green and white socks pulled up to his knees, with white runners and carrying a football.

Those colours were almost sacred to the men in the audience. To be picked to play for Francis Street Christian Brothers' School in a hurling joust against Synge Street or Artane was a proud day, and the green and white strip brought it all back for the fathers present. Paddy advanced to the centre of the stage amid great applause and whistles. One old man began to sing the Franner anthem, as if he was still at a match – 'Folly them up, folly them up, that's the way to win the cup.' Then Paddy put his foot on the ball, and began his recitation, casting his magic over the audience in a modulated accent, and humouring them to the end:

> *I tasted it. It was delicious, and I could not stop until I had eaten it all. When Daddy and Mummy came home and heard what I had done, they were extremely annoyed. Mummy said I was hunger's mother and Daddy called me an unnatural son. I could not bear to listen to their unkind remarks. Oh, it will rankle in my heart for ages.*

He was the gift of a boy, and a friend as well, but I never heard of him again from the time I left Francis Street School shortly afterwards.

Some years later I had got a job in a Dublin office. One Friday morning Nell rang me just after I had begun my day at work and she sounded upset. The festival of Italian opera was about to begin in the Gaiety Theatre. Included among the guest artistes was a well-known baritone, Antonio Manca Serra, and Nell's bad news was that he had unfortunately died during the night, before he even had a chance to perform his role in *Lucia di Lammermoor*. What she said now took away my equanimity, and delivered me back to a personal tragedy and a strange coincidence that had happened during the previous opera season five months earlier.

At that time, the Dublin Grand Opera Society was presenting their season of Grand Opera, running up to the Christmas holiday. Nell was in the chorus, which was drawn from local amateur talent. The music critic for the *Evening Press* was John O'Donovan who, in a display of the self-righteous manner of some such, failed to attend the full performance of the opera he was reviewing. That did not stop him saying that the chorus was the slovenliest he had ever heard, and that he hoped they would have pulled themselves together for the next production.

Nell was annoyed. She collaborated with Martha in drafting a rebuttal of O'Donovan's view, which was published in the *Evening Press* a few days into the opera season. The letter defended the chorus in a reasonable way, and it must have been an easy critique to question, given the circumstances. I sympathised with Nell and forgot about it for the moment.

In the meantime, preparations were being made at home for the Christmas celebrations. Dad had the children practising their singing. My brother Joe was three years younger than me and, like the rest of us, loved to sing. His favourite song was 'Westering Home':

Westering home and a song in the air,
Light in the eye and it's goodbye to care ...

Dad would put him standing on a chair to sing out, as he did with all the children. However, I had noticed before that, in the middle of a phrase, Joe would snatch a breath, then continue. I did not know the importance of that until later. Mam and Dad had been told that Joe had a serious murmur of the heart. The diagnosis was that he had probably been born with it but it had only recently come to be noticed as it worsened. They were told that an operation would be premature, and so had decided to say nothing and to allow him to live a normal life, like any little boy, until the appropriate time.

Two weeks before Christmas, Nature struck, and Joe suffered a heart attack. He was very bad. Our home was devastated. I prayed that he would live, and I told Joe about the great holidays he and I would have when he got better. He was allowed to stay at home, under Mam's care, as his illness was beyond healing now. Mam nursed him by day and night, and tended his every need.

Joe rallied a little. Mam was exhausted. One morning, in the early hours, Joe woke up, but said nothing to Mam, who was sleeping in the same room. We thought afterwards that he did not want to trouble her. He got up, took a drink of water in the kitchen, and went back to bed. Mam found him dead at six o'clock in the morning. It was Christmas Eve. I went downstairs to a broken household. Peggy was sitting sideways on a kitchen chair at the window, with her elbows on her knees, sobbing into her hands. The stricken faces of the family surrounded me. Dreadful loss was on us, and I could not absorb such depths of grief.

I cried; how I cried. Mam was trying to console us in her own anguish, but she cried too, from time to time. I had never seen Dad weep, and I knew that Liberties folk were at their bravest in a tragedy. I looked at him. His face showed his sorrow, and a single teardrop lay on his cheek. The dignity of his upbringing and the depth of his beliefs seemed to give him strength. Now and then my parents would embrace. Mam and Dad laid out Joe's body on a bed in the parlour, and Mrs Dinsmore washed him, and said there was not a mark on him. I was sent for blessed candles to Rosie Flynn's and I could not control my distress. Joe was buried on the day after Christmas, St Stephen's. It was the saddest day of my life.

In the afternoon of the day Joe died, a knock came to the door. It was a heavyset man, in a shabby overcoat, who introduced himself as John O'Donovan, the music critic from the *Evening Press*, and he had called to see Nell. He had no idea of our tragedy, but Nell told him what had happened. He offered his sympathy and left, and when things settled down, we wondered why he had called in the first place. He did not know anyone in our house, and was obviously spurred by the letter published in his paper being critical of his judgement. It was a coincidence that he chose that particular afternoon to call to our home on a mission unknown to us, and his visit became inextricably linked to Joe's death in my mind. In the end, I could not think of Joe without remembering the connection between John O'Donovan, the opera and his death.

Now here was Nell, just five months later, telling me of another death, again connected to the world of opera, and asking me to do something for her. On her way to work she had bought a wreath on behalf of herself and her friends of the chorus in Sheila's flower shop in Baggot Street. However, the shop could not deliver that day, and she had to go on to work. 'Could you collect it and take it to the hotel where Antonio was staying?' she asked me. 'It's the Standard Hotel in Harcourt Street.' It was easy for me, as I worked in the area, and so I agreed, but the news of the death awakened all my jittery feelings that had been caused by Joe's passing.

I was shocked anew anyway, because Nell had been telling me about the great singers like Ebe Stignani and Paolo Silveri who were to perform with Manca Serra. I collected the wreath, a cross of flowers, and carried it in full view through St Stephen's Green and halfway up Harcourt Street to the hotel, ignoring the curious stares. The hotel was really no more than a big guesthouse. The paint on the front door was beginning to flake.

A bell rang out as I entered. The young girl in Reception listened to me sympathetically, but instead of taking the flowers, she asked me if I would like to bring them to the room. I was not expecting this, but the invitation came as an agreeable surprise. I went upstairs to the bedroom. I knocked, but there was silence. I held my breath, opened the door and entered the room very quietly, gripping the wreath and staring at the bed.

Antonio Manca Serra was partly propped up on crumpled pillows, his arms stretched out on the covers. His eyes seemed barely closed, and his round, handsome face was unshaven. His black hair was tossed, and his red and white striped pyjamas were quite open at the neck. He looked as if he had fallen asleep and would awaken shortly. I was amazed at the sight, but I felt privileged, because it was clear that I was his first visitor, and no one had yet come to attend him.

The room filled with stillness, and I was overcome by memories and regret. I slowly approached, and placed the wreath on the end of the bed, never taking my eyes off Antonio's face. I stood still, my nerves flaring in the company of the dead again, and this time I was alone. I was aware of a presence near me but I was not frightened, just sad. I wondered if there was a spirit world after death, and continued to stare intently at his face, and then around the room. Who was this man and what was it that had led him to the life of an opera singer? I thought how brave he was to die for music in this way, in a jaded bedroom far from home.

I said a prayer for Antonio Manca Serra, and touched his cheek, before I sat on the chair beside the bed for a moment. In my state of mind, I wondered if he had died alone, and I thought of Joe dying in his sleep, and what were his last thoughts. Was it true that you forgot who you were before you entered that arbour of swirling light? I rose to leave and, as I did so, I became calm, and I thought the ambience in the room had changed. By the time I reached the staircase, I was consoled, and I marvelled at the things that were beyond comprehension.

8. THE SPARROW'S HOUSE

A knock rapped on the front door. 'That'll be Mr Doyle,' said Mam. 'Billy, get three pints and Seán will give you a hand. Ask him what the weather will be like today.'

Billy fetched the jugs and opened the door, with me in attendance. Mr Doyle, our milkman, was standing ready for action. A small churn with a spout for the loose milk was strapped across his back, and he had a pint measure in his hand. 'Three pints,' Billy said, 'and I've to ask you about the weather.'

Mr Doyle poured the milk, looked thoughtfully at the sky, as he did every time we asked this question, and declared confidently, 'It'll be bright this morning and we'll have a little rain in the afternoon.' We gave him the full status of being a farmer, although his holding was near Clanbrassil Street. The sky was red and the clouds were light. The sun was rising on a lovely, airy day.

As he spoke, a V pattern of birds swooshed overhead. I stared at this perfection, not for the first time, and went back into the kitchen, carrying two of the jugs. Mam had told me about these birds when we first saw them flying in formation. 'That's a little family of ducks going to school,' she said. 'The one in front is the only one who knows the way, and he's showing the others how to get there.' Today she told me to eat my porridge, and to put a plastic mac in the pocket of my short coat before I went out, just in case.

After dinner, I told Mam I would see her later, that I was heading to the Phoenix Park to go bird-watching on my own. She was aware of my hobby and she knew she could trust me not to stray too far. Billy told me not to go near the Hollow outside the zoo as it was too lonely, but I considered it was a grand place for spying on birds. He got agitated when I said so and told Mam, but she said I could use my own discretion as I had already been on one bird-watching trip alone.

I had cycled to Greenhills earlier in the year, and I thought I had reached the heart of the countryside when I came to the Walkinstown crossroads. The green fields stretched out of sight towards Tallaght and the Naas Road. I said to myself that this would be a great place to go picking blackberries in September. I was soon climbing over the nearest five-barred gate, and found myself in a field, very close to a herd of cows that stared at me, and made me a bit nervous. They were more watchful than the beasts I'd seen driven on the hoof down Francis Street. I found a grassy mound to sit on, with a clear view of the undulating countryside rolling away to the horizon. The pattern of the fields was broken only by a few sandpit scars in the distance. I had no idea of the time and it did not bother me. The day was calm and the sky was blue; I had no cares in the world.

I was sitting there for a while, watching for bird activity from my little open hide, when I had an unexpected diversion. A rat came ambling into my view from behind me, and slowly moved away in a narrow furrow in the meadow grass on my right-hand side. He was very close, but quite unconcerned about my presence, and seemed unaware of it as well. I did not move, and felt it was great being so much a part of the surroundings. Linnets darted in and out of the thorny yellow gorse and the antics of a mother yellowhammer, trying to feed all her brood at the same time, kept me amused.

After another few minutes I observed a black-and-white bird in the near distance, and concluded without hesitation that it was probably a woodpecker, as I remembered that the woodpecker had that same colouring. Now there seemed to be two of them and they traversed my line of sight from left to right and back again, staying all the time in my view. They were too far away for me to see what they were doing, but I went home happy with my field trip, and well satisfied with my discovery, even if I was not absolutely certain of the species.

The following day I went into Thomas Street Library to confirm to myself that it was indeed a woodpecker I had seen. There it was, a study in black and white, with scarlet underneath the tail, the Greater Spotted Woodpecker, but only the black and white registered with me. I discovered that the woodpecker is quite rare in Ireland, so I was excited and decided there was no need for me to change my opinion. I hurried back to the same field as soon as I could, determined to learn more about the habits of my woodpeckers. I found them without any trouble, flying across my view so often that I eventually identified the focus of their interest.

Their objective, on my left-hand side a quarter of a mile away, was a tree on a hillside. I deduced that they were taking food to their nest and decided to carry out a proper investigation, so I approached the tree. There was a dark clump that could only be a nest near the top. In the meantime, a few woodpeckers, and crows as well, began to cluster in the tree, squawking and scolding, and threatening to dive-bomb me. I ignored them completely and steadily climbed towards the nest in the interests of science.

When I arrived at my objective I had the company of a discordant black-and-white chorus all around me. The nest was beautifully crafted, a rounded shape like a globe of twigs, with a little entrance to one side. Five or six chicks popped up their heads in curiosity at my arrival. I took stock of them as if I was a Jubilee Nurse. In the meantime, the parent birds and their allies were getting noisier, so I decided to withdraw from the scene, rather than upset them more. Nevertheless, I was fulfilled and pleased, because I had learned the way of the woodpecker at first hand.

A few days after my discovery I happened to be in Molesworth Street on the way to the National Museum. Geoghegans had a little tobacconist shop on that street, and they also sold some books. These were an allurement to me, so I stopped to look. A few sample books were laid out flat at the very front of the window, all in a row, to show that each volume was one of a series. To my surprise, there was a picture of my woodpecker in flight on the cover of every book, chosen as a common logo. Disappointment followed on surprise, because the name, plain to read, was the Magpie Series, with a picture of that bird beside it. So my wonderfully exotic woodpecker turned out to be a magpie after all!

I was consoled in the knowledge that I was the first to discover my mistake, and that I had never seen a magpie in the Liberties, but said to myself that I would not be in such a hurry to identify a wild bird in the future. However, regardless of mistakes, I was determined to continue with my hobby. It had an irresistible appeal.

Shortly afterwards, I wanted to see Uncle Bartle before I went to the Phoenix Park because I was curious about a blackbird that sat high on a bush in the grassyard every evening, outlined against the sky, pouring out his music. I had learned to recognise him from a white streak on the feathers of one wing, and I had never seen a blackbird marked like that before. I loved that bird's behaviour. When he landed on the grass, he would stick his head forward and do a short sprint, listening for worms. If a cat disturbed him, he would shake his wings indignantly and sound an alarm like a spectator's wooden rattle at a soccer match for a few seconds before flying away. I felt close to him.

On the way over to Bartle, I noticed a blue tit doing acrobatics while pecking around the Handkerchief Alley sign on the old brick gable of Mrs Phelan's shop across the grassyard. That sign was the only thing that had survived the demolition of the tenements that had once stood there. Now there was just a rusting corrugated-iron façade facing on to Francis Street.

I crossed the street to the Tivoli Cinema side to touch

the date, 1886, on the granite slab at the Baker Wardell factory entrance for luck, which I always did. I kept moving because the smell of tea and coffee combined, coming from their factory, was very odd, being neither one nor the other, although my brother Tommy loved it. Bartle lived with my grandparents over Durney's butcher's shop a few doors up. Mrs Durney was a nice woman who let us pass through her shop and kitchen to get to the stairs, rather than bring Bartle down to the hall door. On the counter, I could see the marks of the nails used as goalposts in the games of push-penny played there on Sunday mornings by Pat Durney and his pals.

'How are you, Shonny?' said Bartle. 'Your granddad has just gone out for an ounce of Velvan Plug. He'll be back in a few minutes.' When I went to give Granny a kiss, she held up her hand and said not to, as she was putting over a cold on her feet. She knew I would be on bird business if I had come to see Bartle and, like most Liberties women, had nothing to say on the subject. She just left us to it and continued to take in her washing from the short pole protruding through the open window. The range burned with a fiery eye in the corner. That was the source of the striped toast Granny always served with the cup of tea she made for visitors.

Bartle was busy cutting back the nails of someone's budgie. 'Have a look,' he said. 'A budgie has a vein in its claw, and if you're not careful you can cut through it. Plenty of blood if that happens.' Every now and then, he would feed Jinny-Joes to his goldfinch mule, which was standing on the cage, giving us a bar or two of song, and enjoying the seeding heads of dandelion. I told Bartle about the blackbird with the white feathers in the grassyard and he was not surprised. 'There's one in the Natural History Museum that's white all over,' he said. 'It's probably an albino, white with red eyes. We should have gone there when we went to see the birds in O'Connell Street.' He was talking about a trip to town we had made a good while before, as a little present for me. He would not tell me in advance at the time what it was, just saying it was a surprise but that I would like it, and it was in O'Connell Street.

With that, Granddad came in with a man who wanted to have a chat with Bartle about something, so I sat quietly by the range on my own, examining the details of the Sacred Heart picture on the wall. The man was from O'Hora's drapery shop across the street, and it seemed they were having a problem of mice in the budgies' aviary they had erected in the shop to amuse the customers. Bartle started to explain a special way to prepare mousetraps for best results, so I knew it was going to take a few minutes.

That trip to O'Connell Street had been very special. It was just after All Souls' Day, I knew, because Peggy and myself had completed our visits to the seven churches, to pray for the souls of the dead in Purgatory that they would be loosed from their sins, just as the Catechism said. Bartle and I had started off from Francis Street across Cornmarket. Mr Stanley was breaking in a horse outside their little white cottage in Lamb Alley, facing the dilapidated city wall, watched by his son Mikey. The horse was on a long rein, running in circles around him. Every now and then he would crack his whip, and shout, 'Whoa,' or 'Gerrup,' to teach the horse his chucks, and sometimes he reversed its direction. Bartle called out that the Stanleys never raired a jipper, but they were too engrossed to reply, so we went on after a few minutes.

I wanted to go down by the forty steps at St Audoen's Church because I liked to count them as I jumped from one to the next. Yes, there were exactly forty of them, as usual. We stood on Capel Street Bridge and took our time looking downriver: the seagulls were flying low near the grating where the River Poddle joined the Liffey after its long journey in from Tallaght. It was still too early to go on to O'Connell Street for my surprise and, although I was curious, I asked no questions, because I knew there was a treat coming up.

Bartle said that he could not cross the Liffey without seeing what Johnny King had in his pet shop in Capel Street. Since we had time to spare, we headed in that direction. I ran into McQuillan's tool shop, where Billy was a saw doctor, to say hello, and Bartle went ahead. When I followed him up to the pet shop, there was a big African Grey parrot in a cage outside the door. Bartle was inside talking to Mr King about how popular the breeding of zebra finches had become, and remarking that anyone would think that the colours of the Java sparrows were hand-painted, they looked so brilliant, so I went back to the parrot again.

I kept repeating, 'Say "uncle", yeh divil,' to him, because of the story Tommy had told me about a man who had a rich uncle and a pet parrot whose repertoire went no further than that slogan. But this bird just combed its plume with a huge talon and screeched, 'Hello,' before continuing to eat from a dish of spinach. When Bartle thought the time was right to move on, we walked down Mary Street, into

O'Connell Street, and turned left towards the Gresham Hotel. There was a row of trees growing on the island in the middle of the road, with traffic hurtling up and down on both sides of it.

Bartle pointed towards these trees as we approached. The branches were bright with fairy lights for Christmas, and at first I thought these were the surprise that he intended. However, as we passed the O'Connell Hall, my heart jumped when I heard a lovely twittering sound. I ran to the edge of the pavement and stared at the trees. I could see some dark-coloured birds darting about in the intermittent brightness of the fairy lights. As my eyes got used to the glare, it was like looking for stars at night, and more and more birds came into view, until I could see hundreds of them in every tree. This was the best surprise ever!

The birds moved about without rest, just taking short hops from one branch to another and coming in and out of sight, while keeping up a continuous muted song. They showed no fear of humans or traffic, and I thought how they added to the fun of Christmas. The chirping got louder as we stood between the trees on the island in the middle of the road.

'Willy, Willy Wagtail,' Bartle said. 'So you like them?'

I said, 'Deffo, I sure do,' and sang out:

Willy, Willy Wagtail,
Born in a handcart,
Christened in an eggshell,
Willy, Willy Wagtail.

'Pied wagtails,' said Bartle. 'They come here when it gets dark every evening during the winter to keep warm, and there's no sign of them in summer. During the day they go off to the country to find food, but the cold of winter in the fields would kill them, so they come back here.'

I had never heard of birds staying in Ireland and coming in to O'Connell Street to keep warm in the winter. I thought they flew away to Africa if they could not stand the cold. I remembered what Father Byrne had said about 'He that cares when a sparrow falls' and I realised that truly understanding nature was beyond me. I was wondering if I would be able to see the birds standing on one leg asleep, as I had seen with birds in a cage, and if they could keep their balance on the sloping branches, but they were by no means ready to rest.

While I was daydreaming of wagtails and that trip to O'Connell Street, Bartle was seeing off his visitor, who was now on his way for mousetraps to Mr O'Connor's hardware shop close by. That was my opportunity to say goodbye, and I left Bartle planning a visit to the Natural History Museum for us when he got a chance. I set out for the Polo Grounds in the Phoenix Park, waving to my cousins, Dermot and Dorothy O'Connor, as I passed their family greengrocer's shop in Thomas Street. Being intent on my own affairs, I did not call in as I normally would.

When I got to the Polo Grounds, a bicycle polo match was in progress, but it ended just as I arrived. I was pleased about that, because the huge sward was like a nature reserve. A butterfly landed near me on a crushed dandelion, and a trio of swallows took over the polo pitch without delay, speeding along just above the ground. The meadow between the Polo Grounds and the main road had been cut. The smell was sweet, and the birds were foraging there in an excited way, disappearing from view now and then in the stubble. On a previous visit with Billy, I had noticed a song thrush that seemed to be nesting in the trees behind the pavilion, but was very fond of feeding on the lawn of the Polo Grounds. I knew by now that if I approached him directly he would fly away, but if I walked in closing circles around him, I could get within a few feet and see how his lovely dappled plumage ruffled in the breeze. He always flew directly over the pavilion on to the top of one of the trees behind the iron railings.

Whether he sang from the tree to entertain his mate, or from sheer joy, I do not know, but I stood filled with pleasure. He sang a whole melody, then repeated it, and it reminded me of lines I had heard so often:

> *That's the wise thrush; he sings each song twice*
> *over,*
> *Lest you should think he never could recapture*
> *The first fine careless rapture!...*

The day was turning into a damp teatime as I crossed the main road of the park from the Polo Grounds and went towards the Dog Pond to see if there was any bird life to be seen there. A coot emerged from the reeds with her gingery chicks. A mother duck followed in the same corridor a few minutes later, glancing anxiously around at her family of eight, all tiny.

I sat alone on a quiet seat inside the wire fence of the Dog

Pond Park, and I thought I heard a bird singing softly, as sweet a song as I had ever heard before. It seemed to come from far away. As I sat listening, I realised that birdsong brought me calm and peace and that it was a gift from kind and generous Nature. It was there in the sound of the bells of the two cathedrals pealing across the Liberties, and in the loud calls of the dealers in Thomas Street. Birdsong was everywhere, and it brought me happiness.

I recalled the little toy bird strung across the pram for the baby to play with when I was little more than a baby myself, and later, the bird-shaped whistle that was filled with water, warbling when you blew on it. And the time when Uncle Paddy had bought us a little mechanical bluebird. 'Listen to this, Shonny,' he had said. 'I'm after teaching this bird to sing my song.' With that he started to whistle, and when he stopped, he wound up our toy. It sang the very same song! We were astounded.

I believed, in a way, that my own nature was mirrored in that of the wild birds, and I was beginning to recognise desire in myself. I imagined that the intimacy of birds, and the warmth of their family life, must have a human equivalent, for which I had a covert aspiration. As my perception grew, I understood that the tendency of wild birds towards carefree love and bravado about tomorrow were qualities that attracted me to them. It also seemed clear to me that family life in the Liberties was founded on the same audacity: you needed only one day's daring at a time.

It was so peaceful there that I knew the spirit of Nature was present, and was very grateful for it. Here, on my own, all I wanted to do was to share in that world. I remembered a saying I had learned when I asked Dad if there was any mention of birds in the Bible:

> *Yea, the sparrow has found a house,*
> *And the swallow a nest for herself,*
> *Where she may lay her young ...*

I left the Dog Pond, looking for a coppice where I could practise my bird-watching. I found what I needed close to the civil service cricket pitch, a fairly dense thicket of mature trees with crows nesting in the top branches. The peace of the park permeated the coppice, and I was at peace too. Nothing stirred, but I was getting better at catching the swift movement of birds from the corner of my eye. Two big crows were strutting about near me in their stiff-legged way, as if they were on stilts, trying to look unconcerned, but never turning their backs to me. They were picking over the dead leaves on the ground, and occasionally lifting one up.

The traffic noises faded to a hum as I made my way deeper in among the trees. A robin seemed to be following me, making a sudden dart into the grass I had disturbed to emerge with a wriggling centipede. I was looking for a tree big enough to hide behind, so that I would not be seen so easily. I soon found one, a gnarled old specimen with some branches torn by storm and lightning, standing in its own pool of sunlight in the coppice. I settled down to wait, stock still, at arm's length from the tree. I knew the birds would have noticed me and that I would have to be patient until they got used to my presence. The bark of the tree was rough to my hand and spotted with damp patches. The rain had stopped, but the brightness was beginning to leave the sky anyway. The calls from the cricket pitch had gone quiet, and the sunlight shining on the side of the trees was beginning to ascend, being slowly replaced by the evening shade.

A boy and a girl passed me, holding hands and looking warmly at each other, hardly smiling, their faces tranquil. They must have seen me as a fixture, because they ignored my presence. But I was at home, feeling every bit the true observer, even if I had no camera, no binoculars and no picnic basket. I was on Nature's blessed trail; I did not need anything more. As I stood there with attention, I could see bees flying in and out of the trees around the wood, and I had the occasional raucous talk of the crows on their high perch for conversation.

I noticed a sudden movement. It was a little brown bird, perched on the bole of a nearby tree. I thought it was a sparrow at first, but it was behaving oddly. It was darting quickly from one tree to another and, as it did, it alighted very close to the ground every time. Then it started to climb up the tree in a circle, prying into the bark with its beak, which I could see was long and curved. I had no idea what bird it was, but I was content to observe.

As it flitted from tree to tree, it was quite restless and never seemed to be satisfied with what it found. It was like a gourmet at a feast, overwhelmed by choice and not quite content with any of the fare. As it landed on a tree to my left, I slowly turned my head to have a better look. It was not a sparrow or indeed any bird that I had ever seen. It moved up the tree, and I could see that it was mostly brown in colour, with a white breast. It seemed to be solitary, so I thought it might be a young bird making its way in the world. As I was noting how quickly it flitted from tree to tree, it came closer to me. I held my breath. Suddenly, the little bird landed on the tree where I was standing. It was out of my sight but, in the silence of my rapt attention, I could hear the tiny sounds it made as it started to ascend.

I stood in stone until this petite vision came fully into view, still climbing slowly upwards in a spiral. I could now see the delicacy of its plumage, its speckled brown wings and its tail brushing the tree as it went. It rose even higher, moving across the trunk, so that it came right in front of me at eye level, but still had not noticed me. An impulse seized me and, as the bird stopped for a morsel, I decided to try to hold it in my hand. I felt as one with Nature, and it seemed to me to be the natural thing to do, and I was oblivious to anything else in the physical world around me.

Dad had taught me how to catch a bird. In captivity, a budgerigar will cling to the wires of the aviary, and to grab it without injury is an art. You shaped your hand as if you were holding a tennis ball, then straightened the first two fingers. When you approached the bird, you struck with the speed of catching a fly in mid-air, in such a way that your cupped hand was over the bird and it was not crushed by your palm. While you did this, your fingers were directed to miss each side of the neck, so that all the force of movement was taken up by the tips of the fingers striking the wires of the aviary, and there was no direct contact with the bird.

As the little bird was at its nearest to me on the trunk, I moved. I held it in my hand for a second; a moment of joyful wonder. I could not believe what I had done, but I was delighted that I had come so close to Nature, and I hoped I had not frightened the bird too much. When I opened my hand, it flew away quickly, calling softly. I looked at my palm in disbelief. There was a single piece of tiny white down clinging to it, dewy from the rain. When I saw it, I joined in the poet's praise for 'He Who hath made the night of stars', and gave thanks.

The next day I found out that my bird was a treecreeper, common enough in Ireland but one that I have never forgotten. After that experience, I felt sorry for wild birds in their cages and made up my mind not to go to the bird market any more. I missed my walk there on Sunday mornings, through St Patrick's Park, around the corner of tiny Canon Street, and a few doors up into Bride Street, opposite the Molyneux Church. The bird market was in a short and narrow blind alleyway, where the buyers and the sellers stood together, usually all men, with little room to move if it was a busy Sunday. In fact, I never saw a woman there in either role. The birds were mostly wild, except for the occasional canary or mule, which the seller might claim could stand up to the best in the Mansion House shows and could sing the Hollow Roll trill like Ronnie Ronalde, the great whistler.

How we stood for hours doing nothing but staring at the birds, watching who was buying and enjoying the chat! The cages of birds to be sold were hung on permanent nails on one ancient wall, so that the little crowd could face the same direction in the narrow alley. 'How much for the grey pate?' a man would enquire, and when the deal for that young goldfinch was done, the seller would say, 'Ask Mick there. He bought one off me last week and it's turning into a great singer.' Then he would grope around the shallow holding cage where his stock of trapped birds was held, so as to put another up for sale. The only access to this cage was through a round hole in the roof, connected to a long sock, which was normally kept tied until the trapper had to reach in to pick his next bird.

The buyer would say something like 'I only wanted it for my grandson, he loves birds,' being too shy to say that it was for himself. Another man talked, to kill time, about shooting game birds on Luggala in the Wicklow Mountains, and how a covey of grouse when disturbed would always fly away in different directions for their own safety. Then there was the man who cycled in every week from the Naas Road and talked about the people feeding the swans in the Grand Canal up his way. The swans had the company of ducks and water hens, with pigeons on the footpath and seagulls lurking on the factory roof across the road, waiting to clean up when everyone had gone home. I remembered his excitement the day he told us about the kingfisher he had seen flying low over the stretch of canal on Davitt Road, early in the morning when he was going to work.

But the talk was also about the changing times. The lads were saying, 'We won't be here much longer; the law is going to call in one of these days about selling wild birds,' and being answered with, 'But we've done it for hundreds of years, and we won't be stopping now.' It was all so innocent. But I never did visit the bird market again after my treecreeper experience.

Still, I had other adventures, closer to home. It was the

first Monday of January when this one started. 'Here,' said Uncle Joe to me. 'Drown these two rats in the trow on the landing. I'm off to Mass for Hansel Monday. Make sure to set the trap again when you're finished.' I knew Joe loved to go to John's Lane Chapel to hear Dal McNulty play the 'Hallelujah Chorus' on the organ, so I could not demur.

One of Joe's habits was to keep a cage-trap set in the cellar under the house and to inspect it on Sunday nights after tea. Rats were endemic in the broken sewers of the ancient cellars of the Liberties. This week, two rats had been taken prisoner. They had made the mistake of entering the cage and gnawing at the baited mechanism that sprung the door shut behind them. The cellar had no windows and no electric light and, at one end, ran into tumbledown vaulted brick arches stretching under Francis Street.

The only light was provided by the doors at the other end, which opened out into the overgrown backyard. Since I had the job of lighting the fires early in the dark mornings of winter, I was well acquainted with the creepiness of moving through the pitch-black cellar to open the back door for light. It was there that I chopped the sticks and filled the coal scuttle. The content of the cellar was old meat boxes and mouldering sacks that had been used by McCarrens of Cavan to deliver pig meat to the shop. Coal for the fires upstairs was stacked in a heap, mixed with turf and slack.

Water could be heard dripping in the vaulted section of cellar under Francis Street, and the occasional squealing of a sewer rat on his travels through the vaults could stop your heart. No one but Joe went into the back of the spooky basement and then only on Sunday nights.

Joe's command to drown the rats was peremptory. There was nothing for it but to obey. I knew what was expected and, anyway, I had a child's ruthless curiosity. Joe went over to John's Lane Chapel for Mass and I turned to the trap. The rats lay huddled together on the floor of the cage, cowering. One was a bit bigger than the other. I stared at them from a distance, in awe of their reputation for cunning.

Now and again they would bite madly at the bars of the cage, then fall back to a corner. I took a deep breath and picked up the cage by the poker handle. Orders were orders, and it would be forsaking my pocket money for a month if I disobeyed. There was a trow on the landing, so I put the plug in the outlet, and placed the cage in the trow before I turned on the tap. I expected to see the water rise rapidly over the creatures but, to my horror, I saw that they could swim. I thought that only water rats in the canal could do that. I had meant no cruelty, but in seconds the water had risen over the top of the cage.

I was upset by this outcome, but at least I would know what to do if it happened again. I hoped that the rats would die soon, and painlessly. When a suitable time had passed I lifted the cage out of the water. To my guilty horror, I saw that the two rats were still moving, although they had been under water for a good few minutes.

I knew then that I should have filled the sink first and just dumped the cage in, but what to do now? I had no heart to put the rats back in the water, but Joe would return from John's Lane soon and would not be long about drowning them himself.

Maybe I could save them. I grabbed the cage and ran down

to the cellar. This time there was no fear. I lit my way to the place where the cage was normally set and left it there. At least the rats would be safe until Sunday, when Joe did his next inspection. In the meantime, I would look after them.

Every morning after that, I fed the rats on a piece of bread and poured water into the bottom tray to give them a drink. At first they were afraid of me, and lunged at the bars when I appeared, but they ate up when I had gone. However, after a few days I noticed that they had settled down and seemed to anticipate the food I dropped in the cage. I studied them while they ate. I could see that the bigger of the two had a scar on his tail. The second one was unusual in that the markings on the brown skin were slightly different on each side.

I decided to call them Uncas and Cora, after the heroes of *The Last of the Mohicans*, a picture I had seen in the Tivoli Cinema. I felt sorry for that couple after their pitiful end at the hands of Magua, the bad Indian. The way the lovers had died, touching hands and leaving love unspoken, stirred something in me. As the days passed, I was getting to know the rats, and they depended on me for supplies. However, on Sunday I had to solve the problem of Joe making his weekly visit to inspect the trap. So, after Mass, I emptied out an old orange box I found in the shed at the end of our backyard, and made some netting wire do for a lid. Then I dumped the rats into the orange box already prepared with food and water and left them there until the Monday morning.

I re-set the trap for Joe's inspection and he passed no comment. On the Monday morning, I reinstated the rats in the cage before I went to school. I continued to feed Uncas and Cora during that second week, sometimes on bread and other times on the occasional bit of meat from the shop. By this time the creatures had lost some of their wildness, and seemed to know me. I called into the pet shop to ask about rats. I was told they make great pets, and that they can speak to each other. Not only that, but they laugh when they are tickled.

I was very curious about this and could not wait to see if it was true. I took a toothbrush from the bathroom and approached the rats. I reached down through the roof of the cage and began to stroke the neck of the big one, Uncas. The rat stood still and leaned his neck to one side. I continued, and in no time I discovered that he was ticklish all over. What was more, he seemed to show his teeth in a big grin!

I was their source of food and water, and now I had the capacity to relate to them in a friendly way, and it made me happy. Again at the weekend, I repeated my routine of moving the rats to the shed, leaving the trap set and empty for Joe's inspection before bringing them back to the cellar. Things were about to change, however.

At the music class in school one morning, Brother Devitt noticed that Georgie Graham had let something fall on the floor and picked it up. It was a hollowed-out cork like a miniature canoe. However, Georgie had positioned a row of pins along the open side of the cork to make a crude tiny cage. Inside this prison was a bluebottle, fluttering its wings hopelessly. I had often seen this done before. When Georgie was challenged he said it was a pet and all the boys had them.

Devitt was kind, and understood the children of the Liberties. However, he saw God in everything. 'Remember, the best prayer a boy can say is to praise Nature,' he said. 'What you have done shows you have the gift of wonder at God's world. But it would be nicer if you were to let Nature be Nature. No wild creature should be kept in a cage, so let the poor thing out now.'

Georgie had to do what he was told. Class resumed, but I was preoccupied at the admonition to let Nature be Nature. I knew it was equally wrong to keep rats in captivity so I made up my mind to do something about it. I was getting tired of the effort anyway, and was losing sleep at what would happen if Joe found out. The following morning I slipped downstairs to say goodbye to Uncas and Cora. I, too, would let them return to the wild in praise of Nature. My heart was lighter. I took the cage by candlelight to the very back of the cellar and jammed open the door near the manhole with the broken cover. After a few minutes the rats came slowly out of the cage, looked around for a second, then bolted for the escape route.

I was sad to see them go, and hoped that they would be all right. At least I had let Nature be Nature, and I would not be misleading Joe any more. I left the cage back in place and set it again. I knew the adventure was over. There was no one to share my secret and I missed them for a few days. On the following Monday morning I went down to the cellar to chop sticks for the fire and found Joe already there. He had the rat trap hanging by his side.

'Funny thing, Shonny,' he said. 'I thought I heard a rat squeak last week when I was down here and I knew they were around. So I put down poison as well as baiting the cage. That way I had every chance of catching them. The poison must have been taken by two of them and that finished them off. At least, they look poisoned to me, but I can't make it out. I found them dead in the cage last night, although they obviously hadn't touched the bait inside because the door was still open. Why they went in there to die, I don't know. Anyway, go and bury them in the grassyard.'

I took the cage. It was Uncas and Cora. The shadows flickered in the cellar. Let Nature be Nature. Magua had won again.

9. FAMILY VOICES

MAM

January 1978

My dear children,
It's hard for me tonight, when I think of all my lovely kids gone from me, but I know they never forget me and they love me – they show it in every way possible.

I want to say that your Dad and I had a very happy life since we met in the Liberties and I don't regret anything. I can remember a lot of my early days. I was born at 138, Francis Street on the 6th of December 1903. That's where the Tivoli Cinema is now. My mother owned a provisions shop there and my father was a chimney cleaning contractor to the Board of Works, so we were pretty well off.

I remember King Edward the Seventh dying in England in 1910 and the English soldiers lining the streets on the day of his funeral. He had been over here a few times, but when he last came in 1903, things were

*beginning to change, and my mother told me that Dublin
Corporation would not let him make a speech to them.*

*It rained on the day of his funeral and the soldiers' big
Busby hats were a quare sight for the kids. Afterwards,
King George the Fifth and Queen Mary came to Dublin
in 1911 to pray in St Patrick's Cathedral and they had
Prince Edward and Princess Mary with them in an
open carriage. They drove along Francis Street to the
Iveagh Play Centre, in Myra Hall, protected by the Fifth
Lancers. I can remember our neighbour bringing Molly
and me up to the top storey of our house. She got us
to throw down orange skins and apple peelings as they
passed. We did not know it, but the people had begun to
get rid of England altogether.*

*In 1913, my mother bought a bigger house with eight
rooms at number 15 Francis Street, just across the road
from us. It had tenants, but my mother paid them to move
and she kept the house for us. It was a very old, four-
storey house then but, after the collapse of tenements
with loss of life, in Church Street, the Corporation got
nervous and we had to demolish the two top storeys of
our house some years later.*

*Also in 1913, Larkin made his famous speech calling
for a general strike. It was so general that even the boys
in the National School in Meath Street went on strike for
cheaper books. The lockout really started in August of
1913. There were riots in the Liberties and the men were
blocking the tram lines on Thomas Street. I remember
the mounted police charging the crowd down Francis
Street and beating everyone with their batons, but we*

were all safe inside our house looking at them through the windows.

After that, a lot of the men in the Liberties joined the Irish Volunteers and some fought in the rising of 1916. Others later enlisted with the Irish Republican Army, who took orders from the first Dáil of 1918. John Redmond, our MP in the English Parliament, was begging for recruits for the English army, because war had broken out with Germany and poor Belgium was getting it bad. The English promised John Redmond that Home Rule would be put on the statute book, so our men went to fight for the freedom of small nations and for hopes of a united Ireland as well. Hundreds of men from the Liberties were killed or injured with the 16th Irish Division in France, just when the rising of 1916 was taking place, but England broke their promise and we never got any further.

After the 1914 war, the men started to come home, and in our street alone, we had three half-mad men. One would stand at the corner of the street clapping his hands and roaring out 'damn the weather' and he was given that name. Another fellow we called Fiddler Cahill. He came home with a battered cornet which he thought he could play. Well, one day he hit some other fellow and when this chap fell, Fiddler started to play the Last Post over him. Another man named Martin Mulcair sang of John Farrell, who used to make a dartboard of his wife, but never got her with the knife. His habit was to throw his wooden leg on the Armistice Day bonfire.

One of my brothers, William, had gone to fight in the

British Army and another brother, Jim, joined the Irish
Volunteers in 1917 and then became a member of the
Old Irish Republican Army. Jim joined D Company, 1st
Battalion, Dublin Brigade. His officers picked him as
being suitable for promotion to the Active Service Unit
and he went for training in County Wicklow under the
command of Paddy O'Daly.

He was engaged first of all in armed patrols on the
North Circular Road, and about this time his Company
Senior Officer was Peter O'Connor from Oscar Square,
who was no relation. Another Liberties man in the
Active Service Unit was his friend Paddy Rigney, who
lived in Meath Street.

I suppose Jim's most important contribution was in
making contact with British soldiers in different barracks
in the city and buying arms from them. He was able to
do this because my Dad was a chimney sweep contractor
to the various barracks, so access was easier. Some of
the soldiers were sympathetic anyway. He fought for
his country, and he was awarded the Active Service
Black and Tan Medal, with bar, inscribed with the Irish
word, Cómhrac, meaning Combat. My brother Joe joined
Fianna Éireann, and was a founder member of Fianna
Fáil. He later became National Organiser for that party.

Ours was a lively street, with something always
going on. Still, they had great respect for us, and the men
would tip their caps when Molly and I were passing.
After my father died in 1927, I decided to open a little
provisions shop in Summerhill. I had always worked for
my mother in her shop, so I knew all about stock and the

profits that could be made. As my intended husband, Tom, had another year of study to complete before he could claim a man's wages, I felt it was up to me to do something to save for our wedding, which was on the 16th July 1928.

Our first baby, Billy, was born on the 29th April 1929 but, even before the birth, trade was getting bad. I had to leave the shop in charge of your Dad, who had no experience to count on, and we got into so much debt that I was unable to pay the rent on the shop. Meantime, his employer told him he had no work for him, so I made a big decision.

I wrote to an old friend of my mother in Montreal to see if we could go out to stay with them until we found a place of our own. They sent a wire to come straight away and I began to sell off all the things we owned. The wedding presents had to be sold, and also the baby's pram and the furniture had to go back to the shop where we had bought it on hire purchase.

We emigrated to Canada in August 1929, when little Billy was only ten weeks old. It was an awful experience, starting with nothing in a strange country, but we managed. At first, Dad could not get any work, as every man seemed to be idle on account of the Wall Street crash, which happened just a few weeks after we arrived in Canada. So I got work in the pantry of a well known family in Montreal, cleaning the silver and all sorts of jobs. The cook was very good to me and showed me how to do some lovely dishes for dinner. Then, after a while, Dad got work and I stayed home to mind Billy.

On the fifteenth of May, 1930, little Helen Margaret, called Eily, was born, but she died in September of that year, and was buried in the Angels Plot of Notre Dame des Neiges Cemetery in Montreal.

While I was working, I bought a ticket for the Soldiers' and Sailors' Club sweepstake. It cost me a dollar and I had great hopes of winning. Well, it's the 2nd of October 1930, the day of the draw, and I am watching the door all day for the telegram boy to call, but it's now 6 o'clock and your Dad is in. As we sat down to dinner, a knock came to the door and, sure enough, it was the boy. He handed the wire to my husband. By this time my heart was thumping. Tom opened the envelope and the wire said: If we send you your fares, will you come home?

Unknown to me, your Dad had been complaining to his mother about how bad things were in Montreal, so our two mothers in Dublin had decided to send us the money to return. I liked Montreal and was sorry to leave it, but we came home on the last boat in November 1930, before the St Lawrence River froze up for the winter. I was sorry to think that we were coming back home worse off than when we had started.

After we arrived in Dublin from Canada we went to live with your Dad's family in Francis Street, as they had more room for us. We only lived across the road from my mother's house, but all the rooms there were occupied. After a while one of my brothers and his family got a house of their own and when they moved out, my mother gave us their room, so we started a new home just where we had begun in the first place. Later on, Dad got a better job. Things went reasonably well for us and we had another addition to the family, Nell.

Billy, by this time, was very healthy and up to every mischief and when I took Nell out for a walk in the Liberties in the afternoons, he used to kiss every little girl we would meet. One day we were coming from St Stephens Green and he was holding on to the pram. He had a halfpenny and wanted to go in to Fullers, a beautiful cake shop in Grafton Street.

I told him they only served ladies. He then wanted to know what a lady was. I didn't know what to say as he wasn't three years old, so I said ladies were women who wore fur coats and lovely hats. When the first lady came by he stopped her and had a good look and then came running back to me. 'Mam,' he said, 'if you had a hat and coat like her, you would be a lady too.' He made my day for me and often did again, after that.

Nell was born on the 11th November 1931. She was a lovely fair-haired baby and her hair grew very long in a couple of years. She was a very quiet little one and Billy and she loved each other. She loved paint books and pencils and spent all her time at these when she was growing.

NELL

Mam's mention of my hair takes me right back to the front room over the shop in 15 Francis Street, where we lived for much of my childhood. When Mam was working downstairs, a trusted babysitter named Julia Mangan looked after me until she came back. One day, Julia got the notion to cut off my curls. I was more than happy to agree; it was an adventure, after all. However, when Mam came in she was furious and sacked Julia on the spot. But for me that was not the worst. When Dad came in, I was already in bed. He took one look at me and said, 'That's not my little girl, that's not my princess.'

I was terrified. Dad didn't recognise me. He didn't want me without my curls. It was my first experience of rejection and it has never left me. No doubt he comforted me afterwards, but I don't remember that. The memory is the desolation at being disowned, however temporarily. In fact, I grew up in a warm, close relationship with both Mam and Dad, who always greatly encouraged me to believe in myself.

We spent a lot of time down in Nannie O'Neill's kitchen/ living room. It had a small window through which she could watch out for customers entering the shop. I loved watching Nannie in the evening when she would let down her beautiful waist-long hair and, heating the tongs on the range, would curl the front as a fringe, and then make one long plait. In the daytime, the plait would be wound around her head, almost like a crown. Really lovely. She often took me to the Tivoli Cinema where we sat upstairs in the best seats, not in the flea pit. She was also good for the odd penny when she sent one on messages.

Upstairs, bread and jam was a staple, and when you sprinkled sugar on it behind Mam's back, it was a gorgeous treat. For some years bread was rationed and it was necessary to join a long queue for our big daily order. The outer face of the loaf was the 'heel' and it was like a biscuit, so worth fighting for.

But perhaps, for me, the highlight of living in the Liberties was my daily trips to Thomas Street Library where my love of books was nurtured. From there I could see into the back garden of my cousins' house next door, which made me feel even more at home. I loved the smell of the books and the quiet of the room and spent many happy hours there. First I read the fairy stories, and then progressed to the *Katy* books, and eventually to westerns by William C. Tuttle, which I loved. They always had a touch of romance, very subtle, but enough to satisfy the soul of a twelve-year-old. By the time I was sixteen, under the guidance of Sister Carmel at Warrenmount Convent as well as a very helpful librarian, I was well into Graham Greene, Somerset Maugham, Dickens and many more, so that ultimately in later years I was reading anything I could get hold of. I still do!

Throughout these growing-up years, Billy and I were very close, as he was the eldest boy and I the eldest girl. He was so full of life, always out and about, and when he was a little older, endlessly practised his harmonica for the concerts he played in. However, there were a few more siblings to come, with whom close bonds were also forged.

But let Mam herself continue her story in which she had a word for us all.

MAM

Peggy was born on the 4th May, 1933. She was a lovely little one with curly black hair. Peggy was different to Nell. She loved being out playing with the girls on the street, and right through the family, I thank God they were all good children. I am very proud that none of them

*ever got into trouble or came to the notice of the law. Of
course, I can't tell what happened when they were out
playing, but here in the house they were very good. I
know I worked very hard for them at home while Dad
went out to the factory to earn the money to support us.*

PEGGY

Although my name is Margaret, I was called Peggy. I remember
the Liberties well. There was a pub on every corner, including
the two corners of Francis Street at the Thomas Street end.
Five adjoining streets had a chapel in them: James Street,
Thomas Street, Meath Street, High Street and Francis Street.
Poverty was rife, but faith was very strong. The O'Neill
family supported various religious societies and Seán made
a list of these that he used for a composition in school. They
included The Franciscan Missionary Union, The Perpetual
Lamp in honour of the Child Jesus of Prague, The Seraphic
Mass Association, The League of Faith in Honour of Our
Lady of the Rosary, The Association in Honour of Our Lady
of Lourdes, The Novena of Grace in Honour of St Francis
Xavier, The Association of the Perpetual Lamp and The
Apostleship of Prayer.

Children were seen and not heard, but were quite happy
to play ball in the entrance lane at the side of the Iveagh
Market. We spent many hours watching the dealers selling
the old clothes on the market stalls. Picking up each article,
they would shout, 'Come on, girls, offer me sixpence,
fourpence, come on, a bargain for twopence.'

Nannie O'Neill, like a lot of people in the Liberties, would
go to seven o'clock Mass every morning, accompanied by

myself or another of her grandchildren, and then go back again for eight o'clock evening devotions, such as the Rosary or Benediction. Nannie lived simply, prayed simply, ate simply and loved simply. Life was hard for some of our neighbours who might not have running hot water and sometimes no running water indoors at all. Toilets in that case were mostly outdoors and were terrible in winter.

On Sundays we followed the James's Street Pipe Band up Thomas Street and back to their hall, dancing along on the pavement to their pipes and drums, forgetting we would have to walk all the way back to Francis Street by ourselves. Men were hard on their children and women were strict, but softer. Some men were easy-going and humorous, like my uncles Joe and Paddy O'Neill, and would help you with your homework.

There were two display windows in Nannie's pork shop. One contained only pigs' feet, or pigs' trotters, as some people called them. Being a child, I was only allowed to sell on Saturday mornings, there being no school. Best were the funerals. Beautiful hearses with two sides of pure glass, drawn by lovely black horses, with black plumes like large feathers on their heads for married people and white ones for children or single people. You were delighted as a child to hear a neighbour had died, because it meant you could accompany your nannie in one of the carriages and, of course, that meant a day off school. The funeral procession went around the block three times, to pass the dead person's home each time, before going on to the cemetery.

My big brother Billy was always there for me growing up, steady and dependable. He had warm hands, and would hold mine if I was cold. I missed him so much when he got married and emigrated to Australia with Alice on the same day.

MAM

> *We were still living in one room, although a big old-fashioned one, and nothing much happened except we had our fourth baby. Tommy was born on June 1st, 1934. He was a big baby and poor Peggy fretted so much that although she did not often cry, as Tommy grew bigger, she seemed to get smaller and people used to think they were twins. But I nursed her all the more, which made her very happy.*

TOMMY

I was the second eldest boy, and named after my father, Tom, in the custom of the Liberties, where the eldest boy was named for the grandfather and the second eldest after the father. Uncle Joe stored the meat in open barrels in the shop, as there was no fridge. Each barrel was filled with brine, water made salty by the addition of saltpetre, or nitre, which was also a deadly explosive. When the barrels leaked they were taken down to McNamaras, the coopers on Francis Street, next to where Aunt Eileen lived.

I was often sent for fish to the stalls on the corner of Thomas Street. There were five meat shops all clustered together in Francis Street. Starting with us, a pork butchers that sold the cheaper cuts of meat, there was Clarkes across the road, who were also pork butchers but who sold upmarket meat, like chops and steaks. Then there was Durney's shop at 142 Francis Street, where Granddad O'Connor and his family lived overhead, while Matt Moore and McGurks faced each other near the Iveagh Market. In the market itself was Hughie Matthews, a garrulous little forager who would enter into negotiations with his customers, because they would never accept his first price.

When it came to playing football, Baker Wardell's tea and coffee factory was the place to go for the ball. We would call out, 'Mistah, givvis a ball of silvah,' in the loading bay that opened out to Francis Street and, if you were lucky, one of the staff would throw down a ball of aluminium foil, which was used to line the tea chests that came with the tea the firm imported. There was a delicious smell of tea and coffee around the entrance, and I loved to take a deep sniff for enjoyment. Dad kept birds in the very early days, canaries and budgies, and that was the hobby of a lot of men in the Liberties.

Billy was very much the big brother. He left me his beautiful racing bicycle when he went to Australia. It was a French handmade bike and I was walking on air. This model was made of chrome all over and did not weigh much. I used to show how light it was by lifting it by the saddle in my teeth.

MAM

Martha was born on Saturday, the 18th April, 1936. She was to me another bit of responsibility, but I can't say anything that was strange about her, only that she was a real one for getting things done in the house. As she got older, if I wanted a room decorated, Martha did the work and also all sorts of jobs around the house. She was a real lively kid and loved children. On Sundays she

*would make cakes for tea and cut the pastry in all shapes
of horses, dogs and rabbits and the kitchen was a really
happy place with Martha around.*

MARTHA

'A wall of O'Connors against the world' is my enduring impression from childhood years. Behind that wall, utter chaos, teeming with life: laughter and tears, singing and squabbling, jeering and jesting; a school for survival in which you learned to fight your corner or duck and run, give in and adapt or try to change our little world to your liking.

A rough-and-tumble, with no holds barred, with each individual personality tussling for attention or time or space – or even for the top of Dad's egg! And underscoring all this mayhem was a solid sense of security, the unmentioned love and loyalty that spelled trouble for anyone who dared hurt one of the clan.

There was quite a bit of religious ritual as part of the family life. All members of the family, big and small, were summoned nightly to say the Rosary after supper. We would all kneel in the kitchen facing the hearth over which there was a picture of the Blessed Virgin Mary. Dad, in his lovely deep voice, would intone the first half of the 'Hail Mary, full of grace ...' while we children would respond with 'Holy Mary, Mother of God ...'

However, as we approached the end of the prayer, the older siblings would begin to speed up the pace of the responses as they would want to get away to their dates or dances or whatever, and by the fifth decade of the Rosary, the responses would have lapsed into an incoherent garble.

Religion didn't dominate our lives but it was very much a part of them and it did make us aware now and then that there was such a thing as a 'state of grace'. As one of the nuns put it to our class, 'Light a candle in your heart for love and make sure it never goes out.' Well, my candle has flickered now and then over the years but it has never been extinguished and even now, at seventy-seven years of age, it still burns brightly. I could go on but it is enough to know now that, although there are a few bricks missing, the wall of O'Connors is still standing.

MAM

Seán was born on Monday, 11th July 1938, and was a real trouble maker. Even at Warrenmount School he would cause all sorts of trouble. Among his sisters at home, after he got them all arguing, he would slip out laughing and all the girls after him. At school he did very well. The Masters said he was brilliant (that's what he said). I let him stay in Nannie's house when we moved to Keeper Road as he was a help to her and he was attending school in Francis Street Parish anyway. I went into Francis Street every weekday so that he was free to come and go as he pleased to either house. Rita was born on 30th August 1939. She was terribly small, only weighing 5 lbs. but she survived with the help of Dr Fitzpatrick, a family friend and a decent man who charged very little for the work he did for his patients in the Liberties. Rita was just like the others after a year, only she was very nervous.

RITA

Seán, do you remember trying to teach me to swallow tablets? I still can't do it. Also, I had a problem with very high winds and was terrified by thunderstorms. When I played around outside I thought I would lose my hair if it was a windy day.

I enjoyed school in Warrenmount Convent but then went on to Weaver Square Secondary School. I hated it because they compared me with Martha, who was very bright. The nun kept telling me I was stupid. That convinced Mam and Dad to let me go to work. I loved earning a few bob, both for Mam and myself, and I always saved up for nice clothes. Nell was a terror for wearing my clothes (without permission) so Terry Keenan built me a big lockable box to go under my bed.

Paddy Whelan gave me my first pair of skates, hence my love of skating. I wore jeans to the rink but Dad had many a cross word about that. My high-heel shoes were always with me for a quick change, without his knowledge.

MAM

Barry was born on the 18th September, a Friday, in 1942. Barry was a real happy go lucky toddler and sang at every opportunity. He had the loveliest head of black hair, wavy and curly. Joseph was born on the 16th July 1941, my wedding anniversary; and it was he who died suddenly in 1955. He had lived a normal boy's life but it still came as an awful shock to us. Barry and Joe were very close, and palled around together all the time.

BARRY

Well, Joe and I were such good pals that I would like to tell this story for him. He was nine years old and I was eight at the time. One day, we went for a ramble to the Phoenix Park. On our way, we passed a big house and we noticed apple trees growing in the back garden. The gate was open so we decided to go in and get a few apples. We were stuffing them down our jerseys when suddenly the gate slammed shut. The man who lived there had come and caught us red-handed. 'I'll get the police for you boys,' he said.

We started to cry and said sorry. 'Stop your crying,' he said, and opened the gate again. 'Go on home and don't come back any more.' He must have felt sorry for us as he told us we could keep the apples we already had. 'Oh, thank you, mister,' we said, with big smiles on our faces. Then we ran out and headed for the park.

We met some boys from school and had a game of football with them and shared our apples. It was great fun. 'Let's go to the zoo,' said Frank. 'I know a way in where the railings are bent and we can all squeeze through.'

Joe and I said, yes, we would like to go. We had never been to the zoo before. We all got in and it was great to see the animals. We went into the Lion House and saw two big lions. 'It's feeding time,' said the man, 'so stand back.' He pushed big chunks of meat into the cages. The lions must have been hungry as they scoffed the lot in no time.

'It's time to go home,' said Joe.

'Right, let's go,' I replied.

We got home and Mammy said, 'Good boys, now wash your hands, the dinner is ready.'

After dinner we sat down to relax as we were bunched after our long, exciting day. 'Barry,' said Joe, 'that was a very exciting day.' I had to agree.

As for me, Mam was right when she said I was very fond of singing. Most years in Dublin there was a season of Italian opera. Nell and her pals loved the opera. I used to get up very early and go down to the Gaiety Theatre in South King Street to queue for tickets for her. At about eight o'clock in the morning Nell would come down and take my place in the queue, so that she could buy the tickets before she went to work. Nell and her friends bought lots of tickets for different nights at the opera. The thing was, if any one of them could not go, they gave me the ticket.

The first opera I went to was *Rigoletto*. It was great. Nell and her friends later joined the chorus and used to sing in some of the operas. One Tuesday night I went to meet Nell at the stage door and she came along with a man I soon realised was one of the stars. 'This is Giorgio Onesti,' Nell said. I was delighted, and said hello.

'Come on Thursday morning at ten o'clock, as we have rehearsals for *Madam Butterfly*, and I will take you in to see it,' he said.

Nell gave me a ticket to go to the Wednesday night performance. She also gave me some sweets and said she would meet me in the theatre later. I was really happy. *Norma* was the name of the opera. It wasn't as good as *Rigoletto*, but the singing was sweet. I was thinking about tomorrow and meeting Giorgio, and just hoped he would not forget me.

The next day, I went to meet him at the stage door. It started to rain. The doorman came and asked me why I was standing there. I told him I wanted to see Mr Giorgio Onesti. 'Come in out of the rain and wait inside,' he said.

It wasn't too long before Giorgio came in. He told the doorman, 'This is Barry, Nell's brother, so let him in anytime he wants to see me.' Giorgio went to the dressing rooms. He showed me how he put on makeup for the opera. It was soon time for rehearsals to start. 'Come along,' he said. 'Sit near the stage and you will see everything that goes on, and meet the other opera singers.' I was delighted, and had a great time. When it was over he took me to a tea shop. I had a drink of orange juice and a big cake, and he had coffee. We walked to the bus stop and he gave me money for the fare home. 'Come and see me any day at the theatre,' he said. The bus came along and we said cheerio. I felt great and hoped Nell might have a ticket for the opera that night. My luck was in, and she did have. That ended one more happy day for me at the opera.

MAM

Philomena was born on the 18ᵗʰ April 1944. She was a lively little baby and when she would lose her temper she would call everyone a 'Hula hula ba ba'. What she meant, we never did find out. She was always very loving to me and needed to be petted and made a fuss of.

PHILOMENA

I was next to Barry and Joe. One day, they took me to the River Dodder fishing with them. I did not know how to swim and, of course, in trying to get the fish, I fell into the water. It was deep, and Joe gave me the net end of his rod for me to get hold of. That fell off and down under I went again, until a man passing by helped the boys to get me out. I never went fishing again.

At bedtime, Mam would put us to bed with his old army coat on top of the covers in the winter, nice and warm, and Dad would sit and read a story from the Bible to us. He would be breathing very slowly, and taking a breath in between each word, God bless him. On Saturdays I would sometimes go over to see Granddad O'Connor to deliver his pension, which Dad collected, and he would always give me a small coin. We could buy so much with so little in those days. Uncle Bartle, who lived with Granddad, had a few small birds and they would be whistling as Bartle would be painting. It was a lovely, quiet time.

After school, we often went to play in the back garden of 15 Francis Street and sometimes climbed over the wall to the grassyard. When Uncle Paddy would come home from work he would be covered in soot, being a chimney sweep, and pretend to chase us around the garden, but never caught us. After he washed he was fine.

Dad always wore a waistcoat to work. One time, it was ripped, and he asked if anyone could do anything with it. I offered to put a new lining in it, so I took it apart to copy the size and then I cut and sewed it all up again. But I had taken in too much of a hem and now it did not fit him. Being the gentleman he was, he thanked me for trying, and after a few weeks he got a new one. I was about eleven years old at the time.

And what about the fiver I never saw? At that time I had won five pounds in a raffle without my knowing and the money was delivered to our house one Friday evening when I was out. Mam never said anything, but I was told about it on Monday. After I had been told, I daydreamed about what I would do with the money, but when I got home, Mam told me it was already spent on household bills. That's the way it was, and I didn't mind so much.

MAM

> *Rory was born on the 18th October 1946. He was very quiet and studious and still is. Eily, the last baby, was born on the 21st of July 1951. To me they were all happy babies even if I did lose many hours' sleep over them. But I have no regrets, I love them all and I know they love me.*

EILY

Well, I was the last in the line. I was named Elizabeth Carmel, but I was called Eily. I was born five years after Rory, at number thirteen. My earliest memories are of myself in the cot in the kitchen, where babies stayed until they learned to walk. It was probably the safest place for a child in a very big household. Everyone would leave for school or work, and it would be just me in the cot and Mam soaking clothes in the galvanised bath or busy at the washing machine or at the stove, cooking. Always with her back to me, always busy obviously, but to me this came to epitomise our relationship, because emotionally we never really connected.

We actually spent a great deal of time together when I was young. She was an old mother, and I was a quiet child, so I made few demands on her. I understood afterwards just how little desire or ability to connect she would have had left, having reared all those other children, but that was little consolation to the insecure little girl that I was. I was in the family, but not really of it. That was how it felt to live there. We were sent back to the schools she knew, and I went to Warrenmount Presentation Convent as she had gone herself. Being at the end of the family meant I experienced everyone leaving, and the sense of the house becoming emptier and lonelier has been the overriding one of my childhood. At Christmas it would fill up for the annual 'hooley' and then it was back to the quietness again.

In fact, eventually I felt more like an only child as I didn't have the opportunity to share those memories and experiences the older ones still laugh about together. I imagine everyone thought I would have the best deal, having my parents all to myself, but as I listened to them talk about the things that happened 'when all the kids were small' it always seemed to me that the happy times were over and my presence didn't bring much joy to them in those latter days.

It was probably not all so, but in the absence of words or acts of affection, that was how I understood it. Joe died when he was fourteen and I was four and a half. I was with him and Mam in the kitchen when he 'took a turn', which led to his death. We never spoke about what happened, but I am sure that much of the lack of joy that I remember in my young years was probably connected with Joe. I know I carried the grief with me well into my adult years, unrecognised, but very much alive.

Dad was a quiet, bookish man, who worked hard until

his retirement. A religious man, we talked a lot as I got older and was more interested in spiritual things. He died two months before I married Detlef. It has always been a sadness to me that I didn't have time with him as an adult, and that he never met our children, especially the boys, who share many of his gifts and abilities.

When Mam died it was the end of a difficult relationship. I think I cried more for what we might have had than for what was lost. But I am proud of my family and my Liberties heritage, and the many strengths we share. I look now at my older brothers and sisters and am inspired by their strength of character and love of life. They give me great hope for the future.

MAM'S LAST LETTER TO HER FAMILY

18th October 1981

Dear boys and girls,

When you read this I will be gone, but I will be as near to you as God will let me. I don't think I ever told you how much I love you all but I really did and you were my whole life and world when you were too small to understand. Nell being the eldest girl, I was able to confide in her, and she was a great help, for which I thank her now.

I can say that we had a very happy life and I don't regret anything. The troubles you had sometimes within marriage really hurt me and I was worried for your sakes. I thought of the happy family we once were, but I did not let any of you know my worries or make your troubles worse. That makes me happy now. No matter where God puts me, I hope it will be near Dad, as we really did love each other.

That's why I was glad that God took him first, because I knew how lonely he would be. I was lonely too after he went, but thank you all, boys and girls, for all you have done for me in all the years, and I know God will understand your troubles.

And now about the home. I would like the furniture in the parlour to be given to Eily. Seán would like to have the picture of the family and the picture of Granny O'Connor as he is fond of old family photographs. Rory would like the picture of Dad and I at Peggy's wedding. I'd like Therese, Peggy's daughter, to have what's in the kitchen, except Nell might like to have the Sacred Heart over the fireplace, as she brought it from Rome or Spain to me. After that, you can all have a choice of what little things that may be left, such as the small bits of jewellery. I know that you will all agree with me with what I am doing. If no one else wants my frocks and things, St Vincent de Paul will be glad to get them, so use your own discretion.

I'll say cheerio on a happy note. Don't cry when I am not here to comfort you, but say a prayer that the Man above won't be too hard on me. I have had a full and very happy life and I thank God for my boys and girls, for when you were born you were always welcome to our love.

Goodbye and God bless you all.

Mam

x x x x x x x x x x x x x x

PS: I forgot to say that the crucifix set in the china cabinet is for Peggy. I know she would like that. Mam.

PART 3:

Growing Up So High

10. SO FAR THE SHORE

In December 1950, when I was twelve, our class was in the last stages of preparation for the Primary Certificate Examination, which was to follow in the spring. Devane told us that there would be a scholarship class for free entry to Synge Street Secondary School, and other colleges, for the boys who would do well in the Primary Exam and that the Christmas Examination would be a good trial.

He mentioned it to me personally, and it was obvious that he thought I would be a good candidate. My attendance record was perfect now, and my English compositions were read out most weeks, so I happily freewheeled towards the Christmas test. I confidently assumed I would be first or second in the class as usual, vying with Tom O'Neill. The results were announced just before the Christmas holiday. Devane had organised a little ceremony in the classroom for the presentation of certificates to the top five students. I sat there, preening myself, as he started to call out the names. First came Tom O'Neill, followed by Paddy Brereton, as my mood slowly changed. Then Casimer Kane and Francis McPhillips were announced, and he finally called out, 'Fifth place, Seán O'Connor.'

He handed me my certificate, a lurid study in green, white and blue, but it was a show of dross to me. I remembered Martha's impromptu speeches from *The Merchant of Venice* and her frequent declamation that 'A golden mind stoops not to shows of dross'. This was intolerable, and had I lost my chance of being allowed to join the scholarship class? I read my certificate, completed in Devane's baby handwriting: *Christian Brothers Francis Street: Class Room number 8: I certify that Seán O'Connor has passed a successful Examination in Sixth Class. He got Fifth Place. Signed, Bro. T.T. Devane (teacher), Christmas 1950.*

I considered the strength of the boys who had beaten me and had to admit that they were as bright as I was and that they must have worked harder than me. I had just been lazy, so I made up my mind that it would not happen in the Primary Examination, as the reward of a scholarship was great indeed.

The idea of a free education in Synge Street Secondary School was so unlikely that I had not even mentioned the possibility at home, and now I was glad, as I had jeopardised the opportunity. I was willing to forget the arguments we had with the Synge Street boys, and the nasty way they sometimes abused us, calling us dunces for not having a secondary school, while we jeered them as Synge Street Canary Boys. I set about my plan with a desire for learning that I never relinquished. I read the dictionary at home for word meanings, noting the exotic comparisons between an allegory and a metaphor, and imbibed other information with Martha's help and Nell's advice.

I was in flying form on the day of the Primary. The first question on the English paper was: *There are three words with the same pronunciation as the number 2. Put them all in one sentence.* Easy! *I went to the zoo with two friends and my dog came too.* I was on my way! I gave the English composition my ornate best. I wrote about a man returning to his old home after a lifetime away and I managed to paraphrase some of the words of a review by Anthony Cronin of *The Great Gatsby* in the *Bell Magazine*. Both our heroes were trying to find a way back to a life they had lost, but to Mr Cronin and myself it was 'an attempt to capture the butterfly, to extort from life the magic it had once promised'. When it was over I was confident that I would indeed qualify for the scholarship class and my battered self-confidence steadily recovered.

Devane was in great form when I returned to school in September after the summer holidays. The results of the Primary Certificate Examination had been published. 'You've done well,' he exclaimed, with a smile, and told me that I had come first in our school in English and had obtained full marks in arithmetic. I was overjoyed because it meant I could join the scholarship class and that I had beaten off those boys who had been ahead of me in the Christmas test. Devane had done very well too, as the entire class had managed to pass the examination despite the difference in ability of each individual.

When the group was assembled we were divided into the scholarship class and those who were destined to leave.

Some of the boys would go on to attend the Day Technical School from which there would be a prospect of becoming apprenticed to a trade. Others could forage as they might in pursuit of whatever messenger-boy jobs were available, although an employer would not normally retain such a person for long. This was because he became an additional cost burden at the age of fifteen as, at that point, he had to join the national insurance scheme, with both worker and employer contributing to the cost of the weekly stamp.

In the meantime, Devane told the scholarship class that the first week back in school could be spent on getting ourselves organised for hard work starting the following week. 'This is the book list,' he said, handing out the sheet to each boy. 'Get this together one way or another by next Monday.'

When I returned home, I told Mam of my success but she seemed to have mixed feelings. It was great that I had managed to get into the group but, although the thought was unspoken, I knew that if I had a little job instead of continuing in school, the money could be well used. 'Child o' grace,' she said finally, 'all I ever wanted was that my boys would have a trade and the girls would do the Leaving Certificate and get a job in an office. But maybe you're the child the fortune teller told me about. He said that one of you would have a brass plate on your door some day. I'll give you the money for second-hand books and we'll see how you get on.' I thought of the expression about not having a brass farthing, never mind a brass plate, but kept quiet.

Devane seemed to be putting matters to rest in his own mind in that first week. We started on a desultory review of the Primary course, but the class bantered with him to an extent that I had never heard before. He seemed determined that there would be this period of lassitude before the intensity of all-out study. His cry of 'A little nonsense now and then' was heard every day as we aspiring scholars assembled our book lists, but when the serious work started in the following week, he reverted to another of his favourite sayings, '*Tempus fugit*, time flies!'

On Monday he asked Brendan Kelly to tell us a story. Brendan was quite theatrical, not an extrovert but a natural actor who lived his life in class as if it was all part of a script. If someone pushed him, he would slither sideways, as though fatally wounded, towards the nearest wall and, when he made contact, slide down to the floor and lie motionless. He was gifted in his ability to recall a tale he might have read and often enthralled us with the retelling. Now it was time for *his* last hurrah as well.

He rose from the desk, eyes half closed in thought, as he settled the details of the story he had in mind. When he got to the front of the class, his natural stage, he was ready to live this tale and take us with him on the journey. Today it was Zane Grey at his best and he gave it his customary beginning. All stories opened with the words 'It starts,' followed by a pause for a few dramatic seconds, until Brendan broke the tension.

> *It starts ... on a cattle trail in Texas. The Chap and the*
> *Pal and his team have been given the job of leading*
> *five hundred head of cattle from Abilene up the trail*
> *to Dodge City. Danger lies ahead as the Indians are*

on the warpath, the weather is turning bad, there are rivers to cross and the Chap has never been on this trail before. He needs some extra hands to drive the herd but he doesn't know that one of the men he picks is a vicious outlaw on the run whose name is Ross Hite. All goes well as they leave Abilene to begin the long trail. The herd move slowly along, grazing as they go. At night, the drovers sing to the cattle to calm them. Everything seems peaceful on the first days of the journey.

But just as they are beginning to move on, they see Indians in the distance. They're attacking the wagons belonging to the settlers but the Chap and the Pal and most of the team go to their rescue and drive them off. When they get back to their camp they find that the cattle have been rustled and there is no sign of Ross Hite. Soon after, thunder and lightning start and the Chap knows that the stolen herd cannot be moved in that weather so they set out after the crooks. When they catch up with them they circle around the cattle, shooting most of the rustlers as they go, and then driving off the herd, but Ross Hite escapes. When they count the drove they find they have a hundred head more than they had at the beginning.

Ross Hite turns up then with another big gang of men and there's a shootout. The Chap is putting up a great fight, but his team is outnumbered and just as they are about to be overrun there comes the sound of thundering hooves. It's a herd of buffalo stampeding towards the river and Ross Hite and his men are right

in their way. The animals keep going and the crook
and his gang are crushed by the maddened beasts
and that's the end of them. When the Chap and the
Pal finally get to Dodge City, they go to sell the herd.
They find that they still have more cattle than when
they started so it was all worthwhile in the end. They
get their money and on the following day they take
the stage coach out of Dodge City back to Abilene.
The Chap buys a ranch of his own in Texas and settles
down, and never has to go on the trail again.

Applause, bow, and exit Brendan downstage!

Devane was set on showing us the way of the world by song and story, and would then extract the moral for our benefit. 'O'Brien,' he said on Tuesday, 'I'd like to hear some of that poem we were learning, you know the one, "A Noble Boy", just the part you can remember.' And Olly started:

> *The woman was old and feeble and grey,*
> *And bent with the chill of the winter's day,*
> *The street was wet with the recent snow,*
> *And the woman's feet were weary and slow,*
> *She stood at the crossing and waited long,*
> *Alone, uncared for, amid the throng...*

'Now you, O'Connor.'

> *At last came one of the merry troop,*
> *The gayest boy of all the group;*
> *He paused beside her and whispered low,*

I'll help you across if you wish to go';
He guided the trembling feet along,
Proud that his own were firm and strong...

'Burke, go on to the last verse,' Devane said, in a quiet voice.

And somebody's mother bowed low her head,
In her home that night and the prayer she said,
Was 'God be kind to the noble boy,
Who is somebody's son and pride and joy!

Devane coughed and said, 'Now boys, that's the way to behave. Have respect for the old and the sick, and especially your mother. There's nothing more certain than death for all of us and we should help each other on the journey through life. You never know what lies ahead.'

One of the things that did lie ahead was the weekly visit from our drill master, Mr Gallagher. He came on Wednesday afternoons to run our calisthenics class in the play yard. Mr Gallagher was genially chubby, fair of head and face, moustachioed, and given to spitting after preliminary notice of the event by way of a noisy clearing of the throat. This habit had been noticed by the boys with pleasure, as it was strictly forbidden in the school. At his command, we ranged ourselves on the play yard like pawns on a chess board. He called out the tempo for the exercises with precision. 'And one, and two, and three, and four,' followed by, 'And forward, and sideways, and upwards, and down,' as we went through the synchronised movements of lunge, stretch and squat on the spot. Ordering us around was the only exercise he did himself but we were aware that if he told the Head that any particular boy was fit, it was sufficient to get that individual a place on the school Gaelic football fifteen.

This squad was run by Brother Devitt. We knew his heart was in soccer, and that he had once trialled for Belfast Celtic, his home team, but if you didn't show pride and happiness in being picked to play for the school, a bad side of his usually genial nature emerged in a rasping verbal onslaught on your lack of enthusiasm: 'Do you want to play for your school or not? You don't look as if you do. Where's your pride, boy? Get on with it!'

Thursday's treat was a visit from Mr Dobbin, a teacher who wore a blue suit and rode a bicycle. He was fond of the percussive phrase 'bunk, balderdash, baloney and rubbish' in dismissing poor answers from his pupils, but he was popular all the same, as he liked to stroll into some other teacher's class for a chat, then entertain the boys by testing them with some obscure riddle. This was taken seriously because his practice was to give a prize of a thrupenny bit to the first boy with the correct answer. Today it was our turn, and after a few words with Devane, he asked our class, 'What is cursing?' Well, most of us thought we knew that one. Hands went up and voices called out all over the room with some vivid, indeed fairly eye-crossing examples, but Dobbin kept shaking his head and saying, 'No, no.' I had Martha's book of religious knowledge in my schoolbag and, as the boys kept up their efforts, had time to consult the very question. When a pause came in the din, I put up my hand and read out loudly, '"Calling down evil on ourselves or on any of God's creatures."'

'That's it,' said Dobbin, walking towards me with fingers in his waistcoat pocket, but a few growls arose from the disaffected, saying, 'But he read it out of a book, sir.' Dobbin said, 'Where else would you expect to find the answer to a hard question?' He gave me the money and I realised I had only won the prize because I knew where to look for the information I needed. This made me reflect.

As Dobbin implied, all true knowledge seemed to lie in books. I could see more clearly now that, if I wanted to know something, it would be quicker for me to go to the source rather than embarrass people by asking questions they might not be able to answer. If they did respond, their lack of knowledge would not prevent them, in their kindness, from trying to enlighten, and so create an illusion if they were wrong. However, power lay in really knowing. Such power was a valuable commodity, well worth having. The sensible conclusion was that, for me, books were the means of progress. In my simple world they came in only two categories. The first was as a storehouse of facts and the second was as the repository of beautiful language, although I already knew that some contained both facets. With such books being accessible, I thought I could be self-sufficient in the pursuit of knowledge while, on the other hand, I could enjoy the lovely way the words of a book or a poem fell together to cast their spell.

On Friday the choir in the class was invited to sing the harmonised arrangement of 'The Blue Danube' which we had sung at the school concert:

Moonlight gleams,
Like fairy beams,
Where whispering bright,
Thy water streams,
So far the shore, so far the shore,
So sweet thy call, so sweet thy call,
For evermore, thou shall hold
All my heart in silver thrall...

O banks so cool, so green,
That fringe with fern thy sheen,
O rocks so bold so old
Was ever so fair, so fair, a scene...

Now in lightest mood, sing to me, sing to me,
Of plain and wood bring to me, bring to me,
On thy silver breast wing to me, wing to me,
Thoughts of homeland, Danube blue.

There was a silence when we finished. I thought of the boys leaving school whom I might not see again. Whoever wrote those words to 'The Blue Danube' must have been far from home and feeling like some of us.

I arrived in school early on the following Monday morning after paying a visit to the new Lourdes grotto in the front yard of Francis Street Chapel. Devane was talking in a jovial way to another Christian Brother whom I had never seen before. The two of them had the same pleasant country accent. 'This is Brother Moran, Seán,' Devane said, and turning to his friend, 'Seán is good at English composition.'

We nodded hello and Brother Moran asked me in a nice way what I hoped to do when I left school.

'I want to be a printer, sir,' I replied.

'Do you mean a typesetter, like they have for the newspapers?' he asked, but that was not what I meant. I struggled to find the word, and explained that I wanted to be in charge of the printing of books.

'Oh,' said Devane, 'it's a publisher you want to be.' That was it exactly. I would love my own business producing books, not writing them, not printing them, not having a bookshop, but just involved in their creation. Moran looked at me dubiously but Devane told him again that I was good at English composition anyway and that only God knew the future. 'Seán,' he said, as if to vindicate me, 'give us the opening sentence you would use for a comp on "A Day at the Seaside".'

I looked at him in surprised silence and felt my face flush deeper with every second. I could not gather my thoughts to begin the journey into the day he had in mind. After a minute Moran said, 'Ah, he's too shy to answer that one,' and I went away abashed. When I sat down I told myself that no one could give their best answer to such a request while staring at two such inquisitors. Did they not realise that unfolding the opening words of an English composition by way of conversation was impossible? Chatting was a different ability altogether. It explained why some of the boys in the class were good at repartee but wrote indifferent English. No, writing was a special kind of escape, where the reality of your physical world faded away without conscious effort and you could draw on words at will to describe what was happening in your new surroundings. Yes, it was truly 'the voice in my dreaming ear'. You could become any person you wished to be and see a new universe through his eyes. Two Christian Brothers lurking in the foreground had no place in that scene.

However, serious work began when Moran had gone. All thought of frivolity was forsaken. Over the next few weeks I learned to draw the map of Ireland freehand and to superimpose on it the major mountain ranges and rivers, together with the railway system, complete with detail such as showing that Limerick Junction was actually in Tipperary.

The history of Ireland was reviewed and we had much to look forward to in reading about the glory of Rome, the writers of the Renaissance and the invention of the printing press. Working with hard fractions and the rules for removing brackets in algebra were all absorbed. I took particular interest in percentage profit and loss as I intended that such matters would arise in my later life. The scalene triangle and the hypotenuse fell to our learning, and ratio and proportion was easy. If one boy put in two buttons and another put in three so as to go in the bunts playing cards, then the winnings were divided in the proportion of two-fifths and three-fifths. Most of us knew this already. By the end of November I was making good progress but couldn't help noticing that Devane was not his usual cheerful self. I ignored that because I knew he was intent on getting good results and, since he still encouraged us with his *bons mots*, I took no interest in what might be on his mind. Early on Monday, 3 December 1951, Devane called me up to his desk and spoke in a low voice. I had never seen him look so troubled.

'I'm sorry, Seán,' he said, 'but there's a problem about you doing the scholarship exam. There's an age limit for entry and each boy must be under thirteen on the first day of September this year. I don't know how this happened, but you slipped under the net. It wasn't noticed that you were thirteen in July, so you are some weeks overage. I've spent the last while trying to see if anything could be done, but it wasn't possible.'

His words staggered me. 'And do I have to leave the class?' I managed to say.

The reply was that indeed I would have to leave eventually, but I could stay in class for the few weeks until the Christmas holiday if I liked. I thought I might as well leave straight away as there was no point in continuing until then. His voice rang in my ears as if he had been shouting but I knew it was not his fault. A bubble of desolation pressed down on my chest. Devane went on talking to me, but I was elsewhere. 'Fragile fragments fallen from the workshop of the Gods', indeed. I wondered how it was that whenever I was either upset or very happy, a line of poetry would come into my head. I knew there was trouble to come and things were going to change for me. There would be no scholarship. I might as well get used to that. And what would be said at home? 'Will I really have to leave the class?' I asked again. Devane explained it all once more. The only way I could show my feelings was to say that I would like to leave that very day, and he did not object.

I sat down in a despondent rage, which I did my best to hide. Was I now expected to walk out the door never to return, leaving my classmates behind, cosy and safe in a nicely planned future? Devane called me up again, smiling in his pleasant way, and said he would ask Brother Devitt to give me a good reference and that he himself would do the same. He tore a page from a jotter and wrote a note for me to give to the Head. I read it as I went out to Devitt's office. *Give this boy a <u>great</u> reference and forget about the time he got into that little spot of bother.* I wondered what particular event he meant and decided it must have been to do with the school attendance officer years before, as I had never really been in trouble in school.

Devitt was in his room when I got there and looked a bit morose himself. 'Hello, O'Connor,' he said, reading the note and then going on, 'You're off, and so am I, to a school down Limerick way. The new head will be Brother Clancy, who takes you for history at the moment.' I had already attended some of this teacher's classes but I said to myself that *I* was history now. Things were changing all around me and I was rapidly losing interest in what happened at Francis Street School.

Devitt wrote in italics: ... *his intellectual brilliance, no less than his good nature, has endeared him to the hearts of his masters ... trustworthy and honest, plays for the school team and represented us at the Primary School Sports in Croke Park.* By the time he was finished I felt that I had been exalted to a status rivalling that of Edmund Ignatius Rice, the founder of the Irish Christian Brothers. Devitt patted me on the back as he handed me the envelope and said that I could return the school's football boots and jersey when I got the chance.

Devane had his reference ready for me when I got back to the classroom. He told me gently that I might stay for the morning and leave at lunch hour, so that I could tell my pals I was finishing school, but I got his permission to leave at the break instead. The sooner this was over, the better. I sat down and put the two references in my schoolbag. The lesson was on geography but I was already far away, demoralised and shocked, and rage was beginning to take me over. When the break came, I picked up my schoolbag ready to go. 'Seán is leaving us today,' Devane said. 'Let's all wish him well in the future.' My pals were agog as I told them what had happened. Casimer Kane reminded me of the time he had voted for me as class captain and the day some of us had gone to Tara Street baths to learn how to swim. He had had a lovely pair of blue swimming togs on for that occasion and I had had Tommy's white soccer shorts. I'd had to leave the pool when the attendant pointed out that my togs were transparent in the water.

When I saw Tom O'Neill I thought of his stories about the months of the school strike he had spent in his parents' home town in Clare, having to go to school there, while we relaxed. The next time I would see Tom was a few years later when he was in the middle of the degree course in chemical engineering in University College Dublin and enjoying the social life. Seán McQuillan said he would keep my bicycle oiled when I got one, and we talked about the nice times we'd had in his home in Iveagh Flats playing with his pet mice. Olly O'Brien moped sadly that there would be no more races like the ones we used to run from the steps of the Iveagh Market. He loved the Liberties as no other boy I ever met and we were pals because his mother, Abby, who had a little shop in Francis Street, was a friend of Mam's in childhood. *Used* to run, I thought, sure it was only a few weeks since the last time. I was already being treated like a past pupil!

That race was from the steps of the Iveagh Market to the corner of the old city wall in Lamb Alley and back. The time for the run was kept by one of the girls counting aloud and, as we prepared ourselves, there was never so focused a group of athletes. With 'Ready, steady and go', there was a wild rush past Grogan's house beside the market and up Francis Street. Then it was Lambert's pub, jostling for position before we hit O'Connor's Hardware and Miss Phelan's little clothes shop. The corrugated-iron frontage to Handkerchief Alley came next and then we flew past our shop and Johnny Reas next door, with startled pedestrians getting out of our way as we went.

We could hear the noise of the budgies as we fled past O'Horas before we were engulfed by the whiff of fresh brown bread coming out of the Hazelhatch Dairy as Michael Keating stood at the door. Mushatt's busy little chemists was the signal for getting into a good position before skidding around Moran's pub on the corner. Once on Cornmarket, we had the last furious fifty yards dash to complete before touching the crumbling city wall, disturbing the girls playing chaineys on the stone shelves. Back at speed, out of breath and sweating. The winner was John Kenny in a time counted out by our appointed official. The prize was the coveted Aer Lingus winged badge collected from their exhibition stand at the Royal Dublin Society Horse Show. To be seen panting after the event was to bring dishonour, so this was hidden by deep breathing with nonchalant hands in pockets, ready to deny that you had made any real exertion. All of that was over now.

I slung on my schoolbag and headed down the stairs for the last time, my senses awhirl. My days in Francis Street Christian Brothers' School were done. I was disgusted that my place in class had been lost just because of a few weeks, and I was fearful of what my parents might say. But mostly I was still raging at the situation in which I found myself. What was I going to do? As I took the side exit from the school into Chapel Lane and down the granite steps under the old brick arch, the gabled houses of Clarence Mangan Square across the road caught my eye. Noel Fitzgerald and I had played handball there, and I knew this would never happen again. I had to find somewhere to calm myself, so I sought refuge in St Patrick's Park nearby. I nearly got killed by a Kennedy's bread cart coming out of their bakery on to Patrick Street, being so preoccupied, but the driver stood up and hauled on the reins so that the horse just missed me. Then he went on with a cloud of steam coming from the van, shouting at me to wake up.

I found an empty bench at the open space near the entrance with my back to Patrick Street. On my left I could see the Bayno through the leafless trees, and on the other side I was overlooked by the carved faces decorating the cathedral clock on the bell tower. Two crows on the flying buttresses were squabbling over something. Scruffy pigeons were eating from a mound of damp white bread as usual, and little groups of old people sat huddled together talking in the cold air. The park ranger kept looking in my direction. I was suddenly frightened and I began to wonder again what would happen to me. I was too young to work and too old for school. I'm like the Prodigal Son in Luke, I thought. 'To beg I am ashamed, to dig I am not able, and I fain would fill my belly with the husks the swine did eat...' but when I got that far I restrained myself. After all, things were not that bad. My mood did not change when I thought of my parents. I knew I was lucky to have them, but they were going to be disappointed and I was carrying enough of my own regrets without having theirs thrust upon me as well.

I thought about Mam. She often said that respectability started with good shoes and a decent haircut, so we had a walk-in arrangement with Mr McDonnell, the barber in Francis Street, and Mr Cripps, who had a shoe shop on Augustine Street hill. She was so proud of all of us, and it was funny the way she sometimes mentioned that none of her family had ever come to the notice of the police, as if that was a distinction. I remembered Aunt Molly sending me for fish one day to my friend Mrs Welsh in the Iveagh Market and she'd said to me, 'Your mammy is a real Liberties woman and her with all those children.' When I asked her what she meant she just said, 'Did you ever hear her whingeing about anything?'

It was true that Mam was outgoing and bright although Nell told me that she sometimes saw her eyes filling with tears in moments of melancholy. The mood always passed quickly and she would soon be her cheerful self again, humming a tune as she went about her housework. Mam had one habit I didn't understand and that was her offhand way of sometimes referring to an incident involving her brother Jim and then falling quiet. And then there was that brazen gesture she had of showing her contempt for any man she didn't like. This was delivered from a sitting position. 'I wouldn't give *that* for him,' she would say viciously, with the word *that* being accompanied by a two-handed shake of her dress, making the crumbs fly. But if you asked her to do anything for you she would always say yes, if she could, and then add, 'with a heart and a half'.

As I sat there thinking, I could suddenly see her face in front of me, smiling, and I wished she could hug me, but that was not her way with any of us and I shook off the feeling. After all, it was mostly from her that we got our confidence, and when she said, 'Hold on to the pram, we'll be home in no time,' I always felt secure. And her music! How she loved to sing. When she got her noble call at a party, it was always the same, and I could hear it now:

> *Willie Earl met a sweet young girl one day in France,*
> *Her naughty little glance put Willie in a trance,*
> *Willie Earl couldn't understand her talk you see,*
> *He only knew two words in French*
> *That he learned in the trench,*
> *They were 'oo-la-la!' and 'oui, oui'...*

Dad was in many ways the standard Liberties man, proud, God-fearing and yet independent, five foot seven and a half inches in height, minded his own business and never used bad language. He sang 'Believe Me' in a pleasant baritone voice when called upon to do so and loved talking about the Bible. He was religious and hard-working, a staunch admirer of Matt Talbot, the famous Dubliner who went to work with penitential chains around his body and who recovered from alcoholism to lead a devout life. Mam was the love of his life and he never left for work in the mornings without giving her a little kiss on the lips, and my sisters had noted her way of changing her apron and combing her hair before he arrived home. However, I already had trouble understanding Dad because of his literal belief in Divine Providence and the absence of any ambition that I could see. He had become the object of my silent disapproval for not owning his own factory, and I thought that at least he might have aspired to being the foreman of Scott's wood-machine shop where he worked at this time.

However, when I said this to Nell she was quick to explain to me that it was not lack of ambition in Dad, but lack of opportunity. Although he was expert at what he did, unemployment was rife. When occasionally he was out of work over the years, his belief in Divine Providence helped him to bear the misery of not being able to support his family as he would have liked. At least he never lost his sense of humour, and I can still see him leaning back in his chair, laughing and calling out, 'Get up, McGuckin,' in warm response to a juicy bit of repartee.

He got annoyed with anyone who would dare make a remark in his presence that could be taken as a slight on the O'Connors, and his special disdain was saved for any perceived whiners of that ilk within the ranks of the extended family. Although he could be stern with us, he would have considered this to be his duty, and he could also be a kindly and gentle man.

I made excuses for him when he had sometimes given me a few clatters around the shoulders if I got 'a bit too big for your boots', as he put it, but in any event I was too afraid to make any complaint for fear of annoying him. What did hurt me was that he had never taken me out anywhere on my own with him.

Midday bells crashed out and woke me from my daydream. As I trudged along the grassy slope between the path and the boundary railings of the cathedral, I remembered how we had made daisy chains there not so long ago. Oscar Wilde's voice came *sotto voce*:

> *Tread lightly, she is near*
> *Under the snow.*
> *Speak gently, she can hear*
> *The daisies grow.*

I took a deep breath and tried to stop feeling sorry for myself. My gloomy mood began to lift into something like determination. Wasn't I a Liberties boy, after all? Were we not supposed to be brave? Now, at least, I could spend more time with my family in Keeper Road, although I did not want to leave Francis Street and my friends completely. Hadn't I heard enough half-stories about my own family to give me courage? What was it that Granddad meant with his talk of rebels and their connection with that diary? And why was it that he never passed St Catherine's Church in Thomas Street without saying something to recall Robert Emmet and the Rebellion of 1798? I would ask him to take me on that walk to Lucan that he had promised me and persuade him to tell me about those things.

Wherever I looked there seemed to be a mystery. If I was going to get a job and join the world of grown-ups then I should know what the family stood for. My resolve grew and I thought about my future. I had two good references and I was the best in English that our school had produced that year. I must be capable of doing some work in an office where I could earn money and learn about business.

Uncle Joe knew a lot about work, I thought. He had been trained for a career, so why couldn't I? He could tell me how he was so successful at what he did for his political party, and how he went about trying to ensure his candidates would be elected. There was so much I could learn from the family! I began to imagine that maybe I *was* that person that the fortune teller had told Mam about, having a brass plate on the door. What would I call myself in business? Seán Oliver O'Connor? If I did that, then my initials would be SOOC, which I did not like at all. If I called myself John, the initials were not much better, JOOC. On the other hand I had chosen Vincent as my Confirmation name, because that day had fallen on the feast of St Vincent de Paul.

So, JVOC? That was more like it. I would call myself John Vincent O'Connor for business and keep Seán for my family and friends. Once I had gone that far, I knew there was no going back and so it was JVOC for work purposes from that day. I went over to the wire rubbish basket and emptied my schoolbag into it and, after a moment's thought, threw the bag in as well.

I walked slowly back to the shop. Eileen was there on her own and was horrified at my news. She said Mam would be calling in for her daily chat and she fussed me with questions.

When she was satisfied, I said as a joke that I was going out in the world to seek my fortune, just like Will, the man in the tale she used to tell me, who lived in our house in the old days. Now it was time she told me the real story. 'Well, most of it was true,' she said, with a smile, 'but here goes.'

It turned out that Lady Anne was really just plain Anne Grattan, better known as the aunt of Olivia Whitmore, the wife of the first Arthur Guinness. Anne lived in 15 Francis Street after she got married to Will, who was actually William Lunnel.

Their house was three storeys with an attic and the gable faced out on to the street, just like the tenements in New Row, and her daughter Martha was the only child alive when Anne died. Later on, Martha married Thomas Grayson who lived in Marks Alley.

'Now, Seán,' said Eileen, 'this house is very special for another reason. The members of the Methodist Church have a warm admiration for the Lunnels because their founder came to stay here on his first visit to Dublin. His name was John Wesley and he was given a great welcome by William and Anne Lunnel and their daughter.'

Eileen went on to explain that when Nannie had bought the house in 1913 it was a bit rickety so she had it repaired, but she left the big open staircase and the cellar exactly the way it was from the start. Just when she moved in, there was an awful collapse of two tenements in Church Street. Adults and children were killed and other little ones were orphaned, so there was terrible grief. 'After all,' Eileen said, 'this happened during the lockout by the employers so the poor workers had no money and here was their houses falling down as well. It was a shame, what they had to put up with.'

Dublin Corporation ordered Nannie to demolish the two top floors of the house for safety some years later, leaving a flat glazed roof. 'Then,' said Eileen, 'when the glass was whitewashed to keep out the glare, it threw a yellow light all over the old staircase. That's what made it so creepy and, who knows, with all that history, there might very well be a ghost here still. Sure every house in the Liberties has a ghost!'

Eileen was interrupted by Mam coming into the room and I nervously told her what had happened in school. To my surprise she did not make too much of it but just said that God knows best and that it might break a bigger cross, adding that I could keep an eye on the Situations Vacant in the *Evening Mail*. Then she told Eileen her great news. My brother Billy had become engaged to Alice Orr, whose family had a shop on the Coombe. Mam said that we must have a party, as he was the first to get married, and the couple were already talking about emigrating to Australia. As she went on talking about the engagement I knew that she had no regrets about my leaving school and that suited me. It was a good moment for me to ask her about Uncle Jim, and what she had to say made me stare at her in silent amazement.

But more of that anon.

11. OFFICE BOY REQUIRED

Tommy asked if I was going to work in a factory and I twanged the strap of his overalls in a way that made the sawdust fly. 'No,' I said, 'two slaves are enough in one house.' He told me to take it easy, that if anyone heard me there would be trouble. I didn't care. I knew enough about his work to be aware that it was a dangerous life, with long hours at saw machines, making furniture in freezing workshops where accidents were nearly inevitable. I remembered Dad having the side of his thumb sliced off by a circular saw and his stoicism as he waited for attention in Jervis Street Hospital. That life was not for me.

I was besotted with the idea of working in an office, which I visualised as a paradise of short hours, clean clothes and good holidays. 'Oh, sure,' laughed Tommy. 'A pound a week and your chances.' I ignored his brotherly jibes, because I had made up my mind. I even asked Nell to let me practise typing on her old machine and the quick brown fox got better at his jumps over the lazy dog as the days passed. In my spare time I wrote out copies of my references for sending to that precious job opportunity that must come along one day soon. Mam left me to it, as she was preoccupied with making arrangements for Billy's party. I studied the Situations Vacant in the *Evening Mail* every night, awaiting the bugle call to action. The only job advertised for someone like me in that first week was for a messenger boy, but being a 'smart lad' in a fishmonger's shop held no attraction.

Consequently, on most nights I had to turn to the adventures of Mandrake the Magician on an inside page for interest, disappointed for the moment, but willing to believe. I was good at reading, writing and doing sums. These were my weapons for taking on the world and I wasn't going to settle for less than the job I wanted. Uncle Joe had told me that I wouldn't be going far without passing more examinations. 'That piece of paper will open doors,' he had said, and I had believed him. In the meantime I went over to see Granddad O'Connor. He was on his own and he was amused when I asked him if I could go for a walk with him. Dad must have been talking to him about my disappointment at school because Granddad was all sympathy, but by this time I had got over my setback and was intent on progress.

He said that, anyway, he was just on his way up to The Clock pub in Thomas Street to meet Aunt Lily for a drink, and I could go that far with him if I liked. I would have gone anywhere with him just then because I wanted the benefit of his wisdom. As we left, he took down his old diary, and put it in a Woolworths bag. We wandered up Thomas Street and he began to tell me about the shipyard in Glasgow where he had worked for a few years before Bartle was born. When we came to the pub, he asked me to run across the road to see if Aunt Lily had arrived, but there was no sign of her. We walked on, keeping a lookout, as she would have to pass us on her way.

At St Catherine's Church in Thomas Street, Granddad stopped and stared through the railings for a moment, blessing the memory of Robert Emmet as usual. Then he told me that Dad had mentioned my curiosity about the rebel connections in the family. He said that, after the uprising of 1798 had failed, many of the survivors moved to the Liberties to be among sympathisers. Those who came openly were mostly women, as the men were either dead, transported or on the run. 'But these women were warriors in their own right,' he said. 'They wore the green when it was dangerous and fought for what they believed in.' Granddad went on talking like that as we ventured further up Thomas Street.

His brother Johnny lived at number twenty-one, but we passed his shop and approached the brewery. He pointed over at the IAWS building and mentioned that Lord Edward Fitzgerald was captured in the house that used to stand there in 1798. 'Guinness were great employers,' Granddad said. 'They knew that Johnny was a Volunteer who fought in the Black and Tan war, yet they took him back to work there when he was released from internment in the Curragh Camp. They didn't lock out their Larkin Union workers in the 1913 strike either, not like Jacob's Biscuits.' When we came to the arched entrance to the Guinness brewery, Granddad stopped, leaned back on the wall and took out his pipe. 'Now,' he said, 'this reminds me of when I used to take a summer walk to Lucan. From here you could just go straight up through Kilmainham, past the back entrance of the Old Fogeys' Home, you know, The Royal Hospital, and on by the swing gates of the Phoenix Park. Once you were that far you could go to Chapelizod and take the drop road through the Strawberry Beds. It's a good ten miles. My own father used to do the same walk in his time.'

Granddad was too old to take that walk any more, but when I heard him say this, I promised myself that I would follow in his footsteps as I loved the idea of continuing a family tradition. On a number of fine Sundays in later years I did indeed complete the walk from Francis Street to Lucan village with my son Eoin and we made quite a ceremony of it. We would march down to the long-deserted house at 142 Francis Street, knock on the door ritually to call up Granddad's spirit, then walk to Lucan on the same route as he had taken. One Sunday in July 2013 was particularly special: I was in the company of my sons Joseph and Eoin, with my grandson James, as we completed the little expedition.

Granddad straightened himself and faced back down Thomas Street again and I knew our walk was nearly over. On our way past Lily's home, I ran up the stairs to find her absorbed in knitting a multicoloured pullover: she had forgotten about the arrangement to meet.

When we came to the pub, Granddad invited me in, handing me the Woolworths bag and saying, 'Here, have a gander at this. It was written by my mother's sister in the old days. There's something that will interest you on January the eighth, 1880.' I sat at a table on my own in the quiet pub, delighted with myself and, while Granddad and Lily were having a drink and chatting, began to turn the pages of the diary. My first surprise was to find a photograph inside the front cover of a woman with a lovely face and a haughty look. Her eyes were lustrous even in the old picture, but they were sad as well, and the set of her features was relaxed but unsmiling. She had a look of brooding determination, as if waiting for something to happen. I could see a family likeness in her, especially to Aunt Eileen, Dad's sister, who had suffered illness and an unhappy marriage. Under the picture was written 'Mary O'Connor'. I liked her appearance but did not know either the name or the face and I wondered why she looked troubled. I went over to Granddad to ask him about it.

'That's my mother,' he said, 'and, like a lot of the women around here, she would say exactly what was on her mind. Her name was Mary Gavin before she got married.' I somehow wished I had been there to tell her not to be worrying and that everything would be all right, but to find this beautiful lady so close to me in ancestry was a nice treat. 'When you're reading the diary you'll find a man named Tommy Gavin mentioned,' Granddad went on. 'That was her brother and the Tom O'Connor was my father.'

I started to turn the pages, hurrying towards 8 January 1880, but I couldn't resist stopping to read some of the entries in the journal. What was I to make of these? Some of them related to my family, but others seemed to be just a record of events in the tenement home where they lived over a shop in 52 James Street:

January 1879
Tommy Gavin took the pledge and refused a pint of porter.

February 1879
Maggie Cahill's husband went either to Leeds or Australia.

March 1879
Tommy Gavin enlisted in the 8th Regiment and was sent abroad with the British Army. I wrote to him today in Koorum valley in Afghanistan.

This was followed by photographs of two bearded men in army uniform with the caption 'Tom O'Connor' under one and 'Tom Gavin' on the other.

April 1879
I lent Lord Byron's Works today to Mr O'Shaughnessy and asked him to return the book when he has read it. Mr Tutty called to see us.

May 1879
Today I had the chimney swept and my top coat dyed. I had to pull out the tail feathers of my sick canary. Miss King left 52, James's Street for America. She sails from Londonderry in the ship Devonia in a few days.

June 1879
Bridget Ward threw herself into the canal. She was then sent to the Asylum, and when released a few months later, was taken prisoner. When she came out of prison she gave up her room and went away on the same day. A few weeks later she was taken

prisoner again, although she was to marry Mr Allen on the following day. She was released and a month later was fined 5 shillings or 3 days' imprisonment for being drunk near James's Street. She paid the fine but was found on the same night insensible in Dawson Street, from where she was taken to Mercers Hospital. A bottle with laudanum was found in her pocket.

September 1879
Kate went to see Mrs Ward in Mercers Hospital, and saw a medical student sitting in a nurse's lap. Very improper.

October 1879
Some person unknown left a foundling baby in the open hallway of 52, James's Street and went away.

Then suddenly there it was:

8 January 1880
*My Granny died yesterday. Her death notice was in this morning's Freemans Journal: **HOLOHAN** – At 52 James Street, Mrs Margaret Holohan, aged 90 years. She was the daughter of Mr John Tutty of Kilpipe, County Wicklow, who was one of the 25 United Irishmen shot at Carnew on the 25th May 1798 and buried in Kilcashel graveyard at Wingfield, County Wicklow. R.I.P.*

So that was it. But what was the connection with the O'Connors? Granddad explained that Margaret, the dead lady, was his mother's granny, whose father was the John Tutty shot by the Redcoats in the rising of 1798. Then he gravely added, 'The rebels were the bravest of Irish people.' He wrote down the names of our ancestors in a chain from 1798. John Tutty who was executed, then his daughter Margaret Holohan, and on to her granddaughter Mary O'Connor, Granddad's mother. I was at the end of a long sequence but what a heritage! The sacrifices they must have made lit up my mind. When I had got over the excitement of the discovery, I gave the diary back to Granddad and said goodbye, more determined than ever to do my best. Lily reminded me to tell the younger ones in the family not to forget to come to the Christmas party in her flat, which she held every year.

A few days later I was scanning the job advertisements in the *Evening Mail* when my heart jumped: *Office boy required for busy city Consultancy, Box No. M641.* I had eyes only for the words 'office boy', and when I read them the second time, I threw the paper in the air and shouted, '*Hooray!*' This was the first suitable vacancy I had seen. I knew what I had to do. The first thing was to make sure I was called for interview, because it was common knowledge that a company who placed an advertisement under a box number would not bother to respond to unsuitable applicants.

I wrote to this consultancy with the fervour of the needy although I had no idea what its business was. Nor did I care. A copy of my two references went with my letter. I set out, without a blush, the unblemished nature of my character and the brilliance of my youthful intellect. As I wrote, I drew on the best English I knew to swear everlasting fealty to this mysterious empire. I would have been accepted by King

Arthur into the Knights of the Round Table in the zeal of my promises to serve faithfully. Although I mentioned that I had left school, I was careful not to give my age. When I was finished, I signed the letter neatly as 'John V. O'Connor', rather than Seán, the first use of my new business name. Then, after addressing the envelope in my best handwriting, I walked down to the *Evening Mail* office by Copper Alley to leave in my application by hand.

After a few days of impatient anxiety, a neatly typed envelope arrived for John V. O'Connor and I knew it contained good news. The letter inside acknowledged my application of the 14th inst. and invited me to telephone without delay to arrange for an interview in the office of Joseph Mallagh and Son, Consulting Engineers, at 14 South Frederick Street, Dublin. It was signed 'Terence J. S. Mallagh', whom I immediately ascribed as being a good judge of character and an astute businessman. Mam said this was definitely a Protestant firm, with such a surname on its letterhead, and that this was a good start. The Catholics of the Liberties rarely had a bad word to say about those of other beliefs. Joe said it was because we were long accustomed to living in mixed company with Baptists and Huguenots and all the other Protestants over the centuries, not to mention the Jews who lived nearby in the Tenters. If a word *was* ever said by an errant Catholic about a Protestant, another in the company would usually remark, 'At least they're honest,' implying dishonesty a little closer to home.

I consulted our *Virtue's Dictionary* for the meaning of the word 'consultant', and learned it was 'a person who provides expert advice as a professional'. When I looked up 'professional', it made me thoughtful. I saw that it meant 'one who has the benefit of prolonged training and a formal qualification'. This looked all right! After a rehearsal-call to my sister Nell at her work, I dialled the number on the letterhead from a public telephone box, the first time I ever spoke to a stranger on the phone. Nell had warned me not to press Button A until I heard a voice answering, as I would lose my pennies otherwise. If I couldn't get through, I was to press Button B to get my money back.

However, I did get through first time. When I heard a woman's voice I tried to relax as I said who I was and explained my business. She told me to hold on for a moment as she was going through her list and then I was asked if I could come for interview on 20 December at twelve o'clock sharp. In addition, she said that they would like to see the original of my references. The appointment was for just a few days away but I thought it would never come. Mam decided that my Confirmation suit was still wearable as the short coat wasn't in bad condition and she had it cleaned specially at IMCO in Grafton Street. I was bothered about the short trousers giving away my age, as boys took to wearing longers when they reached fourteen, but she said I could carry my raincoat on my arm and pull up my socks so that my bare legs might not be noticed. Mr McDonnell cut my hair, reminding me to tell Mam that it was time to put his name in the hat. Old Mr Cripps, with his white collar standing vertically on his neck, fitted me out with new shoes. When I went home I spent a little while admiring myself in the mirror and was well satisfied with my appearance. Mam said I looked *extra* and Dad said I was very like Nell around the eyes.

When the day of the interview finally came, I set off early from Keeper Road with my letter in my pocket, clutching my references and Primary Certificate in an old foolscap envelope. I got the bus down to the Coombe and called into Joe for his last-minute advice. He told me not to be nervous and that I just needed to speak up and remember my manners.

Although I had absolutely no idea what a consulting engineer did, I was determined to prove to the firm of Joseph Mallagh and Son that they'd do it a lot better if they hired me. Still, I was a little apprehensive as I headed down Francis Street. I was in plenty of time so that I could take particular notice of the familiar places that I might not be seeing so often if I got the job. I crossed Patrick Street and walked around the corner where my favourite barbershop was situated. Tommy White, the proprietor, kept goldfinches flying wild around himself and his clientele; they could land anywhere, although they had a roosting rail on one wall. I thought it was a wonderful idea and never passed by without going in to have a look. It was frequented by the men who sold in the bird market, and the talk was mostly of the latest trapping or breeding coup. The magazines were old copies of *Cage Birds and Bird Fancy* and the schedule for an upcoming bird show in the Mansion House was being passed around. A discussion was going on about the proper size of the spots on a budgerigar's neck for show purposes. A young man with a tanned face was saying that there were plenty of young linnets in the furze at the green road in the forest at Mullaghcleevaun.

In St Patrick's Close I passed the forbidding glower of Marsh's Library, suitably located overlooking a graveyard, with weedy battlemented walls and locked gates that I had never seen open. The lack of welcome there was a byword in the Liberties. The locals claimed that only the ghost of Dean Swift himself had access to the shelves and he showed his disgust by throwing some books on the floor from time to time. Beside it was Kevin Street Garda Station. The old handball alley in the front yard was decrepit, with plaster crumbling off the weathered walls, and it was full of bicycles, mostly wrecked, that had been stolen and remained unclaimed. Policemen were setting them up in rows in preparation for one of the periodic auctions that were of great interest to the locals. I saw Mr Kenny, the father of my cricket-loving friend John, who was a guard himself, having a look over the bikes. I knew he made a little money at Christmas repairing them and doing them up, because there was always a demand for second-hand bicycles. John Kenny had told me that Kevin Street Garda Station had once been the headquarters of the Dublin Metropolitan Police, and before that, the Bishop's Palace, but now it had a moping air of neglect and decay and I hurried on.

Before I got to St Stephen's Green corner I passed Brian Kavanagh's home on Cuffe Street. He had been a pal in school. The bullet-holed stonework of the College of Surgeons came into view just before the Green Cinema and I thought of Kavanagh again. He was about four inches taller than me, but he liked my company and it was partly because of him that I had never taken up smoking.

One day in our last term in school, he'd told me he had a girlfriend and wanted to go to the Green Cinema with her. The problem was that his mam had decreed he could only go with friends, so he asked me to take Rosie, his girlfriend's pal, to make up a foursome. I, being young, had never been on a date, so I was shy, but willing. My extra incentive was that they were showing *The Yearling* again. I loved the story of Jody, the boy whose brothers and sisters are dead but who adopts a fawn for company, with tragic consequences when the deer has to be shot. However, his mammy's love brings the story to a happy end. This was too good to miss, and in Technicolor as well. And Kavanagh was paying for the four of us, after all.

His tolerant mother served us tea and cake in their flat and then we left for the pictures. She gave him Black Magic chocolates in a little box complete with red tassel to take with him and he bought two packets of Craven A cigarettes before we went in. He handed one packet to me, and told me to share them with Rosie, my new friend. She was a little bunty girl, happy and talkative, with a head of black hair, which she had combed out like a Jinny-Joe and she kept humming the first bar of 'Powder Your Face With Sunshine' to herself. I did my best to like her but we didn't seem to have any interests in common.

Rosie lived in Oliver Bond flats, just down the hill from Francis Street, and her parents, who were from Tipperary, had come to Dublin when she was very young. This alone was worthy of curiosity. I had never met a girl of my own age who had come from the country to live in the Liberties. She was an avid smoker and told me that if she didn't have a cigarette she wouldn't know what to do with her hands when she walked into a room. This problem was new to me, and I looked her over as I tried not to stare. But when I *did* catch a glance of her hands, there was nothing wrong with them that I could see. I told her that I didn't smoke myself because I liked athletics and wanted to join a running club.

She did her best to feign interest but simply couldn't understand why anyone would exert themselves chasing around a track with nothing to pursue. Then she said that her father had a racing greyhound, and asked me if I bopped, and had I ever been to Lourdes? I floundered in this flood of worldliness and sophistication and began to wish I was far away, though not necessarily as far away as Lourdes. Kavanagh sparked up when the picture started, then put his arm around his girl's shoulder and kissed her quickly on the cheek. I was embarrassed by this display of adolescent carnality and, to hide my confusion, took out the packet of cigarettes that he had given me.

Rosie suggested that I light one for her as well, but when she saw me in danger of burning myself, she took them both, placed them between her reddened lips, and lit up the two cigarettes together. Kavanagh looked across at me and smiled but he still had his arm draped affectionately around his girl, and I had to look away again, blushing. I pulled strongly on my cigarette and it glowed, just like it did for Humphrey Bogart in *Casablanca*, but the smoke was invading my airways. Halfway through that first cigarette, feeling faint and dizzy, I sagged into my seat, trying to disappear. Rosie misunderstood the signal and put her head on my shoulder, giggling away. Her big black mop of hair enveloped me and I sat disconcerted by this invasion of my territory. After a few more minutes, I excused myself and went out to the toilet, then left the cinema to clear my head, only coming back just before the picture ended.

Nobody minded. Rosie was devouring the last of the Black Magic and Kavanagh was rubbing his lips with his handkerchief as he separated from his beloved. When we got outside I handed him back the packet of cigarettes with eight still intact and swore to myself that I would take a vow of poverty, chastity and obedience before I would ever smoke again.

Now, as I crossed the road to the railings side of St Stephen's Green, on the way to my interview, I felt a long way from my old friend. I took out my letter to confirm the address again and asked a policeman how to get there. He pointed and said, 'Just around the corner down Dawson Street,' and I realised I was near the place where, according to the story Mam had told me, life had changed for ever for Uncle Jim. By now I was coming close to Fusiliers' Arch on the corner of the Green, which was like a monument to a great triumph. However, when I had a good look at it, the soffit of the arch was inscribed with the names of hundreds of Irishmen of the Royal Dublin Fusiliers who had died in the Boer War, fighting for England. Two of them were simply described as Pte J. O'Connor, and I wondered if we were related. One end of the arch was peppered with scars from bullets fired by the British Army at the rebels in the College of Surgeons in 1916, and I thought of my uncle, William O'Neill, who had fought in the British Army in the First World War. Mam had always told us to have respect for all the dead, because each and every Irishman had done his best for Ireland in his own way.

Time was running on, and I found myself hurrying down Dawson Street to my appointment. South Frederick Street turned out to be a long terrace of unkempt Georgian houses with a high-water mark of repaired brickwork at eaves level on most of them. Some had been plastered and painted over as if the owner wanted to make a feature of the numerous cracks in the walls, and one leaking rainwater pipe had grown a vertical swathe of moss on the façade. The sun did not penetrate the canyon of houses although I could see clothes hung up to dry here and there through the railings of the basement areas. Seagulls were screaming on the ashbins awaiting collection and bin men were calling loudly to each other in a way that I found comforting. I could hear 'Danny Boy' being played on the bagpipes from the Trinity College end of the street and, although it was different from what I expected in a centre of business, I felt comfortable in my surroundings.

A row had erupted between the driver of a motor car and a Corporation traffic official in a green-peaked cap. The man had parked on one side of the street before going to work but officialdom had later changed the adjustable sign to indicate that on this particular day parking was allowed only on the other side of the street. As I came to my destination at number fourteen, I stood on the steps to have a look at a group of young women, dressed beautifully, standing on the pavement next door, with one having her photograph taken by a man with a camera on a tripod. The others were awaiting their turn, and each girl threw an unnatural shape as she posed. On the far side of the narrow street a small group of men and women was watching them with appreciation.

One woman called out to no one in particular, 'That's a lovely fishtail skirt that mannequin is wearing.'

A man said, 'Mammy, buy me that,' as a lovely youngwan pouted her lips and showed off her style to best advantage.

The next girl wore a full multicoloured gypsy dress and, when she twirled for the camera, there was the dead silence of true admiration. 'The Grafton Academy of Dress Designing (Miss Prigge prop.)' was painted in white on a black background on the wall forming the backdrop, and the girls seemed oblivious to the excitement they were causing.

The sight of these goddesses was a great diversion for my febrile emotions, but I had business to do. I turned around and gave my attention to number fourteen. The fanlight over the door was in need of cleaning and each dirty black brick on the wall showed a little margin of its original brown colour around the edges. The hall door was punctured with openings for letterboxes, some of them in place and one blanked over with unpainted plywood. Brass plates of different sizes identified the tenants. Whoever did the polishing had managed to get Brasso stains on the brickwork. The surface was patterned here and there with neat little holes where name plates had once been. It made me wonder just how old the house was.

One of the plates read 'The Theosophical Society' and a smaller plaque, in need of polishing, noted the presence of Leslie Condron, Solicitor. Finally there was the one I was looking for, '*JOSEPH MALLAGH AND SON*', and below that, '*Consulting Engineers*'. I wiped the dirt off my shoes on the metal scraper at the door, said a Hail Mary to myself, pulled up my socks, and pushed my way in. The door opened and then slammed behind me as I stood into the big hall. I was in semi-darkness but a man following me with a sack of logs on his back turned on the light, which he said was on a time switch, and told me to watch myself on the stairs. The hall was freezing cold and bare of furniture, except for a grand old table on which lay an untidy stack of envelopes and a notice saying, 'Post no bills'.

The worn stone floor tiles were laid diagonally in a pattern of blue and cream, interrupted by repairs in random colours. The walls were painted a fading maroon, but it all looked neat and tidy. A smiling grey-haired man in a white dustcoat stood at the end of the hall talking to another, who was wearing a brown Crombie and carrying a briefcase. The smell of brilliantine assailed me as I approached. *Henry J. Lyons and Sons, Architects and Civil Engineers* was inscribed in gold lettering on the open glass door to the office behind them. A bell in some nearby church was clanging midday. The man in the overcoat was saying that he had to get down to Amiens Street station to catch the express back to the city. I wondered where he meant. I started to climb the stairs, running my hand on the ornate banisters and gazing all around as I marvelled at the size of the place. Little groups of people were standing on the first-floor landing, making quiet conversation and holding cups and saucers. The door to the Theosophical Society was open behind them and on the wall I could see a poster reading 'THE SOUL OF MAN IS IMMORTAL.'

The office of Joseph Mallagh and Son was on the second floor. I scrupulously wiped my nose before I knocked. The soul of man may indeed be immortal, but the nostrils are subject to the weather. The door into Reception overlooking the street was opened by a young woman, who invited me in with a fleeting smile. She was on the plump side, but not fat. Her face was pretty and she wore full makeup. I couldn't help noticing her shoulder-length red hair, which was shining, and included a calf's lick dropping in perfect symmetry past each ear. She was dressed neatly in black and white and there was a nice hint of musky perfume. I thought she was lovely but she seemed to be agitated about something.

She told me her name was Miss Mellon and, as I handed over my envelope, invited me to hang up my coat behind the door. When I did so, a bit carelessly, she went over and hung it up again, so that it fell in straight folds. On her way back she stopped for a moment to glance at my bare legs, then sat down at the desk, inviting me to sit opposite her. As she did, she touched each set of papers on her desk as if to make sure they had not been disturbed in her absence. An open page of her notebook was filled with the hieroglyphics of shorthand. A cup of tea and a cream slice on a plate kept it company.

Miss Mellon made a sandwich of plain and carbon paper and rolled it quickly into her typewriter before picking up a small disc of blue eraser. Her manner was so officious that I assumed she was carrying out the interview, especially when she began questioning me briskly. She assured me that all the applicants for the job were being asked for the same information and not to mind, it was just routine. Which school had I gone to and had I got a bike? What did my father do for a living? Could I remind her of where I lived and how many were in the family? She looked up when I told her that I was one of thirteen children, including one who had died in Canada, but I was surprised that she didn't bother with my references and seemed to know very little about me. Whenever she made a typing mistake, she went to a lot of trouble to erase it on the original and the copy, then neatly swept the crumbs of rubber into a cardboard box with a little brush.

A bell on her desk rang suddenly. My heart seemed to jump. She grabbed my references and her typescript and darted to a door behind me, knocking before she went through. When she returned empty-handed she made a brief telephone call, confirmed she had Truemans on the line, and asked them to send over their messenger to pick up a drawing for printing. A moment later a boy older than me came out of the other office, said goodbye and went on his way. The dividing door opened again and a genial-looking man with a moustache and glasses beckoned me to enter. Miss Mellon addressed him deferentially and said who I was without telling me his name. It didn't matter as I knew it must be Mr Mallagh. I also realised that the real interview had not yet begun. Mallagh reminded me of Mr Gallagher, our old sports teacher, but appeared a lot fitter. I took to him straight away as he had an air of good-natured authority. He waved to a chair on the other side of his desk, read over my letter of application, then peered at me curiously before he began to check my references.

There was a portrait on the wall of a man who looked the image of him, with the same type of moustache and round glasses, but wearing a chain of office over a lovely suit. Underneath was written '*Joseph Mallagh, President of the Institution of Civil Engineers of Ireland, 1930/1931*', and I presumed that they were closely related. A book entitled

Mitchell's Building Construction lay facing me on the desk with a small square of netting wire beside it, which looked out of place. Mr Mallagh asked me if I had written the letter of application myself as he placed the references to one side. Then he said suddenly, 'What is eleven times twelve?'

'One hundred and thirty-two, sir,' I replied straightaway, because I knew all the tables off by heart as did most boys in my class in school.

He looked up and asked: 'What is twenty per cent of eighty?' I immediately said, 'Sixteen, sir,' because Devane had taught us that in percentages you just multiply the first number by the second and fix the decimal point, making two multiplied by eight in this case.

'I see,' he said, 'and what is twelve per cent of fifty?'

The same principle applied, so I said, 'Six, sir.'

He smiled and asked me to spell 'architect', which I did. After a few minutes of further questioning he began to tell me about the job. They needed someone to light the fire in the drawing office before the staff came to work, the three rooms had to be kept clean and dusted, and messages had to be run. Miss Mellon would look after that side of things. The boy who got the job would be given time off for further education, which the firm would pay for. Training would be given in engineering draughtsmanship, if aptitude was shown. All this depended on passing examinations. In fact, there was a chance that the boy could one day become an indentured pupil for the study of engineering. Taking your chances indeed!

I told him how I could light any fire just by using old newspaper wrapped up tightly with ashes on top, and that

I would not mind coming in early each morning. Then I showed him my Primary Certificate and said that I would have no trouble studying as I was well used to it. As the interview ended, I was informed that they would be writing to all the applicants shortly as they wanted the position filled urgently. When I went through the outer office, envelope in hand, Miss Mellon remained seated at her desk, talking to another boy, and nodded her goodbye, asking me to make sure I closed the front door fully as I left the building. My feelings were a mixture of relief, anticipation and impatience. What a great opportunity this could be. But had I got the job or not? I set off for home trying to put my hopes to the back of my mind.

On the way, I walked along the footpath outside St Stephen's Green until I came to the narrow entrance gate almost opposite Dawson Street and across the road from the Provincial Bank. I put my hand on the railing and remembered again the amazing story Mam had told me about the terrible thing that had happened here on a morning in March 1922. It had come to the notice of the IRA that two men from the Ministry of Labour Finance Branch called into the Provincial Bank at the same time every Friday morning to collect cash, travelling the few hundred yards back to their office by taxi. Three members of the Active Service Unit of the IRA, Laurence Dowling, Augustine Troy and my Uncle Jim, left Francis Street with orders to rob the clerks. Troy was lookout. The hold-up was to be executed by the other two.

Max Green was chairman of the Irish Prisons Board at the time. Although a Catholic, he had enjoyed a brilliant career under British administration. Before his chairmanship, he had acted as private secretary to the Lord Lieutenant, the Marquess of Aberdeen, who was the British monarch's personal representative in Ireland. Mr Green's wife, Johanna, was the daughter of the Home Rule parliamentarian, John Redmond.

Mr Green had left her, unwell, in their home in Appian Way that morning as he walked their twin boys to school before going through St Stephen's Green on his way to work in the city. Jim and Dowling held up the men from the Ministry of Labour and robbed them of their attaché case as they were getting out of the taxi at their office in Molesworth Street. An official of the ministry ran out, jumped into the taxi and gave chase, shouting for help to catch the robbers.

Troy disappeared in the gathering crowd, leaving Dowling and Jim O'Neill running on the footpath opposite St Stephen's Green, near the Shelbourne Hotel. Dowling threw away the attaché case as they were pursued. The two men ran as far as Dawson Street corner and went separate ways. Jim O'Neill headed down Dawson Street, gun in his hand, but was overpowered outside the Mansion House. He had not used the weapon, and he was disarmed by a detective named Gerald Grace, who was a member of the police force which had been set up by the Pro-Treaty group within the IRA with headquarters in the Gresham Hotel. As he was being taken away, some shots were heard. Grace, and many of the onlookers, ran back the short distance to St Stephen's Green, from where the sound of gunfire had come.

They found a disaster. Dowling had run across the road with the intention of escaping through St Stephen's Green. He had a gun in his hand and was being shot at by his pursuers, who were gaining on him. As he made to enter the park by the same narrow gate where I now stood, there were shouts of 'Stop that man.' Mr Green was just about to leave the park. When he heard the yells, he did not hesitate but stood into the exit and held out his arms just as Dowling was about to enter. Two or three shots were fired. Max Green fell with a bullet to his chest. His spine had been shattered by the blast. Dowling ran along the footpath and entered St Stephen's Green by the Fusiliers' Arch nearby. When he was captured half a mile away, he had no gun, but a weapon of the same type that had killed Mr Green was found in a lane through which Dowling had run. Shots had been fired from it and it was jammed in the firing position. The cartridges were the same type as the bullet that had killed Mr Green although, from the first moment of his capture, Laurence Dowling denied ever firing the gun.

He was eventually tried four times on charges of murder and of robbery under arms, but the jury would not convict on the murder charge because of their doubt that he had fired the fatal shot, and the possibility that it was one of the pursuers who had accidentally killed Mr Green. Dowling ultimately received a sentence of ten years' imprisonment for armed robbery.

As for Jim, he appeared four times on the robbery charge, but the jury failed to convict him on each occasion. The only person who could have identified him with certainty as being one of the robbers was Gerald Grace, the man who had disarmed him, but he failed to attend the court, for whatever reason, to give evidence. Some people said he had been kidnapped and others that he was not well. It was also suggested that he had been intimidated or simply sympathetic, having been a comrade of the accused men before the bitter pathos of the split caused by the passing of the Treaty vote in the Dáil, which led to the partition of Ireland. By the time of the last O'Neill trial, not only did Mr Grace fail to appear, but the real evidence had disappeared as well. When the Anti-Treaty Republicans occupied the Four Courts in 1922 at the start of the civil war they were under siege for eight days by the Irish National Army, who took over the Bridewell Garda Station during that period. This happened to be where the guns and attaché case from the robbery had been stored awaiting the trial. These disappeared during the week of the siege.

The result was that the prosecution had lost all of the evidence needed to prove their case and it was no surprise that the charge of robbery under arms against Jim O'Neill was dropped. He had been arrested on 3 March 1922 and was not released until April 1924 and it ended sadly for everyone. Curious crowds had often gathered outside 15 Francis Street during his incarceration. The house was kept under observation by the security forces of the new Free State. Granddad O'Neill had contracts with the Office of Public Works for the maintenance of boilers in various locations, but this work almost disappeared after the trial. Jim O'Neill was warned to leave the country as his life was in danger. Shortly after his release, the family shop in Francis Street was strafed with bullets.

Mr Green left behind a widow and twin boys just eight years of age. There was great sympathy from all sides for the Green family because, in his job on the Prisons Board, he had often done his best for political prisoners, although a few said he could have done more during the hunger strike that led to the death of Thomas Ashe. But his widow had a great love of the Irish and, a playwright in her younger days, had often depicted them in a sympathetic way in her work. Mr Green's death made international headlines. Mrs Green, whose health was poor, died before the year was out and the event was reported in the *New York Times*. Mam said that the Green family was so highly thought of in British society that the House of Commons voted to give the orphaned boys a little maintenance pension payment until they reached the age of twenty-one.

It ended badly for Jim too. The Black and Tans had already raided the shop in Francis Street and had fired shots indiscriminately into the house when they were active. Now Jim had to fear a worse foe. He was told that there were elements within the police force of the new State who intended to kill him if they could, just as they were suspected of doing to others like Noel Lemass, whose riddled body was found in the Dublin Mountains a year later. Jim had to leave the country and was bound for Canada within a few months of his release. He left his sweetheart behind, although they had been very close. Her name was Tillie Murray and, when I heard the name, I understood at last why Mam had always treated her as our aunt.

Granddad O'Neill's health suffered and he died in 1927. This put Joe in the position of having to change his job as a ship's radio officer for the task of minding his ailing mother and running the little butcher's shop at 15 Francis Street, the house where I was born. Mam said that at least Jim was safely in prison during the worst of the civil war and God knows what might have happened to him if he had continued to fight against the Treaty, and that Joe had been right to take the path of peace. Her compassion for the Green family was unbounded.

I stood there thinking of what it must have been like. I said a prayer for Mr Green and his family; and for Jim O'Neill and Laurence Dowling, who was only nineteen years of age at the time. A big man had to nudge me out of his way to get past, muttering about my blocking the gate. People were hurrying in and out of the bank across the road as usual and I could nearly see the railings of the Mansion House in Dawson Street where Jim had been arrested. One man dead, families devastated, children orphaned, a nineteen-year-old imprisoned for ten years, Jim having to leave the country he loved never to return again without fearing for his safety, Granddad O'Neill dying just a few years after Jim went away. Nannie O'Neill was heartbroken at losing Jim and shed a tear whenever she heard his name afterwards. When the proceeds of the robbery were counted, the contents of the attaché case amounted to fifty-one pounds in silver coins. I sighed, and went home.

I told Mam about my interview when I got there, and started to think about study again. Dad thought it would be a great opportunity to join a firm where I would be allowed to advance. Joe told me I was on the pig's back. Two days later I got another letter from Mallagh's office telling me that they were pleased to say I had been successful at interview, and could I start work at eight thirty a.m. on Monday, 11 January 1952? Hours were eight thirty a.m. to twelve thirty p.m. and two p.m. to five thirty p.m. with a half-day on Saturdays. Wages were twenty-five shillings a week. There would be two weeks' annual holiday. Further, I was to telephone without delay to confirm that this was acceptable. The letter was signed by J. M. Mellon p.p. T. J. S Mallagh. There was no happier boy in Ireland on the day I got that job.

12. WHEN McGEE DRAWS HIS FIRST WEEK'S PAY

Martha and I were playing House in the parlour. She had just called *clickety-click* to fill her card and win the game when a knock like a drum roll assailed our front door above the noise of the party from the next room. A voice shouted through the letterbox, 'Hello, hello, hello, a happy new year, everybody.' Uncle Bill, Aunt Eva and my cousin Rory stood there, all apologies for their late arrival to the O'Connor family celebration of the engagement of my brother Billy and Alice. The infrequent Saturday bus service between James's Street and our home on Keeper Road was the culprit. But what matter? They were here with us now.

Martha took their overcoats to lay them on a bed upstairs, which was her allotted job. My task was to keep the ashtrays tidy and mind the little presents for the couple. We also had to wait in the front parlour to entertain any visitors who might like to take respite from the clamour. We had set up our game of House to pass the time while the smaller ones played hide-and-go-seek upstairs. Martha was calling the numbers. We'd had Uncle Bartle and Granny O'Connor for company so far. Granny did not look well and Bartle, who usually avoided parties, had only come to wish a blessing on the happy couple. I was willing to do anything Mam wanted that evening, because I was fizzing with the excitement of going to work for the first time on the following Monday.

When the visitors came into the hall they admired the Christmas decorations, which had been left in place although it was already the 9th of January. I threw open the door to the scene in the smoky kitchen. Cries of welcome added to the noise. Our guests had formed a big circle and were dancing solo with some abandon, in a variety of styles. A couple of disoriented flies buzzed slowly past me, hopelessly trying to find a quiet place to go back to sleep. The room was vibrating to Teresa Brewer's singing and Aunt Dinah vamping percussive chords on the piano:

> *Put another nickel in –*
> *In the nickelodeon.*
> *All I want is lovin' you*
> *And music, music, music!*

Bill and Eva joined the revellers around the circle amid delighted hugs and kisses. 'Make way for horse traffic,' shouted Uncle Paddy, giving Bill a slap on the back.

'How are yeh, Paddy? You're looking like Two Ton Tony Galento,' said Bill, poking him in the belly and laughing away.

Billy and Alice were on the inside of the circle, holding hands at arms' length and smiling at each other as they swayed to the music. Over by the kitchen sink, Aunt Molly was helping Mam to keep up the sandwich supply, which Peggy and Nell were intermittently handing around. Jack Hilliard stood beside them, organising drinks to suit all tastes and setting them up on the kitchen table, which had been shoved out of the way to make space. At the same time, he was telling Tommy about the great win his jockey son, Jimmy, had brought off on his mount Anadir in the Selling Hurdle at Market Rasen.

Uncle Joe was seated at the open kitchen window sipping watery whiskey and running his finger down the condensation on the pane, admiring the rivulets he was making. He loved a singsong, but never danced. Mam called out to Bill, 'What'll you have?' and he responded in a loud voice that he was not really a house-drinker but would force himself to accept a glass of whiskey in the circumstances – but, please, just barely fill it. He lived life to the full, always exuberant, even if he was a bit supercharged. Everyone laughed at his little joke.

The music stopped for a moment while drinks were served. Joe stood up and said, in his serious way, 'Here's to Billy and Alice. Long life to you both and God bless you in the future, so far away in Australia.' Alice thanked him, and told us again about their plans to marry later in the year, preferably December, if they could get a dispensation from the parish priest for a wedding in Advent. This would best suit their arrangements to go to Australia on the Assisted Passage scheme. Mam tugged her handkerchief out of her sleeve, but Paddy proclaimed, 'None of this "Heart Bowed Down" stuff. Hey, Bill, give us an oul' song. I was the last to sing so it's *my* noble call.'

'Of course I will, but I'll let Eva go first,' said Bill, looking at his wife.

'Honest to God, you might have given me time to take off my gloves,' said Eva, 'but sure I might as well go first as last.'

When Rory heard this he begged his mother not to sing *that* song but there was no turning her. Eva said, 'My friend Betty learned it in the Peggy Medlar School and why wouldn't I sing it? It's a poor heart that never rejoiceth.' With that, she started into the story of McGee, a man who had just got a job after being idle for quite a time:

> *All the world will be bright,*
> *Next Saturday night,*
> *When McGee draws his first week's pay.*

When she came to the chorus, Rory groaned and clamped his hands over his eyes in woeful anticipation as Eva broke into a shimmying little-girl tap dance routine, touching her knees and tossing her dress. The great huzzahs from the onlookers added to the mortification of her son. When she was finished she said, 'And now my call is for Joe O'Neill to entertain the company with a song.' This request obliged him to perform, but he needed no encouragement. Joe was in great form because, as Mam had told us, he had met a lovely new companion named Monica Kennan, who worked with him in the Fianna Fáil offices in Dáil Éireann.

Someone wanted to know about the other girl in Joe's life, Lily Cole, but Mam said they were only friends whereas things with Monica were serious. Anyway, Joe looked like a happy man and was wearing a new suit, his receding hair well kept in place with Brylcreem. Tommy assured me that his tie was in a Windsor knot and noted that his smart Fair Isle pullover matched it. Joe claimed that little whiskey devils were trying to get out of his head, but in honour of the occasion, he would certainly sing an old favourite of his from Gilbert and Sullivan:

> *On a tree by a river a little tom-tit*
> *Sang 'Willow, tit willow, tit willow'...*

When he'd finished, he asked Bill to sing 'Trees', his usual offering. 'Dinah,' Bill said in a joke, 'can you give me an A and then follow me?'

Dinah was Mam's sister, resident pianist in the Premier Inn in Meath Street at weekends for the singers in the lounge. She had already played her classical piece for us, a John Field Nocturne. 'Another Liberties man,' she had said. Having discharged her own duty and set the bar high, she was now free to accompany all jumpers.

'Bill O'Connor,' she exclaimed, 'don't get me started. If *you* can sing it, I can play it in any key on the circle of fifths, and Arran Quay as well, if you like. Just you make a start and I'll pick it up.' Dinah never took a drink in her life. Some said it was because Granddad O'Neill was too fond of the juice – but when faced with the new-found talent that topers discovered in alcohol, she knew exactly what to do. Bill sang 'Trees' as though it had been written for him, and the words of Joyce Kilmer came to life in the music:

> *Poems are made by fools like me,*
> *But only God can make a tree.*

Aunt Eileen Copley, Dad's sister, produced a photograph from her handbag. Her face was ashen with the illness that would end her life before the year was out, two months before the wedding. 'Did you know that Billy was my page boy on the day I was married?' she said quietly. 'That's him in the little white suit. He can have this for a souvenir to take with him to Australia.' My heart went out to her, being sick and having a lonely home life, her husband involved with another woman, but she was quite self-possessed.

At the mention of photographs, Jack Nesbitt went upstairs and came back with a box Kodak and the company gathered at one end of the room for a group shot. 'Here comes Karsh of Ottawa,' called out my cousin Eileen, his wife. 'This is for the *Picture Post*. Say cheese.'

Aunt Lily had just been telling them about the day she sang 'South Of The Border' with Jack Doyle, the Gorgeous Gael, in the Limelight Bar. Now she put a caring arm around her sister and announced, 'Eileen and myself are going to sing "Home To Our Mountains", from Verdi's *Il Trovatore*.' When they sang the repeated last line on a slowing diminuendo – 'Away, away, sorrow away: Away, away, sorrow away' – the words hung on the air like an incantation.

Uncle Rory, sitting on the polish-brush stool by the fire, was trying to chat to my sisters as they moved about, telling them they had lovely smiles, but Mam had warned them that he was fond of his hands. 'Yes,' whispered Tommy to me. 'Roman hands and Russian fingers.' Granddad O'Connor was sitting beside Joe, smoking his pipe and telling the singers to open their mouths and let the sound out before he showed how it was done with an old hit: 'If I Had a Talking Picture of You'.

The music started again, and the circle re-formed. Soon Teresa Brewer was exercising her spell once more, but some were getting tired. A few couples joined Billy and Alice inside the circle, lurching together in mutual enjoyment. Afterwards, Billy played 'Star Dust' on the Hohner chromatic harmonica that had been given to Alice by Larry Adler himself when she had volunteered to go on stage at his show in Dublin. Mr Higgins, our next-door neighbour, was prevailed upon to sing and we went down Memory Lane again:

> We set out together, mate o' mine,
> When youth was in its prime,
> Life the path that lay before us,
> Life the hill we had to climb ...

That brought on a few tears. I left and went back to the parlour, where the game of House was continuing with Granny O'Connor and Bartle. Jack Nesbitt and his wife Eileen followed me in, then Joe and Granddad. We each took a card for another desultory round as Martha called out the numbers. Joe began to tell us one of his whimsical stories. 'Did you hear about the man who died last week in the new buildings in Thomas Davis Street? The house was so small that they had to lift the body down the stairs. Halfway down, they let him fall and his leg was broken when he hit the hall.'

Intermittently, he was discussing with Granddad the easiest bona fide pubs to visit if you lived in the Liberties. They decided that taking the tram from Thomas Street to Terenure and going on to the Cuckoo's Nest in Greenhills was probably the best. Jack Nesbitt was a carpenter on a building site. He asked when I was to start in my new job and whether it was true that I might be trained as a draughtsman. I had noticed how many of my relations seemed to be aware of my 'getting a chance', as they put it, and how they went out of their way to wish me well. Mam must have told them about it but they had a real interest in how I got on, and I loved them for it.

Then Jack told us that he had apologised to Dad for his performance on the previous Saturday. I remembered it well, because Dad had been very sarcastic about it. What happened was that Eileen and Jack had made a mistake about the date of the party and had arrived at our house exactly a week too soon. Jack carried his welcome under his arm in the form of a dozen of stout but Mam and Dad were out seeing friends for the New Year. Eileen wanted to wait for a while, and we sat at the kitchen table. Jack had opened a bottle of stout, and the contents of the first one were soon diminishing as he told me about the need for clarity on engineers' drawings. 'You'll have to learn to watch for the two mistakes that are made on a building site,' he said. 'The first is the one the men hide from the foreman, and the other is the one the foreman hides from the resident engineer.'

That was the way the time was spent waiting for Mam and Dad to come back that evening. Jack opened another bottle, more chat, then another, drinking unaccompanied, as he and Eileen began to talk about their plans for going to live in New York and how it seemed that so many people were emigrating. There was still no sign of Mam and Dad at half past ten, so the visitors stood to leave, Jack with some effort.

He did the decent thing and left one bottle of stout for Dad, making no attempt to take away the eleven dead soldiers. It was no wonder that Dad was annoyed that evening, but it was all in the past now, and Jack had apologised.

Bartle asked if I still had the belt he had won for boxing. He had given it to me some time previously, and I was able to show it to him. I knew he had made a spectacular amateur career for himself in the twenties, and this was one of his prizes, the studded belt of the champion. Then he took out a pencil and drew a cartoon of Martha on the back of a cigarette packet. Not long after, he and my grandparents left to go home and Martha went around with them to the 50 bus stop bound for the Coombe. The sound of Uncle John singing 'Mexicali Rose' came through the wall, followed by Lily doing an a cappella version of 'Landlord Fill The Flowing Bowl', with plenty of help from the family, and then a babble of voices broke out. I opened the door to listen.

'I hear they're going to do away with the Holy Hour. Closing the pubs from half past two to half past three in the afternoon is ridiculous anyway. You have some people hiding in the toilets the way things are at the moment.' Marie Harte, Uncle Rory's wife, was telling them about a young tenor by the name of Dermot Troy who lived opposite them on Cashel Road. It seemed that he had taught the 'Chorus of the Hebrew Slaves' to a choir in Inchicore and they made a great job of it. 'Yes,' said Nell, 'that's "Va, pensiero", from Verdi's *Nabucco,* it's lovely.' Thus the time gently passed and the party was nearly over. The Christmas decorations were tattered and some were ready to drop, as were most of my uncles and aunts. Dad sang 'Believe Me' before everyone made ready to go home. Someone said, 'Don't overlook the hostess,' so Mam gave them 'Willie Earl'. John declared that Dad was the best singer there, to murmurs of agreement. 'Except for Lily and Eileen,' Dad said. 'My sisters have lovely voices.' Paddy gave a loud '*tray bawn*' in agreement as Bill started to lead a noisy chorus of 'Show Me the Way to Go Home' and we knew the party had really ended.

Mam served a Dublin coddle with one for the road. Eva said Bill's drink must be for the white line, as they made their way for the last bus back to the Liberties. 'Any of the fifties stopping opposite the Loreto on the Crumlin Road will do you,' called out Mam, 'it's only a few stops,' smiling at the great success of the evening and hiding her feelings about Billy going away.

Tommy and I went to bed that night and talked about our own plans. He was preparing to go away on a soccer trial to Ipswich Town, and I was to start work on Monday. I told him I was going to spend the Sunday in Francis Street with Joe, so as to glean last-minute tips on how to get on in an office, and Tommy just said, 'No better man.' When I had shown Nell my letter of appointment she'd said I would be more like Johannes Factotum than Joannes O'Connor, which she had to explain to me. 'I mean you'll be Jack-of-all-trades, like Figaro,' she said.

Now I was about to find out for myself just exactly what work was like. I dreamed that night of starry skies and steering a ship in waves as high as Marie's shop, a phrase that came back to me from a story we had read in Warrenmount School when I was in Low Babies.

My job meant coming in early, an hour before the rest of the staff. I was to light the fires, sweep out the rooms, dust the furniture and keep the place clean. When the engineers arrived, I was to help in the drawing office and do any message needed, including delivering drawings to the building sites where Mallaghs were acting as consulting engineers. In no time at all I found myself in the company of Messieurs Browett, Ruddock, Sockett, Maddock and Moffitt, all Trinity College graduates and Protestants, with Mallagh as head of the firm. This mix was leavened by Pat Broy, who was a National University engineer, and who soon began to tell me his secrets as though I was his own age. I liked him in particular because he called me 'The Corduroy Kid' when I turned up for work in standard Liberties outfit, zipped top with two breast pockets and short trousers to match. He had a way of greeting people with *yuff yuff*, in place of hello. 'John,' he whispered to me once, with no small pride, 'at one o'clock this morning I was sitting on the bed of a divorced woman.' He drew on his pipe, exhaling without taking it out of his mouth, looking at me for a reaction. I never knew what to make of this kind of impartation but I warmed to him all the same.

Miss Mellon paid me my first week's wages out of the petty cash and I was proud to give it all to Mam. 'Now,' she said, 'would it be fair if you handed up a pound each week and kept five shillings' pocket money?' That was all right with me and I promised I would tell her if and when I received a rise. Mallagh was intent on my getting some education. So was I. He arranged that I would have time off each week to go to pre-specialisation classes in Technical School. The initial examination I sat was in English language for the General Certificate of Education. I passed it easily, and I liked the feeling, so I made it the first of many such outings.

In the meantime, I was Lord High Master of the preparation of all drinks and foodstuffs to keep the staff happy at their tea break. Like most engineers, they were pleasant company. Although from a different culture, they treated this Liberties boy in their midst with respect and good humour. Broy was intent on trying to explain to me the latest designs he had on his drawing board. Another engineer would glance at his work and quip, 'Are you still on the same drawing?' A mock row would ensue because this, apparently, was the biggest insult you could offer. The only time I felt threatened was one day when the engineers were having a tea break and discussing the film of Liam O'Flaherty's novel, *The Informer*. Broy brought me into the conversation by asking if I knew what it was about. I mentioned the name 'Gypo Nolan' as the man who squealed on the chap who was in 'the movement'. At the mention of those words, Browett looked at me in alarm, and said, in a loud voice, 'What do *you* know about the movement?' Perhaps he was just nervous, or reacting to his nickname that had been coined that day, Buckwheat Browbeat McBrowett. Broy had to reassure him that there wasn't a spy among them but I was careful after that just to listen.

Ronald Maddock, the second-in-command, was a benign chap, the oldest of the engineers. He wasn't selective about the jobs he would ask me to do, and one day I was sent to Pims in South Great George's Street. He'd handed me a brown-paper bag and told me that his wife had been in touch with the ladies' department there, and all I had to do was to exchange this parcel for another, which the shop assistant would have ready. When I went over to the department in question, the girl accepted my bag and shook out its cargo on the counter before me. It was a bra. Reportedly, it should have been a size bigger. My face quickly went a size bigger as well, as I had never been so close to an unrelated female as I was that day to Mrs Maddock.

Jeffrey Sockett was the resident engineer on the building of new silos in Dublin North City Milling Company, using a method of support that had been invented by Mallagh. Steel wires were wrapped around the high circular blockwork silos and tensioned like an elastic band to prevent collapse when full of grain. Since I had to deliver drawings to the site, he would explain how it all worked and even let me climb the ladder to the top of the scaffolding. However, things were not going too well back at HQ, mostly because I was losing interest in my cleaning duties and spent most of my time in the drawing office. Nevertheless, Miss Mellon seemed to see my presence as an opportunity for her to exercise her talent in planning, organising, leading and controlling my work schedule, and I had become a reluctant recruit.

It was 'John, do this' and 'John, do that.' Before long, my situation did remind me of *Figaro*, just as Nell had joked it would. Miss Mellon seemed to think haunting the drawing office was not in my job specification, and she might have been right, but I could see no future in Brasso. I learned a lot about human behaviour from her, as she spoke to me, not badly, but in a nagging way I didn't like, while she was quite a different person at the tea break, flirting harmlessly with the engineers and enjoying their risqué remarks.

I can see now that the girl was overworked, and I was hopeless as a help to her, since all I wanted was to make progress in the drawing office. She once showed me the muscles on the back of her fingers, which had developed from thumping her manual typewriter all day. 'I do as much as any engineer in the office,' she said, 'and all I get is eight pounds a week and they get thirteen.' I had not got the courage to tell her she was lucky, considering that my own wages were only twenty-five shillings. One of my jobs was to dust the top of her desk in the mornings so as to remove the debris of her erasing, which grew in a pile under her typewriter each day. If I missed any she would get annoyed and almost take me by the ear to show me where I had erred. Then it was a question of polishing the top of the desk again, accompanied by plaintive requests for me to try to do better next time: I should understand she had to have a lightning start to her day's toil.

Miss Mellon encouraged me to take my bike to work so as to get the messages finished more quickly. On the first such morning, I wheeled it into the building and carried it down the stairs into the basement. I was trying to lock it when the old lady who lived in the basement flat emerged, yelling at me to get out of her apartment and how dare I take such liberties. I laughed to myself at the idea of calling that run-down old area 'an apartment', but did as I was told, and hefted the bike upstairs to our office landing. A few days later, a nice young woman stopped me in the hall. She told me her name was Sadie and that she was a niece of the old lady, Mrs Kennedy, who lived in the basement with her husband, Joe. It transpired that Mrs Kennedy had changed her mind, seeing that I was a boy who worked in the house and I was no threat. In fact, it was now quite in order to leave the bike in the basement anytime I liked.

I was delighted with myself and from the following day I took advantage of the offer. One morning as I came down the stairs I heard a frightened voice calling faintly for help. The entrance door to Mrs Kennedy's front room was slightly ajar so I threw my bike down and ran in to her. There was a blazing fire in the hearth. Her husband, Joe, was nowhere to be seen. A chair lay on its side and Mrs Kennedy was lying just inches away from the flames. She was in mortal danger and she was terrified. I moved the poor old lady away from the fire with little effort and sat her back in the chair in a safe place, where she lay in a faint. Joe came home a few minutes later and she seemed to recover after a drink of water. Later in the day Sadie came up to tell me how much she appreciated what I had done. She added that they had seen me observe the bird life in their back garden and said I could spend as much time there as I liked. I had a warm feeling again that I had first come across in the Liberties. Doing a favour for someone, especially something that money could not buy, made you feel good yourself.

Fred Hanna's bookshop was just around the corner. I spent many a happy hour reading Tennyson and the other Victorian poets from the marvellous display. I loved the romantic poems particularly, and memorised 'A Jacobite's Epitaph' by Thomas, Lord Macaulay, in one lunch hour, thanks to kind Mr Hanna, who never objected to my having a free read of books I couldn't afford to buy. The end of that poem seemed spectacular to me:

> *Forget all feuds, and shed one English tear*
> *O'er English dust. A broken heart lies here.*

Miss Mellon often asked me to go to McGills in Johnston's Court for her. She was very fond of pâté but told me that I would probably forget the French word so I was to call it 'chopped liver' and bring back the receipt. This was a private errand for her, so I didn't exactly hurry. The shelves in McGills were packed with German sausage and dried ham, and the smell in the shop was delicious, spicy and rich, so intense that it made me cough at first.

I felt genteel as I asked for my medium tub of pâté, sometimes remembering Devane's old admonition to 'cutt outt every wordd'. My order was given in a loud voice and an artificial accent, tremendously enunciating my Ts. I had taken to wearing a tie every day, and the result was a noticeable difference in the attitude of the tall, balding shop assistant: he seemed to serve me quicker when I so dressed. I was learning about life in the fast lane.

Grafton Street was hypnotic. I stood outside Bewley's café and watched a man in the window. Dressed in a white dust-suit, he was roasting coffee beans in a huge open drum. The aroma of coffee outside had drawn a crowd of onlookers who couldn't afford to drink it, including the nun who usually stood silently at the door seeking alms, but we all pressed up near the window for the spectacle. From the distance arose a wonderful tinkling sound, like a dulcimer, but I could not place it, so I followed it down Grafton Street towards Trinity College. Just outside Weirs there was a huge Irish harp, heavily decorated with shamrocks and seashells, being tuned by a tiny old lady standing on a chair. I stayed to listen. Soon the mournful strains of 'She Is Far From The Land' fell on my ears. I was enthralled. She played the melody with great feeling and decorated the harmonies with exquisite grace notes. When she was finished her set, the harp was lifted by a man, who, someone said, was her son, and they went up to Bewley's with a few of us following.

After a while I had a look in Dixon Hempenstall's window. Broy had told me that Mallagh always gave a bonus at Christmas, and I had made up my mind to buy a set of Zeiss drawing instruments if that happened. There were stainless-steel pens, dividers and compasses in a beautiful green-padded box, and they bewitched me even though I didn't yet know how to use them. Outside, a policeman was on duty almost opposite the Provost's House in Trinity College. He had long white gloves and was beaming like the mechanical Laughing Policeman in the Bray arcade as he directed traffic past the roundabout of flowers behind him. Workmen were moving the college boundary railings closer to Trinity to make more space on the busy road. I noticed the policeman was standing on a box and many of the drivers waved a salute as they passed by.

While I was there, I tried to find the house in Grafton Street where I had been told the young wife of Robert Emmet had lived before marriage, but the shop fronts did not bother with commemorating such details. I turned around again and walked up to see what was on in the Forum Cinema. George Formby was starring in *It's In The Air*, and I made up my mind to go there when I got paid because I loved to hear him play the ukulele.

In the office, I'd listened to the engineers' conversation to improve my command of English. They behaved as if I spoke some dialect, as to them indeed I did because they had never heard the idioms or the accent of the Liberties. Broy would have no hesitation in correcting any slip, saying, 'There *is* one, but there *are* two,' or 'Neither takes *nor*, and either takes *or*'. Their courtesies towards each other were fascinating. The gentle exchange, 'No offence meant' followed by 'No offence taken' was often heard. If something was funny, then it had to be either 'funny peculiar' or 'funny ha-ha'. They often spoke laughingly about the nonsensical definitions of people being either U or non-U, meaning 'upper class' or otherwise. This ranking depended on the way certain words were used to describe objects. It was U to say 'scent' and non-U to say 'perfume'. 'Lavatory' was the word rich people used for 'toilet'. They had great fun over a list of such words that Broy produced one day.

Once finished, the engineers' drawings on tracing paper had to be copied in either Truemans or Thompsons in Commercial Buildings in Dame Street. Mr Thompson was a jovial man who once had been a naval architect. In the construction professions, being an architect gives a person a teasing right to look down on engineers, and he was no exception. On the day he claimed that most engineers knew nothing about literature, I was able to tell him that the ones I worked with, graduates of Trinity College, had completed a degree in arts at the same time as engineering. Furthermore, if he liked I could recite Tennyson's 'Mariana'. I promptly started:

With blackest moss, the flower-plots
Were thickly crusted one and all:
The rusted nails fell from the knots
That held the pear to the gable wall ...

When I went back to the office I made a little plan. I had read an article there about a famous engineer named Pier Luigi Nervi. He had perfected a method of building lightweight structures in concrete, and the piece was about his latest creation in the Exhibition Building in Turin. I absorbed it until I understood it, asking Broy to explain as needed, and the next time I saw Mr Thompson I asked him what he thought of Nervi, entering into a discourse on what I knew. That improved things, and he offered to show me how copies of drawings were made from tracing-paper negatives on one of his dyeline printers. In fact, he became one of my informal guardian angels, of which I am lucky enough to have had a few.

He made suggestions to help my progress, such as changing the way I said 'Mr Mallagh's office' so that it didn't sound like 'Mr Malice office' when I was on the phone. There was a sign on the wall of his room that read 'Some Day My Prints Will Come' as a joke against himself, but he always seemed to have time to give advice to the little underling from Mallaghs and he enjoyed passing on his lore. He told me about the difference between drawing on Whatman paper, which created a single original and was going out of fashion, and tracing paper, from which any number of copies could be made. On another day he told me that if I was tinting one of our prints in watercolours for easy reading on site, to make sure that the edge of the wash never ran dry because it would create a high watermark on the paper. 'Now,' he would say, 'green for go: green is the colour for concrete in section, and yellow is for concrete in elevation,' taking the pipe out of his mouth and laughing loudly through his nose.

Back in administration, there never was an office with a brass plate that glowed so brightly or fires lit so promptly as in that silent Georgian building each morning, not to mention the dull beauty of the polished lino. Miss Mellon's desk shone like the pool of still water that had attracted Narcissus, and reflected her power over me in a mirror image of herself, but my heart was with the engineers.

I thought she was inclined to be harsh, but Nell would have none of it, telling me that the girl was doing her best and to make allowances for her. Nevertheless, there would be remarks, probably correct, about the tea being too cold, no toilet paper, no receipts got for messages and no cream slice for her break, all of which I translated to mean that I was useless. I was getting fed up with this, but things got worse when Broy set me up with a drawing board where I could improve my lettering skills when I had time. He taught me to use a soft 4B pencil for sketching and a 2H lead for drawing on tracing paper, and I absorbed his wisdom for future use. I was far too interested in that to bother overmuch with my polishing and dusting. Trouble was inevitable, but I was learning as well.

Before the year was out I could see the shape of buildings on Broy's general arrangement drawings when he pointed them out, and could help him by checking the spelling of his notes in the margin. There was a little corridor with a tea station, which separated Mr Mallagh's room from the drawing office, and it was in this area that Miss Mellon continued to fill my unwilling ears with unheeded advice as to how I might get things done better. It was 'A watched pot never boils,' as I stood by to make tea for some jaded engineer, or 'Have you nothing else to do while you're waiting? I'm sure if you looked around there would be something.' Now, where I was brought up, this kind of nagging by an adult towards a boy was seldom heard, and I had not encountered it directly before. In the Liberties, if your mother told you what to do then you did it with alacrity, fearing the outcome if you didn't. But if a stranger did likewise you might tell her to mind her own business, unless you were in good humour, in which case you might be silent and simply do nothing.

What I could not understand was the contrast in her conversation with the engineers. They sometimes made double-meaning remarks in her presence as engineers would, and tea break was always convivial. To them she was great fun, sunny and willing to spark harmlessly, like saying, 'I'm not going out tonight, washing my smalls,' with a playful leer. When I asked Nell with some trepidation what she was referring to, Nell said she was just flirting with the boys as girls do, making the point that at least she was in fashion and didn't wear passion-crushers. This was all news to me.

I thought I could tolerate her, but listening to complaints over a period of months eventually broke me down. One day I was sweeping the floor in a corner of the drawing office when she suddenly emerged from the small corridor beside me and started into a rant again. She seemed to think that the administration was in a state of minor crisis, listing my failures as the reason why. I took this badly, with my O'Connor temper rising and my Liberties foundation of tolerance sinking fast. My little world flashed before me. *Damn her and her job. There was more to life than this! I would have her guts for garters!*

I surveyed her position. She was four feet away from me and standing in a corner beside the wall, which had a deep, hollow skirting board. I had often knocked against it by accident with the end of the sweeping brush in the ordinary course of duty, and it gave a loud echoing sound. But this was different. This time I intended to release my childish anger in a spontaneous manoeuvre, even if it cost me my job. I used all my concentration and nervous energy in calculating the velocity and arc needed to give her a good fright. Then I swung the brush along the floor with great force and gathering speed, with the same timing and energy that had netted me many a gudgeon. I was moving quickly, under the influence of hot anger. The brush skimmed by her toes and the end of it struck the skirting with a terrible *bang*, and all the intentions of what I really would have liked to do with it were evident in my stance. The poor girl jumped up shrieking and ran down the corridor, calling out to Mr Mallagh and the individual members of the Holy Family for help as I waited to face annihilation.

A few minutes later Mallagh came in with a dark face. 'Miss Mellon is complaining that you attempted to hit her with the brush,' he said, to which I replied honestly that I had had no such intention and in fact had not hit her. He told me that the services she provided to the firm were more important than mine and that, if we could not get along, there could be only one outcome. I accepted this judgement, and I was appropriately grateful, but I was also demoralised.

When I got home I asked Mam if I could go to work in the factory with Dad, and if not, might I join the Royal Air Force as a cadet, but she was adamant. 'You're being given a great chance where you are so there's no question of you leaving the office. I'll get Dad to speak to Mr Mallagh.' Over the next few weeks, letters travelled between the two, and Dad actually showed me the last note he sent. Its concluding words were... 'and you, Sir, would be the best judge'. I thought it was too respectful and was leaving Mallagh to make up his own mind as to what might befall me without providing much of a defence. That was the way it was with Dad, I told myself, Divine Providence again, noting that at this stage he had purchased the burial habit of the Third Order of St Francis for future use.

The incident left me unhappy. Miss Mellon and I got on better for a while afterwards, but it still rankled with us both. I had misled her about my age as a necessary step to getting a job, implying I was actually fourteen. She might have had her suspicions, but now, nearly a year later, she reminded me of the necessity of putting me on national insurance stamps to comply with the law, 'Since,' she said mistakenly, 'you are nearly fifteen years of age. Now,' she repeated, 'bring in your birth certificate before Christmas,' giving me a few weeks' grace. Things were beginning to close in on my little domain. I decided there was no point in worrying about it for the moment and my thoughts turned to the excitement of Billy's wedding in a few days' time and having a day off to celebrate. Nevertheless, what happened when I went back to work led me to a different path.

13. Leaving the Liberties

By the day of Billy's wedding I had achieved my plan for being well dressed on a limited budget. Mr Barber, whose sons Eric and Davey were known to me, was the manager of the Blackrock Tailoring Company in Chatham Street. His suggestion was that I buy a pair of slacks for two pounds and a sports coat for five, and replace them separately in the future as they wore out. Not only that, but a discount was available for friends of his sons. This transaction was to be financed by a Provident cheque that Mam arranged, which she could repay by the week until I was able to do so myself.

On Fridays after tea, Mr Halpin, the Provident man, would be one of a succession of people who arrived at the door in the hope of being included for payment that week. He wasn't always successful, as he had to compete with two insurance men, Messrs Grace and Pounch, and the spectral pleadings of the milkman Doyle and the barber McDonnell were also heard, along with representations from Cripps shoe shop and Nortons of Francis Street, who held our ration books. 'My word is good,' Mam would say defiantly, after disappointing a creditor, 'and if you're not careful you won't even be in the hat next week.' Removal from the hat was the darkest of threats. That was how, on the day of the wedding, I was resplendent in a pair of smart grey slacks and a brown herringbone tweed sports coat with dappled leather buttons.

I was well shod too because Billy had asked me to break in his new shoes for the day and I did so, even though Martha said that they looked like canal boats on me. Nevertheless, I was happy to do it for a brother who was set to emigrate on the same day as he got married. I was in high spirits that December morning. I had few cares and I was about to embark on a lovely family outing. What could be more enjoyable? The day was bright. The weather was good but, somehow, when I mixed with the guests on the way into the church, an atmosphere of impending gloom permeated the happiness of the occasion, and the light-hearted conversation I'd been expecting was muted.

Billy and Alice seemed unaffected. They had an air of serenity about them. If anyone passed a remark about the pity of having to go away, Alice replied that it didn't matter because at least they would be together, whatever might happen. I was coming down the stairs behind Billy later in the day and, as he passed her going in the opposite direction, they touched hands without stopping, in a love-signal that was clearer than speech.

We knew that Mam was upset at the thought of losing her eldest son, but there was a dismal atmosphere over the whole of the Liberties. Even Uncle Joe was subdued. Before we had left the churchyard after the wedding I heard him say to Aunt Dené, 'Dublin Corporation needs our side of Francis Street for road-widening. If that happens it'll be the end of us. O'Hora says he'll have to close his drapery shop because he's going to lose his front windows.' I was sorry to hear this because O'Horas had been a place I'd loved to hide in when I was small. It had a fascinating overhead transport system that whirred the customers' payments to a central cashier and the noisy aviary of budgerigars of every colour in the middle of the shop was a further allurement. It was easy to lurk behind the racks of cloth and enjoy the show without being noticed when I was supposed to be out playing on the street.

But I knew what Joe meant. The change was not curtailed to road-widening. Now when I returned to Francis Street at weekends to see my friends, I would discover that some had moved out to the new suburbs, like our own family. How I missed my old school pal McQuillan in Iveagh Flats, even if I had made a new buddy in Seán Swain, but most of the class in my last year in school had vanished. I happened to meet John Burke in town one day, carrying books in a cardboard box for Easons where he had managed to get a job, and he told me about the scholarship examination that I had missed. Francis Street School had won twelve of the eighty places in Dublin, including first place in the city, but I was surprised at how little it meant to me. It seemed very far away.

Now if I went to the Tivoli Cinema after work, nobody shouted, 'Show the picture,' when the reels were being replaced in mid-film, and I emerged to a quiet street with few people and little traffic. And were the street lamps a bit dimmer? Even Mrs Fox and the other dealers had given up trading at the top of Francis Street and had retreated to a busier pitch around the corner in Thomas Street. The friendly bedlam of the Liberties was dying in a social upheaval that was being re-enacted over the whole country. It was only at weekends that life really returned, as the natives came back to their old home place to shop on Saturday mornings.

Uncle John said that the decline had begun a long time ago when the rich business people of the Liberties had moved out to the new houses in Blackrock and Dalkey to be near the sea. 'Canon Hayden told me himself at the opening of the girls' school that when the rich went away they left behind mostly the working class and the poor, draining the parish of money. Sure they even had to reduce the number of priests because there was not enough income to support them.'

Granddad, too, was sad, these days, because Aunt Eileen had died in October, and our beloved Granny, the quiet core of the family, had passed away just three weeks before the wedding. 'My poor Maggie and Eileen,' I heard Granddad say, 'how I miss them.' Dad gently reminded him that at least they were now sleeping side by side at peace in Mount Jerome Cemetery. 'Billy is lucky,' Granddad said. 'There's nothing here for anyone any more. What we have is a motherland, not a fatherland, and it's not a way of living now, but a way of dying.' I attributed that opinion to his feelings about Granny and Eileen, but a horrible malaise had indeed struck the country. In the decade of the fifties, almost half a million people went away when they despaired of finding work in Ireland.

When Mam talked about it, it was like *Gone With The Wind*, where Melanie Wilkes relates to Scarlett O'Hara the names of the beaux who were the latest to die in the American civil war, except for us it was not the Tarleton twins, and not death, but the emigration of boys and girls we knew as friends. 'The Mastersons and the Bellews are gone, the whole family, and the lads in O'Byrnes and Careys,' she would say, but that was only a part of the bleak recital because the same was true of every parish in the country. All the same, when Mam spoke like that it troubled me. Martha and I had once tried to count the number of relations we had in the Liberties and had stopped when we reached a total of fifty. I was afraid that most of my own brothers and sisters might have to go away and I could not bear to think of that.

I began to appreciate how right Joe had been all along. That 'piece of paper', the examination certificate, was the key to survival and I internalised that message when I saw the havoc its absence seemed to create in the lives of my friends. Seamus Meates had derided my new job and called me 'Office Boy' to tease me, bragging that he was only a few years older than me and earned eight pounds a week as a plater in Smith and Pearsons, the steel fabricators. A few months later his company ran out of orders and he was sacked, forcing him to go away to Moss Side, Manchester, along with many more.

I thought about my own job. I knew I was safe because Mallagh said I had potential, but now I decided, almost in desperation, that I was going to become an engineer and one day I would be a consultant just like him. I remembered the way Dad had been treated by indifferent bosses, and it led me to believe that being self-employed was the surest means of survival. But first of all I would have to learn enough in Mallaghs to get a job elsewhere, because I could see little hope of promotion in an office where I had begun as junior. I knew I would hate to emigrate, unlike Bill and Alice, who were happily facing the unknown in Australia.

Their wedding reception was in Alice's home on Downpatrick Road. They had erected a marquee in the back garden and, after the breakfast, the party had divided into lovers of singing, who took over the main bedroom in the house, and those who preferred to dance to a three-piece group. When I went upstairs, a young man was claiming that he could sing higher than Mario Lanza. He gave us 'Granada', making a brave effort, but somehow the party did not ignite and, as the day lengthened, a sense of dismay seemed to dull everything. At seven o'clock a white double-decker parked outside the house, with the words 'THE WEDDING BUS' emblazoned on the sides. It might as well have been a hearse, with hushed voices saying, 'They're here.' We filled it to its limits, ready to take our last collective journey with Billy and Alice.

He had been the only child when Mam and Dad had gone to Montréal in 1929. Billy was there to give them hope when our baby sister, Helen, had succumbed at the age of four months when they were far from home, and he was their unwitting consolation. Now he was on his way to board the liner *Oronsay* bound for Sydney from Tilbury Docks and no return was imaginable. The tears began to flow. A girl with a voice like Gracie Fields's started to sing 'Now Is The Hour', a sad song of farewell.

When the bus travelled down the Coombe and passed her old home on the corner of Hanover Street, Mrs Orr, the bride's mother, began to cry, sighing deeply as she tried to control her feelings. Billy and Alice glanced at each other in wonderment, then looked at the faces around them as if they had just realised the significance of leaving the Liberties and Ireland for ever. The quietened bus drove on to the quays and we crowded around, hugging and kissing them a sad goodbye that had no words of expression. Then someone started to sing again, a song that initiated a happy-go-lucky ritual practised in the Liberties when a newly married couple were leaving their wedding party. The guests assembled in a double line facing each other and formed a tunnel for Billy and Alice to run through, and they sang 'Wish Me Luck as You Wave Me Goodbye' as they did so. When the couple emerged from the arch there was a convulsion of grief. Billy and Alice departed, not to return for nearly thirty years, and then only on holiday. As a sequel, when Billy died in 2012, long after Alice, he was surrounded by his Australian family and three of his siblings. He had lived sixty years in Australia but his obituary notice in the *Sydney Telegraph* began:

O'CONNOR, William (Billy)
Born 15, Francis Street, Dublin, April 29th 1929, passed
away on March 12th 2012.

❧

When I returned to work in the week before Christmas everyone was in good humour as Mallagh had given a double week's pay. I was included in the largesse, and I also got a rise, taking me to two pounds a week. It seemed like an opportune time, so I took a deep breath and told Miss Mellon that I had made a mistake about my birthday and that I was not yet actually fifteen. She was like the beadle when Oliver Twist asked for more: '*Whaaat?* You forgot your own birthday, I'm sure you did. Do you expect me to believe that? What'll it be next?' Her lips curled in derision, but I had no defence and said nothing, although she would have known what I thought of her by the glare of contempt on my face. Certainly, Miss Mellon must have realised that she was facing unfamiliar forces, for she did not mention my birth certificate again until I produced it in July, when I became fifteen years of age.

I had indeed got a double week's wages, but my funds did not extend so far as to cover the cost of a new set of drawing instruments. Broy advised me that Meredith's pawnshop on Cuffe Street specialised in goods belonging to impoverished engineering students and I would surely find something there. I went into the shop not knowing what to expect as this was my first such transaction. Mam hated pawnshops so much that she would not be seen in public carrying any sort of parcel on Mondays, but I had no such unease.

There were two men behind the counter, one talking on the phone and the other haggling with a duffel-coated lad who was trying to pawn a double-elephant sized drawing board. As he did so, the assistant turned to me and said, 'The boss will treat with you in a minute,' and in just a little time I had bought a nice set of second-hand Wild drawing instruments in the original green-padded box. The pawnbroker told me how to fill the open pens with Indian ink, and warned me always to put the stopper back on the bottle or it would dry out almost immediately. It made a nice Christmas present for myself, and was my first financial investment in my future profession.

Later, in January, Mallagh called me into his room one morning and asked me to arrange his bookshelves in alphabetical order of author's name, then resumed a conversation he was having with Maddock. 'It certainly was a case of *in flagrante delicto*,' he said, with a laugh. 'It's a wonder he wasn't arrested.' I tried to concentrate on the musty old books, most of which seemed to belong to his father, Joseph Mallagh, who had once been chief Dublin Port engineer, but couldn't help being intrigued by what I was overhearing. They were discussing a report that had come in from a clerk of works on one of their projects about an incident on site that had caused a neighbour to complain, but Mallagh seemed to think it was funny. When I had completed the rearrangement of the books, he asked me to take the report in to Moffitt for his comments, and when I gave it to him, he laughed and showed it to the others.

It seemed that the mother superior of an adjacent convent had written to the architect looking for an explanation in respect of an incident where a man in a state of undress was seen running across the site. The architect in turn had requested a report, which had now come to hand. I had been on that site delivering drawings and it always seemed to be very well organised. The men were respectful of their devout neighbours and, for modesty's sake, had been warned not to go bare-chested on site and to do their best not to swear. The foreman was a former navy frogman who was given to petulant moods blamed on his war experience, but I discovered that this irritability was not unusual for men in his job, as it was sometimes difficult to please both the architect and their builder bosses. 'God and Mammon,' Moffitt slyly suggested.

However, on this occasion the problem seemed to have been caused by the clerk of works, whom I knew as a gentleman, and unrelenting in his condemnation of shoddy workmanship, so I could not wait to read what had happened:

CLERK-OF-WORKS OFFICE, NEW ROSS PROJECT
REPORT ON INCIDENT OCCURRING ON SITE ON 10TH INSTANT
I acknowledge receipt of your letter requesting a Report on the incident in question. The facts are as follows: I arrived on site at 8:00 a.m. on 10th inst. A short time later I had reason to use the toilet facility, which is set apart from the main block. The toilet building comprised lightweight timber frame and felted roof construction, and was scheduled for demolition.

The Contractor had brought on site a mechanical digger of the JCB type with a large bucket. At approx 8:15 a.m. I entered the dilapidated toilet block and took off my overalls as far as was necessary to utilise the facility. I then divested myself further in order to shave myself and continue with my ablutions. I heard the sound of a machine being started up, which I took to be the Volvo Dump Truck, and thought nothing of it as I was occupied at the time.

As I proceeded with my toilet arrangements, the sound came nearer and I felt a loud crash and the toilet building was shaken to its foundations. At the same time, the toothed bucket of the JCB came through the wall at floor level and slid under the toilet bowl which I was using. Some of the timber supports to the back of the building were sheared off and the roof commenced to sag at a dangerous angle over my head. I called out to the driver and tried to escape, but the door was now jammed by the impact. As I heard the digger reversing and moving rapidly toward me again, I jumped on to the toilet in the hope of being seen, but the machine struck again, demolishing most of one side wall and causing me to fall from my vantage point.

Unfortunately, the supply pipe to the cistern had been broken, resulting in a deluge of water, saturating myself and my clothing, which I had left on a shelf. I called out loudly for help again, but with the continuing noise of the JCB I could not be heard, and I could not be seen in the debris and the cloud of dust, but when there was a lull in the work for a moment I readied myself to leave the scene.

The next moment, I found myself inundated by a high-pressure hose in the hands of a ganger, who could not see me. I was told later by the Foreman that this was intended to keep the dust down on the demolished material in accordance with the specification. Being saturated to the skin and only partly clothed, I was nevertheless forced to run from the building immediately and seek the shelter of the Foreman's office.

*I trust the above explanation of what happened is
accepted. I have entered the incident in the site log under
'accidents' and I can say with conviction that there will
be no repetition of the event.*

Edward Brosnan, Clerk of Works.

At that time it happened that a mining engineer named Cogan
had taken a room on the top floor above Mallaghs and had
noticed me sweeping our landing. He offered me half a crown
a week to tidy his office, to which I rapidly agreed on condition
that it was done on one day only and then after hours. My
calculations were simple. A budgerigar cost ten shillings. At
half a crown a week I could buy one every month. These birds
are gregarious, and will not breed if there is only one couple.
In fact, the more birds in the flock the better. With his half-
crown I could buy budgies in Johnny King's pet shop, and keep
them in a cage until I had bought enough birds to populate an
aviary, the procurement of which was a second-stage problem.

Things went well for a few months, and I bought a nice
nest of green-split-blue hens and a stylish cobalt blue cock,
but on one fateful Wednesday lunch hour my scheme for
development was liquidated. I was seen coming down the
stairs from Cogans by Miss Mellon, whose searchlight eye of
suspicion was trained on me until I stood at landing level. I
explained the situation, but she pointed out that I was using
the office equipment. My difficulty was that I had not told
anyone what I was doing because I wanted to keep it secret.
Now she was in a position to make life awkward for me, so I
felt it wiser to stop, fearing retribution if I continued.

My entry into the cult of the budgerigar was therefore halted, at least for the moment. However, Mam had a saying that 'It is better to be born lucky than rich' and so it was. Mallagh was building a yawl, a long, open boat with the hull made of individual planks, in his back garden in Clonskeagh. I was enrolled to help on Saturdays for which he would pay me, yes, half a crown. With that steady and flawless source of income I was determined to acquire, not just the birds, but an aviary as well. And it happened that, one Friday, Mallagh sent me out to buy turpentine for use the next day on the yawl.

The nearest supplier was McKenzie's hardware shop in Pearse Street. As I went about my business I took time to have a look at their display of garden sheds and idly thought I would ask the assistant if they sold aviaries. I took my place in the queue, ordered the turpentine, and made my enquiry in a manner that suggested I was a person of means. Before the assistant could answer, a woman standing behind me touched me on the shoulder, smiling. She said that her husband had until recently been a member of the Dublin Zoological Society, but had retired now and had an aviary he did not need any more. Would I be interested in it?

Praise the Lord and pass the ammunition! I turned right around to speak to her. She was a decent woman from Sandymount, quite old and genteel, who looked remarkably like Our Lady of Fatima, I thought. She gave me her telephone number and told me that it was quite in order to call if I could make arrangements to have the aviary collected. It sounded like a difficult task, but when I told Dad about it he could see no problem as his love of birds matched my own. He rang the man in Sandymount, who told him that the aviary was sectional, which meant that it could be easily dismantled once the bolts that held the parts together were removed. He would treat them with penetrating oil and we could collect it when all was ready. Furthermore, in the circumstances, he would let us have it for nothing, provided we met the cost of taking it away.

A few weeks later we were on our way to Sandymount, sitting on a four-wheeled dray with a Clydesdale for locomotion, all hired, with driver, from Stanleys in Cornmarket. After a few hours the aviary was on the back of the cart and assembled by a work party of O'Connors in our back garden. This gave me the opportunity to experiment with line breeding of my stock, and even exhibiting them in the Éire Budgerigar Show in the O'Connell Hall, although that cobalt blue cock disgraced me by lurking on the floor of the show cage just when he was being inspected by the judge.

Time passed, and the months fled. In the office, my week was divided between improving my drawing skills, attending Technical School and my mundane duties. But my knowledge was slowly increasing. The discipline of work and study was interrupted for leisure. I played soccer in Danny Lacey's team, St Finbarrs, and continued to train for athletics in the Army Grounds. In quieter moments I listened to classical music from Martha's collection of second-hand records, and wondered why Beniamino Gigli continued singing until his voice had such a wobble. Martha's secondary-school poetry book had its delights too, but I still yearned to be able to read music.

I was inspired in that desire by the wonderful tenor Dermot Troy, who won the Irish round of *The Great Caruso* competition in 1952 and in May of the same year was placed second in the finals, which were held in England. All Ireland was looking for a hero. The national atmosphere was one of rejoicing, and on the evening of his return to his home on Cashel Road in Crumlin, I was in the excited crowd who gathered there to greet him. The road was decorated with bunting as bright as a May procession. A man was telling anyone who would listen that Mario Lanza, who played Caruso in the film, had sent Dermot a telegram of congratulation.

There were so many of us there that the public roadway was not wide enough to allow us all to congregate outside the Troy home, so the kind neighbours allowed the overspill into their front gardens for a better view. The pride in our local boy's success was immense. Even the parish band was there to welcome him, and I saw two men holding up a banner on which was written 'GOD BLESS YOU OUR IRISH CARUSO'.

There was a sudden hush in the crowd when the top-floor window of the Troy home was thrown open, and Dermot appeared. That was the signal for a huge roar of approval, as we all shared in his triumph and some called on him to give us a song. When it was plain that Dermot was actually going to do just that, the delighted crowd gave him silence. The beautiful free voice of the natural lyric tenor rippled through the air and was carried over our heads in a delightful warm vibrato. It held us in a spell, what with the occasion, the words and the haunting melody of Toselli's 'Serenade (Come Back)':

Like a golden dream in my heart, ever smiling,
Lives the image fair of happy love I knew in days
* gone by,*
Still I seem to hear your laughter beguiling,
Still to see the joy,
The love light beaming from your radiant eye.

In the uproar of applause I looked around to share my delight with my neighbours. I noticed a girl about my own age standing on the edge of the crowd talking to somebody. She looked slightly familiar, but it must have been wishful thinking. She had the prettiest face I had ever seen, with an easy grace about her. Her brown hair was tied back in a white ribbon, and I remember that she had a tiny waist. I stared in her direction, fascinated, and kept her in sight as long as I could without being noticed. When she had gone, I thought again how beautiful she was and imagined that maybe we would meet some day.

Back at work, I took stock of my position. I was bored with some of the tedious duties of my job, so I decided to leave Mallaghs at the end of the college term if I could get a position elsewhere. I planned to move to some small consultancy as a draughtsman, staying there until I had perfected my drawing technique and then joining a high-powered engineering design office, which would give me the experience to prepare for professional examinations. I rationalised that I would have better wages and so could afford music lessons, and other luxuries, as a bonus.

My plan was precipitated when Mallagh suddenly offered to make me an indentured pupil shortly afterwards. This meant that they would employ a new office boy and I would enter into a formal agreement to undertake the study required to become an engineer in that firm. The conditions were that the training period would be five years and, at that point, my salary would be twelve pounds a week and I would also be allowed to join the new pension scheme. When I heard this I knew it was time to leave. In fact, I felt threatened by the conditions offered. A pensionable job signified to me low wages and a boring life. I had no intention of needing a pension when I got to retirement age as I intended to be a self-employed person of means long before then. I realised, too, that I needed the excitement of opportunity. I would have to go as soon as I could.

Shortly afterwards, I got a job as a junior draughtsman in the office of Sir Hugh Molony, Bart, at six pounds a week, a man whose father had been the last Lord Chief Justice of Ireland and coincidentally had been the presiding judge at one of the trials of Uncle Jim. At least this post was full-time on the drawing board so that I could prepare myself for moving to a big consultancy when time and chance presented itself. A new phase of my life began when I told Mallagh I was leaving. He seemed to understand and gave me his blessing, and I made a sentimental last journey into town to run errands for the engineers.

Maddock had sent me to the Gate Theatre for tickets, and I found it dusty and dark, like 'Satis House' in *Great Expectations*. I thought of Miss Havisham in her mouldering mansion as I walked up the stairs and into the theatre itself, and I would not have been too surprised if a latter-day Estella had greeted me. Everything was memorably dowdy, and some years later, when I saw Lord Longford standing on O'Connell Bridge with a flag day collection box seeking aid for the restoration of the theatre, I better understood the indomitable will possessed by people with a mission, and I learned from it.

Passing the Metropole Hotel on the way back, I went in to collect two dress-dance tickets that Moffitt had ordered. As I approached the restaurant, I heard a deep voice singing with piano accompaniment, syncopating 'A Nightingale Sang In Berkeley Square'. A waitress saw me listening and said, 'That's Peggy Dell warming up to entertain the diners later on.' I knew her name well because she was famous in Dublin for once being the lead singer with the Jack Hylton Band in America. I crossed the road, trying to avoid being run over by the pantheon of cyclists, and made my way through the stalls of the flower-sellers at the foot of Nelson's Pillar.

I had always wanted to meet Nelson, with his one arm and one eye: whose statue had survived the bombardment of the General Post Office across the street in the Rising of 1916, a feat which, according to Dubliners, made him one of our own rather than a great Englishman. The ancient handrail on the platform, lumpy with bad painting and wear, did not look strong and I hoped the balcony would not collapse just then. Nelson looked gigantic and, being quite fed up with exposure to decades of public scrutiny, I suppose, did not reply to the friendly salutations of myself and others who had managed to climb the cramped spiral staircase. An American tourist with a Hasselblad camera squeezed past me and stopped at an opening in the protective mesh surrounding the balcony and waited for his moment. Down on the quays, the gasometer stood like a gigantic pint glass, with a mile of unkempt roofs between us. Away to the city's west, the Duke of Wellington was remembered by his Phoenix Park eyrie. When I saw the grand sweep of the lovely Featherbed Mountains in the distance, I thought of John Locke and said to myself, 'O Ireland, up from my heart of hearts, I bid you the top o' the mornin'!'

I could not pass the Paradiso Restaurant in Westmoreland Street without calling in to see Kirwan, who was a waiter there. I had developed a taste for their apple strudel, which I couldn't afford, but my friend saw to my needs occasionally. Lord Nelson was not the only one who could turn a blind eye. I loved to admire the photographs of the stars who had dined there, framed on the wall of the twisting staircase. The menu had a blank space inviting the customers to insert the name of a person to whom they would like to have it sent, so I promptly filled in Broy's name and the office address for the pleasure of hearing him wonder whom he knew who could patronise such a swanky place. Finally, in honour of the occasion of my new job, I treated myself to afternoon tea in the DBC café beside the Shelbourne Hotel, where the custom of the house was to set out a platter of six delicious cakes on every table. The clients ate as many as they desired and paid for them on the way out, in a singular display of trust that I did not breach.

I had made friends with Mr Corway in Henry J. Lyons, the architects on the ground floor in South Frederick Street, and when I told him I was leaving, he smiled and said, 'Fresh fields and pastures new.' Then, in his decent way, he gave me his advice, telling me that the best engineers tried to visualise the finished building from the drawings, then integrated the structure into the architect's concept of the design. He reminded me to consider the lovely Victorian buildings in Dublin, framed with just the use of the masonry arch and the rolled-steel joist long before reinforced concrete was in common use. Then he offered me his hand in a formal way, and bade me, '*Au revoir* but not goodbye.'

I left Mallaghs without regret, and started work on a drawing board in Molony's office. My plan was in operation! I was fully employed as a draughtsman, my wages had improved and I could afford music lessons. The maestro, Miss Russell, lived in a tiny flat on Aylesbury Road. A Steinway piano took up the centre of her living room, nearly covered with neat piles of sheet music, some of them ring-marked from teacups. 'I'm just back from Italy,' she said, 'and I specialise in *bel canto*, that lovely old way of singing. Let me hear you on a few scales.' I did what I was told and she said I had a light voice, not good for opera, but suitable for *bel canto* training. With that, we started straight into 'Caro mio ben' by Giuseppe Giordani. 'This is an exquisite example of a *bel canto* song, and the *tessitura* will suit you,' she said. 'Get a recording of it by a lyric tenor. All the flourishes are there, *mezza di voce*, octave leaps and lovely cadenzas.' When she discovered I was from the Liberties she told me that Giordani's brother, Tommaso, had once been the musical director of Francis Street Chapel and in fact had died in Dublin after a long career here.

Every time I went there I learned something new. 'As for practice,' she would say, 'don't bother too much with singing for the moment. You'll only roughen your voice. I want you to do some simple breathing exercises for ten minutes each day, and you'll be surprised at how your breath control improves.' The technical aspect of what she was saying appealed to me and I loved to sing, but my real ambition was to be able to read music and I told her so. 'Then you'll have to study music theory as well,' she said, 'and take it up to grade five of one of the London schools. At that level you'll be able to read anything on the page. No need to go higher than that unless you want to start learning to compose as well.' Her words were the entry for me into the relaxing pastime of trying to read vocal music from the comfort of an armchair, which I have been doing fitfully now for many of my seventy-five years.

Now, perhaps in the middle of reading a haunting Schubert song, my mind's eye hubbles back in time and lingers on my schooldays in the Liberties; that unique place where I grew up. I say to myself, 'These were thy charms, sweet village,' and I imagine I am once again in the clamorous streets with the people who taught me the virtue of resilience and brightened my path in life, and I thank them for it. Then I might stray to the happy memories of childhood in the bosom of my own family, and I can see Mam, the well of our delight, smiling and consoling and holding out her arms to us in joy.

After all, the Liberties was the place where many of the most important and life-changing moments of my youth had happened, including what would turn out to be the most momentous of all. One evening, not long after I had got my job in Molony's office, I went to see Granddad in Francis Street. When we were finished chatting, he asked me to go to Findlater's shop for him, because he needed a bag of sugar. I swung around the corner into Thomas Street and when I had just passed McDonald's dress shop I heard an urgent voice calling my name. I stopped and turned. When I saw who it was, I was shaken. My cousin, Betty Hilliard, stood there, smiling in her usual friendly way, but she was not alone. 'How're you, Seán?' she said. 'Here's someone I work with who wants to meet you. She lives on the other end of Keeper Road, but when I was telling her about you, she says she doesn't know you at all. This is Marie O'Grady.' I recognised the friend. It was the beautiful girl I had seen outside Dermot Troy's house on that night in May 1952 when he came back to Dublin in his fame.

The traffic stopped. The Liberties fell silent. We spoke for the briefest of moments. I walked the few yards to Findlaters, with a stanza of Tennyson's 'The Princess' trying to push into my mind. But I couldn't think straight, I was so beguiled.

Not long afterwards, on my fifteenth birthday, I got a surprise. An envelope arrived to the house containing a birthday card and it felt like velvet to the touch because it was from Marie O'Grady. The rhyme filled me with wonder and pleasure:

> *Sharing in your happiness,*
> *And fondly hoping too,*
> *That future years will surely see,*
> *Your hopes and dreams come true.*

I wrote a card in return, remembering that verse of 'The Princess' this time, but I hadn't the nerve to send it:

> *Now folds the lily all her sweetness up,*
> *And slips into the bosom of the lake:*
> *So fold thyself, my dearest, thou, and slip*
> *Into my bosom and be lost in me.*

All the same, I had no intention of letting her go and a week later, one day after work, I met her by seeming chance in Thomas Street. We stood alone outside John's Lane Chapel in the heart of the Liberties. I was too nervous to say much. Her lovely face was bright as an apple of gold and in her grey-blue eyes I saw sign of our children, Joseph, Éimear, Sinéad and John. I resolved then to make her as the apple of my eye, no matter what might befall us, and to love her until all love in the world had come to an end.

GLOSSARY

aililiú!: wonderful! (In the Irish language, *Gaeilge*.)

alligations: misbehaviour. 'Stop your alligations.' Usually directed at a bold child. Not to be confused with 'allegations'.

***An Óige*:** The Irish Youth Hostel Association.

Auburn: the subject and setting of the poem 'The Deserted Village' by Oliver Goldsmith.

Baby Power: a miniature bottle of Power's whiskey.

Back-of-the-Pipes: a lane that provided a short-cut between James's Street Basin (also known as Grand Canal Harbour) in the Liberties and Dolphin's Barn.

Bayno, the: the Iveagh Play Centre, built 1913, in Bull Alley Street facing St Patrick's Park. Its first location was in Myra Hall, Francis Street.

bazz-off: time out for rest and recreation.

bona fide pub: the official closing time for pubs was ten thirty p.m., but the publican was allowed to stay open until midnight to attend to the needs of bona fide travellers. To be a bona fide traveller you had to be at least three miles away from the place where you had slept the previous night and not travelling just for the pleasure of drinking alcohol after hours. The law was changed in 1960 to end this practice.

bowsie: a trouble-making drunk. A hard chaw.

box car: a handmade timber box with two wheels on a single axle and shafts for pushing in the style of a rickshaw.

bunking in: unlawful entry into a cinema to avoid paying to see the film.

bunts, in the bunts: in partnership, usually in playing cards for buttons.

bunty: squat.

Buttoner, the: a north city button factory.

'butts on you': a request to a boy eating an apple to leave you the core, or butt, as it was known.

cess: a tax or levy on roads and sewers originating in the fifteenth century.

chaineys: fragments of old broken china, preferably highly coloured, used by little girls, and sometimes boys, to play a make-believe tea-party game.

chandlers: the white maggots of the bluebottle.

chip: a light basket, with metal handles, made from raffia.

chucks: a means of controlling the movements of a horse by changing pressure on the reins.

clickety-click: slang for '66' in calling numbers in the game of House, an early version of Bingo, often played in the home.

clocks: woodlice.

Cobaloes: more correctly, Coppolas, an Italian ice-cream shop in Cuffe Street, well known for its delicious ices. It was the venue for special treats.

coddle: a Dublin dish made mainly of sliced pork sausages and thin rashers.

cogging: stealing the ideas or plagiarising the work of other boys.

combo: short for 'combination'. A street game of football in which the boys practise their skill as distinct from playing a match.

common rossie: rough and tough girl.

commoner: a feral pigeon. Also, a rough and tough girl, see *common rossie*.

comp: short for composition or essay.

Conamara Gaeltacht: a region in the west of Ireland in which the vernacular language is Irish.

coort: kiss and cuddle.

DDT: an insecticide powder once in wide use to control fleas and lice.

deadener: a punch to the arm halfway between the elbow and the shoulder, which has the effect of deadening the nerves and preventing movement of the arm for several seconds.

dohiyi: Cherokee word for 'peace'.

double-elephant: an old standard size of drawing board measuring *circa* 28 inches by 42 inches and approximating to the metric A0 size.

feis: a traditional Gaelic festival of arts and culture.

follyinupper: a serial adventure film shown in weekly episodes, the most popular in the Liberties being about Flash Gordon and his nemesis Ming the Merciless.

Francis Street Chapel: the colloquialism for St Nicholas of Myra Church, Francis Street, our local Catholic parish church.

Gaudeamus: more commonly known as *Gaudeamus Igitur* (Let Us Rejoice).

ghen-eye-nox: money.

gig: a flat board on four wheels with the front two wheels on an axle turnable by reins held by the driver sitting on the board. The driver had to be pushed in order to move the vehicle.

gone on: as in 'I'm not gone on him,' meaning, 'I don't like him much.'

gouger: a very rough man. The term 'an oul' gouger' was a kinder description reserved for the man (never a woman) whose behaviour was unkind or reactionary.

gowdle harbour: street language for 'Great!'

green road: an unpaved narrow road typically running through forested areas at the foothills of the mountains.

hansel: a good-luck gift for a special occasion such as Hansel Monday, the first Monday of the New Year, when Liberties folk gave a small cash present to a child as a token of good fortune for the year.

hard chaw: tough man (never used in reference to a woman).

hogger: a term of slight disparagement for a youth or man whose identity is unknown, as in 'This hogger came up to me and asked me what I was doing.'

Hollow Roll: the finest song in the canary's repertoire.

Holy Hour: the closure of public houses between 2:30 p.m. and 3:30 p.m. on Sundays in accordance with a law now repealed.

IAWS: Irish Agricultural Wholesale Society.

IMCO: Invisible Mending and Cleaning Company.

imprint: in common use as an alternative word for 'impertinent' or 'impudent'.

in the cod: to fight in the cod, a friendly sparring match with a pal.

IRA: Irish Republican Army.

Jackstones: a game played with five small pebbles, and an extra one to throw, called the jack. The players sit on the ground. The game begins when the first player throws the jack a small height in the air and attempts to swipe the five stones into his hand while awaiting the return of the jack, which he catches in the same hand. The game proceeds with more difficult throws.

Keevesenackers: the colloquial name for O'Keefes, the knackers in Newmarket.

Kitty the Hare: a character created by Victor O'Donovan Power. Kitty was a famous travelling woman who told her stories in an Irish brogue. Both author and character were well known in school circles from the tales appearing in the *Our Boys* magazine.

Liberties: Lands lying outside the city walls which were granted by the Crown to a favourite. The administration of these areas was independent of the city authorities and was the responsibility of the holder of the Liberty.

louser: a derogatory term comparing a person to a louse.

lurching: dancing carried out by an embracing couple swaying to the music without moving their feet.

mitching: failing to attend school without the permission or knowledge of the parents.

mule: a cross between a canary and a finch.

noble call: a person who sang at a party had the privilege of selecting the next singer. This right was called his 'noble call.'

'No nagoes': words of refusal to share whatever was being eaten by the speaker when asked to do so.

oirick: the chapping or chafing of the skin typically caused by wet clothing.

on gur: staying away from school without the permission or knowledge of the parents with no intention of returning home; in other words, running away.

on the jare: mitching. Staying away from school without the permission or knowledge of the parents, with the intention of returning home after school hours.

onit: 'I'm onit.' The name of the person playing the chief role in a children's game. In hide-and-go-seek, for instance, the child who does the searching is 'onit'.

oul' gouger: see *gouger*.

pinkeen: minnow. From the Irish word *pincín*.

planxty: the meaning of the word is lost but its common use is as a name for a piece of music dedicated to a person, for instance, Planxty Lord Inchiquin.

Praigue: the Liberties pronunciation of Prague.

'Praise The Lord And Pass The Ammunition': the title of an American patriotic song written by Frank Loesser in 1942. It became a catch-phrase later.

pure crackt alive*:* a typical saying from the character Kitty the Hare, meaning very much in love. See *Kitty the Hare*.

*qui vive***:** from the French. Be on the *qui vive*; be on the alert.

raired a jipper: reared a jibber, i.e. a horse that refused to jump a fence.

ralleyers: two pieces of comb-sized slate held between the first two fingers and played by children to keep rhythm in music, the clacking sounding like castanets. To play a rally was to play a solo, rather like a drum solo, keeping the beat of the music with embellishment until the melody was heard again. The other instrument involved was usually the comb with tissue paper over it, played by mouth, called a kazoo.

ruggy-up: a row or fight on the street.

salong: as in 'so long'.

scabbled: roughened stone.

scunched: specifically, the state arrived at when all one's buttons have been lost playing cards.

scutting: joyriding. The verb 'scut' can be distinguished from the noun 'scut' as in 'Stop scutting, you little scut,' meaning 'Stop joyriding, you little nonentity.'

slindge: foot-dragging. Typically, a child dragging his feet noisily on the footpath while walking slower than his accompanying mother in a show of mute protest.

spalling: chipping and splintering.

spin spout or black out: 'Are you spin spout or black out?' Words directed by one child to another to query the state of a childhood friendship. 'Spin spout' refers to the rotating cap on a chimney keeping the fire going, so 'Spin spout' as an answer meant that the two speakers were still friends. However, if the answer was 'Black out' it meant that the fire was extinguished, thus the friendship was over.

splitten: spit and image. Or exact likeness.

squealers: young pigeons.

stand for: 'My aunt stood for me', meaning that the said aunt was the child's sponsor in baptism, otherwise known as the child's godmother.

stand out: 'Will you stand out?' This was a challenge by the speaker to fight the boy so addressed.

Tenters: an area of the Liberties once famous for its manufacture of silk and poplin.

***tessitura*:** the range in which a given type of voice sounds best.

Three Stewdies: the Three Stooges of film fame whose special line was farce and slapstick.

took the pledge: a vow not to drink alcohol, either taken formally as a member of the Pioneer Total Abstinence Association or informally with the same effect.

trow: sink. 'Put it in the trow.' The word 'trow' may be a corruption of the Irish word *troch*, meaning 'trough' or perhaps an old English word still surviving.

waxed end: a needle threaded in advance with shoemaker's stitching cord and then waxed for durability; it was used to repair the rips in the seams of a leather football, etc.

Yawke: York cabbage.

youngwan: a young girl.

ACKNOWLEDGEMENTS

This book would not have been written but for the interest of my commissioning editor, Ciara Considine. I thank her for her stalwart support and expertise at all stages. My gratitude also to the entire team of Hachette Books Ireland for their professional skill and enthusiasm in delivering *Growing Up So High*.

I thank Seán Kavanagh, editor of *Ireland's Big Issue* magazine, who published my short stories *Uncas and Cora* and *Small Don* in May 2008 (Issue 71) and February 2010 (Issue 100) respectively. My only other publication was a short piece for *You'll Ruin Your Dinner*, by Damian Corless, published by Hachette Books Ireland in 2011.

Many old and new friends shared reminiscences with me over the period of writing and I warmly acknowledge the happy conversations we had about childhood days. My thanks to Seamus Byrne, Tony Byrne of the Tivoli Theatre, Clive and Angela Conway, Finbar Callanan, John Callanan, Cliona Cassidy, Rev. Dudley L. Cooney, Harry Gorman,

Francis Harman, Graham Hickey, Mary Jones (née Durney), Commandant Victor Laing (then Officer in Charge Military Archives, now retired), Kevin and Eleanor Lee of Carnew Historical Society, Tony Lyons, Una Noon, Tom O'Neill, Thelma Pope, Pat Quinn, Tom Reilly, Mrs L. Rankin (née Risk), George Stuart, Margaret Taylor and Peter Walsh. The recent image of Seán on the jacket of the book was taken by John Searle, Photographer. The front cover of the book shows Seán at the age of ten in a school photograph, together with a picture of The Coombe, in the heart of the Liberties, courtesy of The National Library of Ireland.

Memory and oral tradition are fallible and I have taken pains to verify these as much as is reasonably possible. Arising from that, I wish to express my gratitude to the personnel of the following research centres for their unfailing help: Central Catholic Library; Dublin City Library and Archive Research Collection, Pearse Street; the Irish Military Archive at Cathal Brugha Barracks; Dublin Civic Trust; Engineers Ireland Library; John McDermot Research; The Registry of Deeds, Dublin; St Nicholas of Myra Parish Centre; and my old Primary School, CBS Francis Street.

I found the Google search engine a boon. The *Irish Times* Newspaper Archives and the Irish Newspaper Archives were consulted under licence and I verified the history of 15 Francis Street by consulting the online archive of The Huguenot Society of Great Britain and Ireland, for which facility I thank them. The picture of 15, Francis Street is reproduced with kind permission of the Methodist Centenary Church, Dublin.

I owe a special word of thanks to Rita Kavanagh, the

sacristan of St Nicholas of Myra Parish Church in Francis Street; to Fíona Collins and Catherine Cole, principal and secretary of Francis Street Christian Brothers' Boys Primary School respectively; and to John Gallagher, chairman of the Parish Centre Committee in Carman's Hall St. Nicholas of Myra who is an ever-present force in advancing the interests of the people living in the Liberties.

My cousins in Ireland and elsewhere were greatly interested in my efforts, and I wish to acknowledge them one and all for their support. In particular, I thank Kay Holland, my aunt, Monica O'Neill (widow of my Uncle Joe), Dermot and Dorothy O'Connor, the late lamented Rory, and Nuala O'Connor, Fergus and Tina Copley, Philomena Lawlor (née O'Neill) and Maureen Laursen (née O'Neill) in Canada, Marie Logan (neé O'Connor), all of whom made materials and/or photographs available that gave life to what had been oral tradition before.

I wish to specially thank my siblings who contributed to the chapter 'Family Voices'. Particular thanks to my sister Nell, who not only contributed to that chapter but was an indispensable guide and mentor in respect of the accuracy of my memories. My friend Enid Mayrs gave marvellous practical help in checking archival facts.

I thank my children and stepchildren, the O'Connors (Joseph, Éimear, Sinéad, John and Eoin), and the Suiters (Jane, Lisa and Kate), for their background support in my writing the book. My son Joseph gave me invaluable advice and stressed the need to allow the reader to enter my little domain, and reminded me that a book will live for a long time and thus demands its author's best efforts. I hope I have discharged that responsibility; but any shortcomings in the telling of my story are my own. The contents of the book are a personal memory of my happy childhood among the lovely people of the Liberties, for whom I have a warm respect and affection.

My wife Viola, to whom this book is dedicated with love, was a great strength during the period of writing and made it easy for me to undertake the task. I now express my thanks to her with gratitude and, for her easy-going ways, I praise the Lord.

ACKNOWLEDGEMENTS OF POETRY AND MUSIC

Ch.4: Franner. The quotation beginning 'the boundary lines have fallen for me' is from Psalm 16:6 in the *Holy Bible, New International Version*, published by Hodder and Stoughton.

Ch.5: South of France-cis Street. The last line of the poem 'Ozymandias' by Percy Bysshe Shelley is misquoted for effect. The actual line reads 'The lone and level sands stretch far away'.

Ch.7: Westering Home. The words 'O Listen, Listen, Ladies Gay!' comprise the first line of the poem 'Rosabelle' by Sir Walter Scott. The song 'Stone Cold Dead in the Market' was written by Frederick Wilmoth Hendricks otherwise known as Wilmoth Houdini. The song 'Miya Sama, Miya Sama' is from *The Mikado* by Gilbert and Sullivan. 'Westering Home' was written by Sir Hugh Robertson. The song 'She Moved through the Fair' is very old but the modern version was written by Pádraic Colum.

Ch.8: The Sparrow's House. The quotation 'He that cares when a sparrow falls' is based on Matthew 10:29. The quotation 'He Who hath made the night of stars' is from the penultimate stanza of 'The Ballad of Father Gilligan' by William Butler Yeats. The quotation 'That's the wise thrush' is from 'Home-Thoughts, from Abroad' by Robert Browning. The reference 'Yea, the sparrow has found a house' is from Psalm 84:3 of the Old Testament.

Ch.10: So Far the Shore. The poem 'A Noble Boy – Somebody's Mother' was written by Mary Dow-Brine. The words 'Fragile fragments fallen from the workshop of the Gods' are from the poem 'The Old Bush School' by John O'Brien. 'The Blue Danube' was composed by Johann Strauss II, and I have been unable to identify the author of the lyrics we learned in Francis Street CBS as printed. The quotation 'And the voice in my dreaming ear melted away' is the last line of 'The Soldier's Dream' by Thomas Campbell. The song about Willie Earl was called 'And He'd Say Ooh-La-La!', melody by Harry Ruby and George Jessel. The citation of Oscar Wilde is from his poem 'Requiescat'.

Ch.12: When McGee Draws His First Week's Pay. The words of the song 'Music, Music, Music' were written by Stephen Weiss and Bernie Baum and are published under licence. I was unable to discover the author of the song 'When McGee Draws His First Week's Pay'. 'If I Had a Talking Picture of You' was written by B. G. DeSylva with words by Ray Henderson. The song 'Mate o' Mine' was written by Percy Elliott with words by Leslie Cooke. James Campbell and

Reginald Connelly wrote 'Show Me the Way to Go Home'. 'A Jacobite's Epitaph' was written by Thomas Babington Macaulay (Baron Macaulay).

Ch.13: Leaving the Liberties. In the song 'Serenade' the music was written by Enrico Toselli and the words are by R. H. Elkin. The song 'Now Is the Hour' is usually credited to Clement Scott, Maewa Kaihau and Dorothy Stewart. 'Wish Me Luck as You Wave Me Goodbye' was written by Harry Parr-Davies. The novel *Great Expectations*, which featured Miss Havisham and Estella, was written by Charles Dickens. The quotation 'these were thy charms, sweet village' is from the poem 'The Deserted Village' by Oliver Goldsmith.

About the author

Seán O'Connor was born in the Liberties of Dublin. He attended the local school, Francis St CBS, and afterwards began work with a firm of Consulting Engineers.

Later, under the name of John V O'Connor, he became a Consulting Engineer himself, qualifying as a Chartered Engineer in 1971, and a Fellow of the Institution of Structural Engineers in 1973, winning the award of the President of the Association of Consulting Engineers of Ireland for General Excellence of Design in that year and a second time in 1976, for Innovation in Building Design.

He gained a Master of Science degree from Trinity College in 1978 and became a Fellow of the Institution of Engineers of Ireland in 1982. After further study at Trinity College and King's Inns, he passed their exams for the Barrister-at-Law degree and became a member of the Irish Bar in 1985. Having practiced in the courts for three years, he returned to Engineering Consultancy in 1988 as one of the founding partners of O'Connor Sutton Cronin, a business employing 90 people. He retired in 2002.

He has five children: Prof. Joseph O'Connor (novelist), Dr Éimear O'Connor (art historian), Sinéad O'Connor (singer/songwriter), John P O'Connor, (counsellor/psychotherapist), and Eoin O'Connor, (marketing manager, Sony Music Ireland). He is married to Viola to whom this, his first book, is dedicated.